God's
Grand Finale
and the
End of the Age

GARY D. LONGBRAKE

WESTBOW
PRESS®
A DIVISION OF THOMAS NELSON
& ZONDERVAN

This book is a work of non-fiction. Unless otherwise noted, the author and the publisher make no explicit guarantees as to the accuracy of the information contained in this book and in some cases, names of people and places have been altered to protect their privacy

Scripture taken from the New King James Version®. Copyright © 1982 by Thomas Nelson. Used by permission. All rights reserved

WestBow Press books may be ordered through booksellers or by contacting:

WestBow Press
A Division of Thomas Nelson & Zondervan
1663 Liberty Drive
Bloomington, IN 47403
www.westbowpress.com
1 (866) 928-1240

Because of the dynamic nature of the Internet, any web addresses or links contained in this book may have changed since publication and may no longer be valid. The views expressed in this work are solely those of the author and do not necessarily reflect the views of the publisher, and the publisher hereby disclaims any responsibility for them.

Any people depicted in stock imagery provided by Getty Images are models, and such images are being used for illustrative purposes only. Certain stock imagery © Getty Images.

ISBN: 978-1-9736-1899-7 (sc)
ISBN: 978-1-9736-1900-0 (hc)
ISBN: 978-1-9736-1898-0 (e)

Library of Congress Control Number: 2018901621

Print information available on the last page.

WestBow Press rev. date: 02/20/2019

Table of Contents

INTRODUCTION

Although this book is about the end of the age, it also takes a peek through a window at the age about to begin; great things are happening as we transition from one age to the next. As the transition begins, God wants us to know what is happening and the wisdom in His plan; He said, "Wisdom and knowledge will be the stability of your times" (Isa. 33:6). Knowing God's plan as it is revealed in the prophets imparts spiritual wisdom and will keep His people stable in a time of upheaval among the nations.

We know through His Word what is happening in the spirit realm; in the world not seen. The birthing of a new age is coming, and we are seeing the birth pangs of it in our world. To this end, He informs us of these things, that we may not be shaken by all we see taking place in our world today. The apostle Paul said, "While we look not at the things which are seen, but at the things which are not seen. For the things which are seen are temporary, but the things which are not seen are eternal" (2 Cor. 4:18). Heavenly things are not seen with the natural eye but through the eye of faith: "Blessed are those who have not seen and yet have believed" (John 20:29).

The most important subject the Bible addresses is eternal life. It speaks of a life in a realm not seen with the natural eye, but it is a life that is without end. Eternal life was at the forefront of my mind when I read the Bible for the first time. If we all must die and be buried, it does not make sense to leave any stone unturned in our search for what happens after we die. We know beyond all shadow of doubt that this natural life has to end, but yet that is not the end of us, we merely transition from the natural realm to the supernatural realm.

The Bible has the most intelligent and reasonable explanation; it teaches that we have three dimensions, we are spirit, soul, and body (1 Thess. 5:23). It teaches that our bodies will die but our spirit will live on. Notice in Genesis, when God spoke to Abraham about his death, He mentions two destinations: "Now as for you, you shall go to your fathers in peace; you shall be buried at a good old age" (Gen. 15:15). After death, his body was buried, but his spirit went to be with his fathers in the unseen realm. This would refer to *Sheol*, the Old Testament Hebrew word that means the abode of the dead. Sheol is the equivalent to the New Testament Greek word Hades, which means the unseen world.

The Lord gives us a story that is a window to see beyond the grave, a window where we can view the abode of the departed, where Abraham had been gathered to his fathers. Only through the divine Words of God are we permitted to view this unseen world where the dearly departed had gone in those days. Jesus tells us this story in Luke 16 which I believe is an actual conversation that took place in the unseen realm and He reveals some very interesting facts.

> There was a certain rich man who was clothed in purple and fine linen and fared sumptuously every day. But there was a certain beggar named Lazarus, full of sores, who was laid at his gate, desiring to be fed with the crumbs which fell from the rich man's table. Moreover the dogs came and licked his sores. So it was that the beggar died, and was carried by the angels to Abraham's bosom. The rich man also died and was buried. And being in torments in Hades, he lifted up his eyes and saw Abraham afar off, and Lazarus in his bosom. "Then he cried and said, 'Father Abraham, have mercy on

me, and send Lazarus that he may dip the tip of his finger in water and cool my tongue; for I am tormented in this flame.' But Abraham said, 'Son, remember that in your lifetime you received your good things, and likewise Lazarus evil things; but now he is comforted and you are tormented. And besides all this, between us and you there is a great gulf fixed, so that those who want to pass from here to you cannot, nor can those from there pass to us.' "Then he said, 'I beg you therefore, father, that you would send him to my father's house, for I have five brothers, that he may testify to them, lest they also come to this place of torment.' Abraham said to him, 'They have Moses and the prophets; let them hear them.' And he said, 'No, father Abraham; but if one goes to them from the dead, they will repent.' But he said to him, 'If they do not hear Moses and the prophets, neither will they be persuaded though one rise from the dead.'" (Luke 16:19-31)

Notice that Lazarus died but his spirit was carried by the angels to Abraham's bosom. The rich man also died and was buried, but his spirit was in torment in Hades. When Lazarus's spirit arrived in the unseen abode of the departed, he was gathered to his fathers, he was comforted in what the Lord called, Abraham's bosom. I don't know how people could read these words of God that give us eyes to see what happens after death and not be moved to do something about where they will go after they die. The Bible says: "It is appointed for men to die once, but after this the judgment" (Heb. 9:27). After this life, there is more. The rich man was not concerned about his life, until he was in torment without access to water to cool his tongue. Realizing it was too late for him, he became very concerned about his five brothers, who he knew were on the same path that brought him to that place of torment.

Our bodies will die and be buried, but our spirits have a destiny in the unseen world. We should take note that this testimony comes to us from the One who said, "I am the way, the Truth, and the Life. No one can come to the Father except through Me" (John 14:6). Only Jesus has the words of eternal life, and He speaks the truth about what happens after we die. He said, "It is the Spirit who gives life; the flesh profits nothing. The words that I speak to you are spirit, and they are life" (John 6:63). He demonstrated the power of His Words when He raised a different Lazarus from the dead by crying with a loud voice, "Lazarus, come forth!" (John 11: 43). Later, He was raised from the dead as well to confirm the truth and the power of life in His Word.

God prepared a natural body for Christ to come into this world, so He could give us the words of eternal life. He came in the power of an endless life to impart that life to us: "For God so loved the world that He gave His only begotten Son, that whoever believes in Him should not perish but have everlasting life" (John 3:16). Jesus, the Word of God, was with God when the world began. (John 1:1-5,14) He came to us from the spirit realm which we cannot see with the natural eye, but He came to give us eyes to see a world that is not visible, which is more real than the world we can see. The world that is not seen is supernatural and eternal while the world that is seen is only natural and is passing away. The new body that God has promised us is supernatural and eternal, while the body we now have is natural and is passing away. As it is written: "All flesh is as grass, and all the glory of man as the flower of the grass. The grass withers, and its flower falls away, but the word of the Lord endures forever" (1 Pet. 1:24-25).

Some may say they don't believe in God because they can't see Him, but unbelief cannot change the truth. If one stands on the edge of a great cliff and declares he does not believe in gravity because he cannot see it, his belief cannot save him after he takes that first step. What he believes is irrelevant; the truth takes authority over his belief. Once he passes the point of no return, it is too late for the fool to change his mind about what he believes, though he may earnestly desire to.

That is the place the rich man found himself in, and at that point, he thought about his five brothers and sought to warn them of that place. But it was beyond his power to help them. We now have Moses, the prophets, and the words of Christ, who was raised from the dead, and they tell us the truth. He who has ears to hear, let him hear.

Because this book is addressing the end of this age, it is very important that we understand to some degree certain spiritual matters. Death is not the end but the beginning of everlasting life. The spiritual life is not first; the natural life is, then comes the spiritual, supernatural, and eternal life. Being familiar with these things, we know we do not need a body to live forever because we are spirit beings like God, who made us in His image. Our bodies are just our house, our dwelling place in the natural world, until the time of our departure.

After Jesus's resurrection, the apostle Paul said that to be absent from the body was to be present with the Lord (2 Cor. 5:8). The body is condemned to death because of sin, but when we accept His Word we are alive forevermore because of Christ. When those who have been born again, born of the Spirit of God, die the natural death, they leave the body and go to heaven, where those who have predeceased them gather to greet them. It is a time of great joy!

But for now, we have a great task. As we consider the many things God has revealed to us through His Word concerning the end of this age, we must not see an end coming but a new beginning. We must not see darkness and gloom but joy and gladness for what is about to come. Remember that the joy of the Lord is our strength; the more joy we have, the more strength we have to stand and not be shaken. Without an understanding of eternal life, we would see only a dark world with no hope.

The wickedness of humanity is becoming great; Christians will be persecuted more and more, but we have been called to rejoice and be strong. We are coming to the pinnacle of evil in this world, but we should be of good cheer; all the evil we see is about to pass away. God has given us the Holy Spirit to comfort us in our time of trouble, but as the persecution increases, angels will also minister to God's people to encourage and strengthen them.

I will share an experience a friend and I had concerning angelic visitations but not so I can appear better than anyone else; it is so those who don't know anything about spiritual things can become familiar with how God works. This book will address supernatural and spiritual things, so I want to familiarize you with some of these things first. To those who say, "I don't believe in spiritual or supernatural things," I say that what you believe can be changed in an instant by a single encounter with God, so don't believe your unbelief. You can see things with your eyes that your mind cannot believe. Remember, unbelief cannot change the truth. Jesus said, "You shall know the truth and the truth shall make you free" (John 8:32).

My journey with God has been spiritual and supernatural. Jesus said, "But the Helper, the Holy Spirit, whom the Father will send in My name, He will teach you all things" (John 14:26). I don't know if you have ever experienced Him teaching you as this scripture says, but I believe I have experienced His teaching many times, and it is awesome! I have to share this with you because that is why He does these things, so we can all learn.

I was first acquainted with the teaching of the Holy Spirit in this manner. I once heard a speaker at a certain church many years ago speaking on the coming of the Lord and some of the signs of His coming. When the service was over, as I got up to leave, I heard these words, "That day shall come as a thief in the night." I knew these words were scripture, and I believed the Holy Spirit was speaking them to me, but they didn't seem to agree with what I had just learned. However, the words were so clear that they stopped me in my tracks; I thought about what I had just heard—*Yeah, how could the speaker be telling us things to come if that day will come as a thief in the night?* But I realized she had given us many scriptures in line with what she had said, so I dismissed it as nothing.

But the Lord was about to deal with His servant in a supernatural way. In those days, I was working at a truck repair shop in Oakland, California. During my morning break, I would open my little New Testament to wherever it happened to fall and begin to read. That day, I happened to open it to 1 Thessalonians 5:1. The first thing I read was:

> But concerning the times and the seasons, brethren, you have no need that I should write to you. For you yourselves know perfectly that the day of the Lord so comes as a thief in the night. For when they say, "Peace and safety!" then sudden destruction comes upon them, as labor pains upon a pregnant woman. And they shall not escape. But you, brethren, are not in darkness, so that this Day should overtake you as a thief.

The first sentence had my full attention, and when I read the last sentence, a great light went on inside me. I could not contain myself. I busted out in laughter, and those nearby asked, "What's going on?" I told them the Lord had just spoken to me through the Bible, and it was awesome! Then I realized the Lord had spoken those words to me the night before to get my attention. God's people are not in darkness, so that day will not overtake us like a thief in the night. I understood what that scripture said; He didn't need to show me anything else.

But He wasn't through. At lunch, I opened my Bible as at first and began to read Hebrews chapter 10 when I came across these words.

> And let us consider one another in order to stir up love and good works, not forsaking the assembling of ourselves together, as is the manner of some, but exhorting one another, and so much the more as you see the Day approaching. (Hebrews 10:24–25)

By that time, I was in the clouds! The glow of His blessed Holy Spirit was upon me, and I was experiencing times of refreshing in the presence of the Lord. I was high without drugs; I was filled with joy without possessions! In His presence, there truly is fullness of joy! Nothing on earth can compare to what God has in store for those who love Him.

I was in great expectation as to what the Lord would do next. During my afternoon break, I opened my Bible by chance to Revelation chapter 3 and read these words,

> Be watchful, and strengthen the things which remain, that are ready to die, for I have not found your works perfect before God. Remember therefore how you have received and heard; hold fast and repent. Therefore, if you will not watch, I will come upon you as a thief, and you will not know what hour I will come upon you. (Revelation 3:2–3)

If He had not spoken those words to me the night before, this would not have made such a great impact on me. I'll never forget the way He taught me these things. From that day on, I have not believed that the Lord would come out of nowhere like a thief in the night. He was teaching us that if we watch, we would see the day approaching, but that if we did not watch, that day would come as a thief in the night. This was also how the Lord confirmed the call He had on my life. I always studied with this intent, that we might see and know how close we are to the Lord's coming. I have been watching and recording what I have seen in scripture and in our world, and now it is time to share it.

Another thing the Lord supernaturally showed me was visitations from angels who are telling us the time is short. Sending angels is a wonderful way God has chosen to show His people things in the past and He is still showing His people things in this manner. This story is true and correct to the best of my knowledge; I will not keep silent about it but will speak of the wonderful works of the Lord. Knowing our Lord has given us signs, I thought it seemed good to write an orderly account as an eyewitness of what I have seen and heard. I believe angelic visitations will greatly increase as the time of the end approaches.

It was after an ordinary Sunday service with a good message from the pastor. I was waiting in the car for the kids (I have four) to come out from children's church when as they were climbing into the minivan, they began to shout, "Gabriel's lips are wet! Gabriel's lips are wet, Dad!" I asked, "What in the world are you talking about?" They told me the story they had heard from their children's pastor. It sounded as if God had done something supernatural; I knew I would not have any rest until I heard the complete story from the children's pastor. I went back into church and asked her what had happened. Apparently, she had a good friend who was a Christian and a trustworthy person who had experienced a very strange phenomenon.

It took place in Los Angeles right after the Northridge earthquake in 1994. Freeways had collapsed, and many people had died in the earthquake. The fires that ensued created a feeling of emergency the day following the quake. In such a setting, this friend of the children's pastor was driving down a freeway in the LA area after the quake, and she picked up a hitchhiker. She explained later that she did not know why she had picked up this hitchhiker because she never picks up hitchhikers. But she picked him up and was driving along when the guy said, "The Bible said this would happen in the last days. There would be earthquakes in different places. This is a sign of the times." She was puzzled why he had said that. Then he said, "Gabriel's lips are wet!" and he vanished right before her eyes.

It so traumatized her that she began to get sick. She couldn't believe her eyes. *People don't vanish before your eyes*, she thought. She pulled over to the side of the freeway, got out, and threw up. Just then a police officer pulled up and asked her if she was okay. She told him she was; she also said something very strange had just happened to her.

He asked, "What?"

She said, "You wouldn't believe me if I told you."

He said, "Miss, I've already heard some strange things today, so try me."

She told him the whole story all the way up to where he pulled up to her car.

"Miss, you're the fifth person who has told me a similar story today."

It must have been quite an experience for that officer to hear so many testimonies of what the Bible says about earthquakes being a sign of the times and then have it confirmed with a supernatural sign. I believe this hitchhiker was an angel sent to give us a supernatural sign that the Lord's coming is at hand. A short time for the Lord may be many years for us. Angels announced that Christ was born in Bethlehem, but it was thirty years later that He came.

The scriptures say, "Do not forget to entertain strangers, for by so doing some have unwittingly entertained angels" (Hebrews 13:2). She might have thought of this scripture when she saw the stranger hitchhiking, but rather than entertaining that angel, he entertained her.

The earthquake was a sign of our times just as the Bible says, and then the angel vanished to demonstrate that this was not a casual conversation but a visitation to emphasize that the Word of God is true. So many earthquakes are occurring all over the world—an unparalleled number in history.

The pastor told me her friend had been in California for only a short time and then had gone back to Oklahoma, so she was not readily available for an interview. However, I knew the Lord our God does things like this, so I wanted to get as much of the story as I could down, but her testimony was all I had.

But again, the Lord wasn't finished yet. Not long after that, I was at work one day when I overheard my foreman telling a customer a similar story; he said, "She doesn't pick up hitchhikers, nor is she a religious person." He was getting to the part about the man vanishing and how she pulled over and got sick.

He said, "Then a police officer pulled over and asked her if she was all right. And she said, 'Yes, but something weird just happened.' And again, the officer asked, 'What?' And this woman also said, 'You won't believe me if I tell you.' And he said, 'Try me. I've heard some strange things today.' So she told the officer her story, and he said, 'Miss, you're the seventh person to tell me a story like that today.'"

"Mike!" I said to my foreman. "I heard a very similar story, and the officer said she was the fifth person!"

That set my foreman off; he said, "No way! You gotta be kidding me!"

I said, "No! I tell you the truth!" I told him as much of the story as I could remember. He wanted to get the two women together and compare stories, but I said that this other woman was in Oklahoma. The person he had heard his story from was a close friend of his wife's. We tried for a while to get the two stories from each source but were not successful. To the best of my knowledge, this happened just the way it is told here.

Our Lord does not want us to be ignorant concerning His coming, which will be soon. The message I get from the Lord is that Gabriel's lips are wet—he's about to blow the trumpet for the resurrection! Trumpeters always lick their lips to make blowing the trumpet easier. Gabriel is about to blow the trumpet for the resurrection, praise God! This is a sign that the resurrection is very near. Has God not sent angels to His people in times past to prepare them as a great event was approaching? He sent angels to shepherds out in the fields to announce that Christ had been born. They are messengers from heaven to inform and warn us of what is to come.

In the days of Moses, the Lord had the trumpets sound loud and long to announce that He was about to speak.

> Then it came to pass on the third day, in the morning, that there were thunderings and lightnings, and a thick cloud on the mountain; and the sound of the trumpet was very loud, so that all the people who were in the camp trembled. (Ex. 19:16)

That was God's trumpet! "And when the blast of the trumpet sounded long and became louder and louder, Moses spoke, and God answered him by voice" (Ex. 19:19). The trumpet was used to announce when God was going to speak. In heaven, trumpets are sounded to announce when God is going to speak. The trumpet is also used to announce things that are about to come.

Paul told us by revelation of the Holy Spirit that the trumpet would sound when the time for the resurrection has come: "For the Lord Himself will descend from heaven with a shout, with the voice of an archangel [Gabriel], and with the trumpet of God. And the dead in Christ will rise" (1 Thess. 4:15–16). "Behold, I tell you a mystery: We shall not all sleep, but we shall all be changed, in a moment, in the twinkling of an eye, at the last trumpet. For the trumpet will sound, and the dead will be raised" (1 Cor. 15:51–52).

An angel has been sent to tell us that the time is short. Gabriel's lips are wet; he is about to blow the trumpet of God loud and long for the resurrection! The carnal bodies of the saints will be raised at the resurrection. When the flesh dies, it decays and returns to the dust from which it came. For dust it is, and to dust it will return. But when it is raised, it is raised an incorruptible and supernatural body. It is sown in the earth as a mortal body, but it is raised an immortal body. Then the born-again spirit will reunite forever with the new immortal body God has promised. How exciting that will be!

We must not be afraid of what is to come. We must be strong and courageous because the Lord our God is with us. Go and tell your friends and neighbors of the wonderful things the Lord has made known to us. For it is written,

> One generation will commend your works to another; they will tell of your mighty acts. They will speak of the glorious splendor of your majesty, and I will meditate on your wonderful works. They will tell of the power of your awesome works, and I will proclaim your great deeds. (Ps. 145:4–6 NIV)

When the Lord performed this sign—two similar stories of events that took place more than four hundred miles away—came together, I considered that a sign and a wonder. The story itself is a sign that makes us wonder, but I believe it is not a coincidence but a confirmation. It is not the only time the Lord has done something like this to confirm His plan for my life. I have always believed that God would put me in the right place at the right time to fulfill His plan, but it is another level when you actually see it happen.

One divine encounter after another has confirmed what I believe God has called me to do. I see and observe things of a supernatural nature so I may proclaim them. But who will believe our report? And to whom will the arm of the Lord be revealed?

What you will read in these pages has come together over the span of about thirty years. It is not meant to be my work or content but what has come to us by revelation of the Holy Spirit. If we look at it as the work of a human being, we will miss what God is saying. I call Him the coauthor of this book because I know more than anyone else that I can of myself do nothing. It is only in times of prayer, meditation, and worship that revelations of these things come to me, and I write them down. This book is going to be good news concerning the end times—not darkness, gloominess, and horror. The Lord has great things in store for His people, and He wants them to know what they are. He has not given us a spirit of fear but of power and of love and a sound mind. (2 Tim. 1:7) He is teaching us through His Word that we need to prepare ourselves for what is to come. If we are prepared, we will not be shaken by the things the prophets have forewarned us must come to pass.

According to the prophets, God will do all He has ever done before and even greater things. He has made Himself known by His mighty hand and outstretched arm before, and He intends to do it again. He has caused His name to be declared in all the earth by His mighty power before, and He intends to do so again. He has delivered Israel from greater and mightier enemies in the eyes of all nations, and He intends to do so again. The earth has shaken at the sound of His voice before, and He intends to shake it again but in a greater manner. He has poured out His Spirit on all flesh before, and He intends to do it again but on a much greater level. It is God's Grand Finale, and His people need to be watchful and prepared.

There is great joy and excitement in heaven over what is to come, and there should be the same among God's people on earth. The church in heaven and the church on earth are about to merge and attend the marriage supper of the Lamb. Therefore, heaven is communicating with us right now to teach us what we should do. Heaven is sending messages to us to tell us what is to come. Prepare the way of the Lord; make His paths straight. He keeps His Word to tell us all things beforehand that we might prepare ourselves for what is to come: "See, I have told you all things beforehand" (Mark 13:23). "Therefore you also be ready, for the Son of Man is coming" (Matt. 24:44). Jesus wants us to know all these things beforehand, but He does not want any of His people to be fearful. He exhorts His people several times in His Word not to fear but to be strong and of good courage. He instructed us to set our minds on heavenly things, not on earthly things that will perish.

> If then you were raised with Christ, seek those things which are above, where Christ is sitting at the right hand of God. Set your mind on things above, not on things on the earth. For you died, and your life is hidden with Christ in God. (Col. 3:1–3)

We have a lot of junk in our minds—concerns and worries about earthly things. But we are citizens of heaven; this place is not our home because we are children of God; He has prepared a place for us in His home. We have to deal with things in this world to an extent, but they should not be what fills our hearts and minds.

> Do not lay up for yourselves treasures on earth, where moth and rust destroy and where thieves break in and

steal; but lay up for yourselves treasures in heaven, where neither moth nor rust destroys and where thieves do not break in and steal. For where your treasure is, there your heart will be also. (Matt. 6:19–21)

Do not love the world or the things in the world. If anyone loves the world, the love of the Father is not in him. For all that is in the world, the lust of the flesh, the lust of the eyes, and the pride of life, is not of the Father but is of the world. And the world is passing away, and the lust of it; but he who does the will of God abides forever. (1 John 2:15–17)

The key to remaining grounded and unshaken in these last days is not just hearing God's Word but doing it. What God is saying to us in His Word is the most important thing we have ever heard in our life. Those who love God as He loves us have no fear and have been perfected in love: "There is no fear in love; but perfect love casts out fear, because fear involves torment. But he who fears has not been made perfect in love" (1 John 4:18).

Those who love the world have not been perfected in the love of God and can be tormented by the enemy with fear. But when they have been perfected in the love of God, His love casts out all fear, even fear of death. No fear! God is love, and there is no fear or death in love; the more we love God, the less we fear worldly troubles. "You shall love the LORD your God with all your heart, with all your soul, with all your mind, and with all your strength ... and, You shall love your neighbor as yourself" (Mark 12:31). Those who are spiritual love God with all they are. Most of us have not arrived, but we must aspire to this level of love.

God is greater than all and should be placed before all.

He who loves father or mother more than Me is not worthy of Me. And he who loves son or daughter more than Me is not worthy of Me. And he who does not take his cross and follow after Me is not worthy of Me. He who finds his life will lose it, and he who loses his life for My sake will find it. (Matt. 10:37–39)

The time to love the Lord with all your heart, all your soul, and all your strength, and yes, even more than your own life is now. The time to grow in love to full maturity is now. The time is coming when lawlessness will abound and the love of many will grow cold. (Matt. 24:12)

The Lord warns us not to love the world or things in the world because we will have to leave it all behind: "In that day, he who is on the housetop, and his goods are in the house, let him not come down to take them away. And likewise, the one who is in the field, let him not turn back. Remember Lot's wife" (Luke 17:31–33). God rewards even in this life those who have forsaken all because they love Him. The apostles forsook all to follow Jesus and learned of their rewards.

Peter said, "See, we have left all and followed You. Therefore, what shall we have?" So Jesus said to them, "Assuredly I say to you, that in the regeneration, when the Son of Man sits on the throne of His glory, you who have followed Me will also sit on twelve thrones, judging the twelve tribes of Israel. And everyone who has left houses or brothers or sisters or father or mother or wife or children or lands, for My name's sake, shall receive a hundredfold, and inherit eternal life." (Matt. 19:27–29)

They had to set their minds on things above, not on the things on the earth if they were to follow Jesus. But Jesus said everyone who has left houses or brothers or sisters or father or mother or wife or children or lands, for My name's sake, shall receive a hundredfold! Therefore, we need to be doers of His Word and not hearers only, deceiving ourselves (James 1:22). We need to set our minds on heavenly things as God has instructed us, and we will be in peace through these trying times. It is inevitable that some will set their minds on earthly things and be in fear. For the Lord has said,

> And there will be signs in the sun, in the moon, and in the stars; and on the earth distress of nations, with perplexity, the sea and the waves roaring; men's hearts failing them from fear and the expectation of those things which are coming on the earth, for the powers of the heavens will be shaken. (Luke 21:25–26)

> But the LORD will be a shelter for His people and the strength of the children of Israel. (Joel 3:16)

"Blessed are the eyes which see the things you see; for I tell you that many prophets and kings have desired to see what you see, and have not seen it, and to hear what you hear, and have not heard it" (Luke 10:23–24). Blessed are the people who make God their strength and the Holy One of Israel their shield. "Blessed are all those who put their trust in Him" (Ps. 2:12). "Blessed are those who hear the Word of God and keep it" (Luke 11:28). Blessed are those who hear the words of the prophecies in this book and blessed are those who are not offended because of His Words.

It is imperative that the reader of this book be introduced to the author, (his walk with God, spiritual things and spiritual wisdom) before reading further. Paul said,

> However, we speak wisdom among those who are mature, yet not the wisdom of this age, nor of the rulers of this age, who are coming to nothing. But

we speak the wisdom of God in a mystery, the
hidden wisdom which God ordained before the ages
for our glory. (1 Cor. 2:6–7)

We speak not the wisdom of this world but the wisdom of God
among those who are mature. It is a mystery to those who do not
know Him. It is hidden wisdom which God ordained before the
ages for our glory. It is not persuasive words of human wisdom,
but hidden wisdom which God reveals to those who love Him.
The natural man does not receive the things of the Spirit of God,
for they are foolishness to him, they are spiritual and cannot be
discerned without His Holy Spirit. But we have received the Spirit
who is from God, so that we might know the things of God, even
deep things of God, that have been freely given to us by God. He
who is mature in spirit judges all things, yet he himself is rightly
judged by no one. Those who are spiritual have the mind of Christ.
See also: (1 Cor. 2:12–16)

PREFACE

It has been a long time coming, but events taking place today have been known only as prophecies until now. What we see in our world today is fulfilling the words of many prophets. Many generations before us have desired to see the things we see but did not see them. And yet, before we were even born, the Lord said these things shall be: "I have declared the former things from the beginning, they went forth from My mouth and I caused them to hear it. Suddenly I did them and they came to pass" (Isa. 48:3). "Before it came to pass I proclaimed it to you" (Isa. 48:5).

Many generations have studied prophecies in God's Word and wondered when these things shall be, but many have already come to pass! We are on earth in the last days, we were chosen for such a time as this. It is God's will to declare things that shall come to pass so when we see them, we will know it is He who is doing these things. He demonstrates through His prophetic Word that He is God and there is none like Him in all the earth! "For I am God, and there is no other; I am God, and there is none like Me, declaring the end from the beginning, and from ancient times things that are not yet done, saying, 'My counsel shall stand, And I will do all My pleasure" (Isa 46:9-10).

Events appointed for the last days are of profound importance to us, who may very well be the last generation. The Lord Jesus said, "When you see all these things, know that it is near, at the doors! Assuredly, I say to you, this generation will by no means pass away till all these things take place" (Matt. 24:33–34). Jesus was very specific here; there is a last generation, and they should know who they are by the signs they see.

The Lord has given us many prophecies that speak of what will take place in the last days, and each has a place in God's plan. As we begin to journey through these prophecies, it will become obvious that there is one at the epicenter of them all, an event the Lord specifically declares would happen in the latter days. We are in the last of the last days, and it is clearly an event that has not yet taken place. It is an event that could not take place until the children of Israel were gathered back to the land God gave them in the last days, and that is Israel today. The stage that must be set for this event, as we see it in the prophets, is strikingly the same as the set we see before us today as we cast our eyes on Israel.

The gathering of Israel to their land and the rebuilding of Jerusalem are the keys to understanding what the prophets have said. The prophet Micah says,

> In the day when your walls are to be built, in that day the decree shall go far and wide. In that day they shall come to you from Assyria and the fortified cities, from the fortress to the River, from sea to sea, and mountain to mountain. (Mic. 7:11–12)

When He said, "In the days when your walls are to be built," He is referring to a specific time—when Israel would be gathered back to their land, so they could rebuild. Through His servant the prophet the Lord describes the return saying: "The decree shall go far and wide. In that day they shall come." When Israel became a state in 1948, the decree went far and wide, to the farthest parts of the earth, that Jews from anywhere in the world could come home to the land the Lord their God gave them and their fathers for an everlasting covenant.

After two thousand years of Jewish exile the gates of Zion were opened, and large numbers of Jews came from all over the world to Israel. We must understand that they could not have come back unless the Lord their God had ordained it. Today, multitudes of Jews from all over the world have come back to the land of their fathers. They have rebuilt the cities of Judah, they have raised up the former desolations, and they have rebuilt the holy city of Jerusalem. This is a sign of the coming of the Lord.

In this prophecy in Micah, the Lord describes an event that He compares to the great show of His power that took place when He brought Israel out of Egypt. For such a show a stage must be set, Israel must be gathered back to their land. What Micah describes could not happen until the Jews were gathered back to their land. The only gathering of the Jews in the last days is the one we are watching today. That is why it is very important for us today to watch what is happening in Israel. Notice what the Lord went on to say in this chapter of Micah.

> As in the days when you came out of the land of
> Egypt, I will show them wonders. The nations shall
> see and be ashamed of all their might; they shall put
> their hand over their mouth; their ears shall be deaf.
> They shall lick the dust like a serpent; they shall
> crawl from their holes like snakes of the earth. They
> shall be afraid of the LORD our God and shall fear
> because of You. (Mic. 7:15–17)

Since the days of Moses, the Lord God has not performed such a great and mighty show of His power as He did when he parted the Red Sea and brought Israel out of Egypt. But here in Micah, the Lord said that when Israel was gathered to their land, He would show them wonders according to those He had performed when He brought them out of Egypt. He says the nations will see His great show of wonders and put their hands over their mouths in astonishment. They would be ashamed of their power to make war because it would be useless in the face of such an infinitely superior power. Some of them would fall to the ground and slither in the dirt like serpents for fear of the Lord and the glory of His majesty when He arises to make Himself known.

This event is so big and magnificent that it is mentioned by several of the prophets; they too compared it to the days when God parted the Red Sea and led Israel out of Egypt. Just as He destroyed Egypt to demonstrate His great power, mighty hand, and outstretched arm that all nations would know Him, He intends to show His great power in these last days. According to all the prophecies we will consider, it appears He intends to perform a great show once again in the sight of all nations, and the prophets agree with this.

> For who has stood in the counsel of the LORD, and has perceived and heard His word? Who has marked His Word and heard it? Behold, a whirlwind of the LORD has gone forth in fury, a violent whirlwind! It will fall violently on the head of the wicked. The anger of the LORD will not turn back until He has executed and performed the thoughts of His heart. In the latter days you will understand it perfectly. (Jer. 23:18–20)

He was not speaking of His anger against all humanity but His anger against His enemies in the latter days.

Most people do not want to hear of the anger of the Lord because they immediately think it is against them when in fact it is not. This passage declares that it is on the heads of the wicked, it is against them, it is the thoughts of His heart, and it is His plan for the latter days. Who has perceived what the Lord is saying about the last days? Who has marked His Word and heard it? Many have ears, but do they hear what He is saying? Should we be numbered among those who shut their eyes and stop their ears lest they understand with their hearts what the great and awesome God is saying? This great and awesome show will be a great destruction on His enemies just like the destruction of the Egyptians in the day Moses led the children of Israel out of Egypt. Therefore, it is written in the prophets that when the Lord lifts Himself up, the nations shall be scattered.

God has enemies today, those of whom He says,

> have given My land to themselves as a possession, in order to plunder its open country ... They have divided up My land ... They have said, Come, let us cut them off from being a nation, that the name of Israel may be remembered no more. (Ezek. 36:5; Joel 3:2; Ps. 83:4)

When the Arab nations claimed the Holy Land, it was not because they didn't have enough land—it was because they did not want the Jews to have any. When Israel became a state in 1948, all the Arab states around Israel vowed to wipe the new Jewish state off the map so there would be no land for the Lord's people. Why do they disdain them so and speak such things against the Lord and His anointed?

And the United Nations general assembly has taken sides with His enemies. They have taken counsel together, divided His land, and given half to the Jewish people and half to a mixed Arab people who call themselves Palestinians. Yes, they have taken crafty and deceitful counsel together against the Lord and His people. Even now, they take counsel together against Israel and pressure them to make peace with those who hate them and vowed to wipe their state off the map. The United Nations cannot prevail when it takes counsel together against God: "The LORD brings the counsel of the nations to nothing; He makes the plans of the peoples of no effect" (Ps. 33:10).

The UN has gathered a counsel and voted to agree with those who rage against God, but all their effort will come to nothing. Do they forget the words of the prophets? "Why do the nations rage, and the people plot a vain thing? The kings of the earth set themselves, and the rulers take counsel together, against the LORD and against His Anointed" (Ps. 2:1–2). Do they forget that He has said, "Do not touch My anointed ones, and do My prophets no harm" (Ps. 105:15). Can God's enemies destroy His people and plunder His land? Can the nations set a snare for Him? Can they catch Him in a trap? Indeed, it would be in vain to try. Therefore, "He who sits in the heavens shall laugh! Then He will speak to them in His wrath and distress them in His deep displeasure" (Ps. 2:4–5). It appears this psalm is prophesying an event that agrees with what Jeremiah said about the whirlwind of the Lord's anger. By these scriptures, our attention is being drawn to what God said in His Word against His enemies who surround Israel today. Could the world stage be set for a demonstration of God's awesome power to be revealed in the last days? Are these not the signs of our times?

Evil and wicked people are doing many great injustices and horrible things to the Lord's anointed people today. Not being content with that, terrorists have also stretched out their hands in rage against the rest of humanity who do not believe what they believe. Many have wondered, "Where is God in all this? Is God not greatly angered by these things? Why doesn't He do something?" But we could also look at it in a different manner. Could all that is happening in the world today be leading us to a great climax? When God demonstrated His mighty hand and outstretched arm in the eyes of the nations when He brought Israel out of Egypt, didn't the stage have to be set? Didn't there have to be enemies who took counsel among themselves against the Lord and His anointed people? Yes.

> Now there arose a new king over Egypt, who did not know Joseph, and he said to his people, "Look, the people of the children of Israel are more and mightier than we; come, let us deal shrewdly with them, lest they multiply, and it happen, in the

> event of war, that they also join our enemies and fight against us, and so go up out of the land." Therefore, they set taskmasters over them to afflict them ... And they made their lives bitter with hard bondage. (Ex. 1:8–14)

Then they also began to kill their children.

> Then the king of Egypt spoke to the Hebrew midwives, and he said, "When you do the duties of a midwife for the Hebrew women, and see them on the birthstools, if it is a son, then you shall kill him." (Ex. 1:15–16)

They took counsel together against the Lord and His anointed and dealt treacherously with them without a cause. But notice that the stage was set years beforehand for the mighty show God performed the day He brought Israel out of Egypt.

Today, a similar stage has been set, and many scriptures confirm that an event such as what took place in the days of Moses should come to pass in the last days. It is an event compared by several prophets to the days when the Lord brought Israel out of Egypt. According to the prophets, it is scheduled to take place in the latter days, and that means it could happen at any time. It will parallel several aspects of the great and awesome acts of God when He brought Israel out of Egypt. It is His plan for His purpose that these things should come to pass. The main underlying reason for this show of His power is so all nations will know that His name is the Lord God almighty.

The prophets indicated that God intends to make Himself known as the great and awesome God of the whole earth. We know this by what He did in the days of Moses and what He said to the prophets. All the prophets, the Law, and the psalms testify to what God is about to do. It is something He has hid in plain sight to be revealed now, in the last days. It is a new prophetic word that could not be revealed by flesh and blood. He gives His people warning that they might prepare themselves and not be afraid. The Lord has always warned His people of what was to come so they might be prepared. Remember what the scripture says of Noah: "Noah, being divinely warned of things not yet seen, moved with godly fear, prepared" (Heb. 11:7). We can expect nothing less for our generation. This show of His power will coincide with such a great outpouring of His Spirit on all flesh that the earth will shake at His presence.

The Lord sets a watchman that he might see what is coming and give warning. As it is written, "Son of man, I have made you a watchman for the house of Israel; therefore, hear a word from My mouth, and give them warning from Me" (Ezek. 3:17). "I have made you a watchman for the house of Israel; therefore, you shall hear a word from My mouth and warn them for Me" (Ezek. 33:7). Today, the principle and the purpose are the same. If the Lord warned His people of things not yet seen, will He not warn His people today of things not yet seen? If His people needed to prepare for what was coming in the days of old, shall they not need to prepare for what is coming in the last days? The Lord is revealing things today that are not yet seen so that His people might be moved with godly fear and prepare for what is to come.

The Lord said, "Go, set a watchman, let him declare what he sees" (Isa. 21:6). Not everyone in the body of Christ is called to be a watchman, but everyone in the body of Christ is called to watch. Jesus said, "And what I say to you, I say to all: Watch!" (Mark 13:37). The Lord anoints the watchman, but we will not know him by a label but by his fruit. He must know and speak according to the Word of God: "To the law and to the testimony! If they do not speak according to this word, it is because there is no light in them" (Isa. 8:20).

What I believe the Lord is saying is that if one comes with revelations (light), it must be according to the Word of God. And it will be easily seen in the prophetic Word of God as something in God's character and something He has done before. Therefore, let us pursue the knowledge of the Lord: "Let him who glories glory in this, that he knows and understands Me" (Jer. 9:24). If one does not speak according to His Word, it is because the revelation did not come from God. When the Lord appointed His servant, He gave him Ezekiel 40:2–4 revealed in this manner.

> In the visions of God He set me on a very high mountain and said to me, "Look with your eyes and hear with your ears, and fix your mind on everything I show you; for I have anointed you for such a time as this, that I might show you all these things and that you might declare to My people all you see."

In the Spirit, the Lord sets His watchman on a very high mountain to see what is in all directions and then declare what he sees. Therefore, everything I see in scripture and in the world today, if you are willing to receive it, I declare to you.

The great and marvelous prophetic event about to take place is like a huge prophetic mountain in the Spirit we will climb. When we climb up one side, we have one view, and when we climb up another side, we have another view. There are many views, but they are all from the same mountain. So it is with all the different prophecies in this book; there are many different views, from many different prophets, but they all speak of the same great and awesome event.

The watchmen firmly agree that the regathering of Israel to the land of their fathers is a sign of the coming of the Lord. There are more prophecies about that regathering of Israel than any other event in scripture. It is a sign that we are in the last of the last days. All prophecies about the last days are about to be fulfilled. Watchmen all over the world began to rejoice and celebrate when Israel became a nation. It signified the end of the Diaspora, the scattering, and the beginning of their time of restoration, favor, and blessing: "Your watchmen shall lift up their voices, with their voices they shall sing together; for they shall see eye to eye when the LORD brings back

Zion" (Isa. 52:8). Zion in prophecy refers to the people and the land of the Lord. Scripture also references Zion as the city of the living God, the heavenly Jerusalem. However, the reference to the earthly Zion in the prophetic Word of God is our point of interest here. When Israel was carried away captive to Babylon, they wrote of earthly Zion,

> By the rivers of Babylon, there we sat down, yea, we wept when we remembered Zion. We hung our harps upon the willows in the midst of it. For there those who carried us away captive asked of us a song, and those who plundered us requested mirth, saying, "Sing us one of the songs of Zion!" (Ps. 137:1–3)

When the Lord began to bring back Zion, the watchmen took notice and lifted their voices. This is the sign we are looking for! This is the sign that the time has been fulfilled! The prophecy says that Jerusalem should be trampled underfoot by the Gentiles until the time of the Gentiles was fulfilled (Luke 21:24). The coming of the Lord is at hand! The watchmen are watching the gathering of God's people Israel and watching the rebuilding of Jerusalem knowing what the prophetic Word of God says concerning these things.

However, the people who have taken possession of the land are resisting the return of God's people to the land He gave them. The watchmen are watching all this—what the nations are doing and whose side they are taking in the matter.

Remember what the Lord of Hosts has declared to all nations: "Hear the word of the Lord, Oh, nations! And declare it to the ends of the earth and say, He who scattered Israel will gather him and keep him as a shepherd does his flock!" (Jer. 31:10). "Thus says the Lord GOD: 'Surely I will take the children of Israel from among the nations, wherever they have gone, and will gather them from every side and bring them into their own land'" (Ezek. 37:21). The Lord God is gathering His people Israel to their own land in the sight of the nations, so whose side should the nations be on? Why would they resist the hand of God when they should rejoice? The watchmen are rejoicing over the things they see because they are telling us of things not yet seen.

It is the appointed time to know these things, and at the time appointed, the Lord reveals these things according to His own will. He has kept these things hidden and untarnished for the times in which we live. It is how He does things; it is His plan. He said, "Shut up the words and seal the book until the time of the end" (Dan. 12:4). Things concerning the end of the age have been shut up and sealed. They could not be known or understood by humanity until the time had been fulfilled; then, the Lord should reveal His plan by His Spirit through His Word. It is amazing how He can open the scriptures to us when the appointed time has come. Many good and godly men have studied the Word for many years, and all have come up with what they believe is God's plan for the end of this age. The problem is that there are many different plans by many scholars, and they cannot all be right.

Humanity has many versions of how the last days and the end of the age will play out, but God has only one version. I believe that if we are to hear His plan, we must set aside our ideas and pursue His ideas. His plan is as established as the rising of the sun. I had to set aside all I had studied and believed before I could hear His voice directing me through His Word. We must keep an open heart toward anything new He shows us. His plan will no doubt be new and different from anything we have heard before. I believe His direction is new now—new understanding, new revelation, new wisdom—and we have been given a new plan for the last days.

If we try to hold–on to the old ways of thinking, we will miss the new thing God is doing right before our eyes. It is a sad state when we listen only to what fits into our old theological boxes. When the Lord bursts forth with new revelation, we are not to patch it up with our old reasoning, so that it fits into our box. Remember what the Lord said,

No one puts a piece from a new garment on an old one; otherwise the new makes a tear, and also the piece that was taken out of the new does not match the old. And no one puts new wine into old wineskins; or else the new wine will burst the wineskins and be spilled, and the wineskins will be ruined. But new wine must be put into new wineskins, and both are preserved. And no one, having drunk old wine, immediately desires new; for he says, "The old is better." (Luke 5:36–39)

The Lord addresses our tendency to hold on to the old, though He said it was no good. Jesus was speaking of what was before He came, the Old Testament, and what He was establishing that was new, the New Testament. It caught the learned and wise Jewish scholars off guard. We must take notice that it is the Lord's way to do something new.

The Lord is doing a new thing with this book. To see the revelation it presents, you will need to keep an open mind for the new things it reveals, and one may have to let some old things go. As it is written: "Do not remember the former things, nor consider the things of old. Behold, I will do a new thing, now it shall spring forth; shall you not know it?" (Isa. 43:18–19). Every disciple who has been instructed by the Lord is like a householder who brings out of his treasure things both old and new (Matt. 13:52). We may need to let go of some things in our old theology—our old box—to embrace the new. But there are also treasures in the old that will come into a new light. As we begin our journey through this new and powerful revelation of God's Word regarding the last days, let us keep an open heart and listen for God's voice because at times, He will utter things kept secret from the foundation of the world. As you read what is noted in the scripture of truth, He will speak to you because He is no respecter of persons.

The people Jesus ministered to had to give up some of the things they used to believe and live by before they could receive the new thing God was doing. They inevitably desired to hang–on to the old when God was doing something new. We must not make the same mistake: "I have made you hear new things from this time even hidden things, and you did not know them. They are created now and not from the beginning, and before this day you have not heard them" (Isa. 48:6–7). It is the Lord's way to do a new thing—to hide His plan in plain sight only to be revealed at the appointed time. It is His way to reveal something new that before this day we have not heard. It is the Lord's way to appoint a watchman to hear a word from His mouth and see what He is doing in this hour and then declare it to His people.

Jesus explained that the new would not match the old; it was not compatible with the old because it was new. But people tend to hold–on to old things rather than see what God is doing new and run with it. He chooses to reveal His plan to the humble because they are quick to hear, slow to speak, and always teachable. They can accept the fact that God's ways are higher than ours and His thoughts are higher than ours (Isa. 55:8–9). His ways are outside our realm of thinking and understanding; they are outside of our box. He may speak through someone we deem incompetent and stupid to test our hearts to find out if we hear a person or Him. Those who hear a person fail to hear God.

I do not consider myself anything of value, simply an instrument through which God can shine His glory. The following should encourage those led by the Spirit to speak in His name because it has encouraged me to write this though I am least among His people.

Some things in John 9 will help us understand how God speaks through us; these include a perfect example of men who failed to hear God when He spoke to them. Notice how a simple, uneducated man who had been born blind and had received his sight from God through Jesus tried to teach some Pharisees what was obvious to everyone else. But because the man was uneducated and had been born blind, the Pharisees could not receive his teaching though it was full of God's wisdom. The blind man first stated he knew only one thing—that though he was blind, he now sees (John 9:25). He was uneducated and illiterate and the last person in the world through whom anyone would expect to hear God speak.

But the poor man received God's anointing and taught the pompous Pharisees. The Lord Jesus explained this was how God chose to speak: "Do not worry about how or what you should speak. For it will be given to you in that hour what you should speak; for it is not you who speak, but the Spirit of your Father who speaks in you" (Matt. 10:19–20).

Let's see how the formerly blind man answered the Pharisees.

> Then they reviled him and said, "You are His disciple, but we are Moses' disciples. We know that God spoke to Moses; as for this fellow [Jesus], we do not know where He is from." The man answered and said to them, "Why, this is a marvelous thing, that you do not know where He is from; yet He has opened my eyes! Now we know that God does not hear sinners; but if anyone is a worshiper of God and does His will, He hears him. Since the world began it has been unheard of that anyone opened the eyes of one who was born blind. If this Man were not from God, He could do nothing." They answered and said to him, "You were completely born in sins, and are you teaching us?" And they cast him out. (John 9:28–34)

It's funny how they could know God spoke to Moses hundreds of years before but; could not discern when God was speaking right in front of them. The Pharisees were scholars and well educated, but because the wisdom of God came through a simple-minded man who had been born blind, they could not receive it. The Pharisees only heard a person when it was in truth, the Spirit of the Father speaking through him. Jesus taught us that this is how He ministered: "I have not spoken on My own authority; but the Father who sent Me gave Me a command, what I should say and what I should speak" (John 12:49). When we are ministering for God; we are not to speak on our own authority, with our own words; but with whatever the Father gives us in that hour, that we speak.

This is how the Pharisees responded to the wisdom of God, "You were completely born in sins, and are you teaching us?" It is not by human reasoning that we know the voice of God when He speaks through someone but by knowing God, and we know Him through knowing His Word. Therefore, He who knows God hears His voice when it comes through a man; as it is written: "We are of God. He who knows God hears us" (1 John 4:6). He is going to send us messengers speaking His word: "Most assuredly, I say to you, he who receives whomever I send receives Me; and he who receives Me receives Him who sent Me" (John 13:20). It is important that we hear God's voice in these last days no matter whom it comes through. He who knows God knows whom God has sent, and he whom God has sent speaks the words of God.

Jesus said that when He, the Spirit of truth has come, He would teach us all things and bring to our remembrance all that the Word of God said. He is the Spirit of truth, so He will always speak according to what is written in the scripture of truth: "But the Helper, the Holy Spirit, whom the Father will send in My name, He will teach you all things, and bring to your remembrance all things that I said to you" (John 14:26). And again: "When He, the Spirit of truth, has come, He will guide you into all truth; for He will not speak on His own authority, but whatever He hears He will speak; and He will tell you things to come" (John 16:13). Jesus only spoke what He heard from the Father, the Holy Spirit only speaks what He hears from the Father, and that is how His disciples are instructed to speak.

Therefore, if God can speak through a poor blind man who received his sight, He can speak through any of His children who walk not according to the flesh but according to the Spirit. I do not count myself to be anything special, but I know that when one cleanses himself from the old ways, he is a vessel of honor, sanctified and useful for the Master, prepared for whatever God's plan may be. It helps tremendously to be filled with the Spirit, speaking to yourself as well as others in psalms, hymns, and spiritual songs, making melody in your heart to the Lord and communing with the Holy Spirit as we walk in the Spirit.

What we are about to look at in scripture is a great and awesome act of God He has planned for the last days. It is something He has done with His people Israel before and something He speaks in the prophets of doing with them again. He has used Israel before to make Himself known by His mighty hand and His outstretched arm, and He intends to do so again! You are about to see in scripture why things are set up the way they are in the Middle East and what God intends to do for His people Israel in the last days. Many have wondered why Israel is surrounded by enemies who hate and despise them. You will see in scripture how what God did in Egypt thousands of years ago was a type and a foreshadowing of what He is about to do. It is obvious that He is about to do a mighty work again because the children of Israel have been gathered to their land and are surrounded by enemies. The world stage is set for this great show. These are the signs that all things written in the prophets concerning Israel are at hand.

The time has come to fulfill the promises God made to the children of Israel of the coming of the Messiah in a great show of power whereby He will deliver them from their enemies and bring them into the new covenant. All Israel will be saved in this tremendous event we can refer to as God's Grand Finale. This event will set the stage for end-time events and the soon coming of Christ for the resurrection on the last day. When you see all the prophecies from Genesis to Revelation concerning God's grand finale and the time of the end, it becomes clear that the time has been fulfilled and His end time opening show is at hand.

CHAPTER 1

The Voice of Prophecy

Before addressing what the Lord is saying through the prophets concerning the last days, there are some things that need to be understood about prophecy. Prophecy is not fulfilled the way the natural mind thinks it should be. When we look at how prophecy has been fulfilled in the past and how it was received by the people who witnessed it, we get a picture of what to expect.

Our generation is no different from others; there has always been the same striving, arguments, and unbelief among the people when the scriptures are fulfilled before our eyes. When Jesus came the first time, some people could see, understand, and accept what God was doing. But some did not agree and were against what God was doing because they had a different theology, if you will, than what they saw God doing before their eyes.

Remember, Jesus was doing God's will, but who believed His work was from God? Who believed His report? Who believed all that was spoken by the prophets? Seeing miracles does not always cause people to believe. After the people had seen Jesus do many mighty works, they still wondered whether Jesus was the Christ.

> On the last day, that great day of the feast, Jesus stood and cried out, saying, "If anyone thirsts, let him come to Me and drink. He who believes

1

in Me, as the Scripture has said, out of his heart will flow rivers of living water." Therefore, many from the crowd, when they heard this saying, said, "Truly this is the Prophet." Others said, "This is the Christ." But some said, "Will the Christ come out of Galilee? Has not the Scripture said that the Christ comes from the seed of David and from the town of Bethlehem, where David was?" So, there was a division among the people because of Him. (John 7:37–43)

Each of them had a reasonable argument, but God chose what confounded the wisdom of the wise. He reserved a new thing they did not know, and it caused division among them because some perceived in their hearts what God was doing while others could not reason in their minds how these things could be so.

If God were doing something today, would there be a division among God's people? Have people changed? They were looking to the prophet's writings, but did they get it right? Would the Christ come out of Galilee? Has not scripture said that the Christ would come from Bethlehem? As far as they could tell, the scriptures said nothing about Christ coming out of Galilee. Notice what the Pharisee said.

Nicodemus (he who came to Jesus by night, being one of them) said to them, "Does our law judge a man before it hears him and knows what he is doing?" They answered and said to him, "Are you also from Galilee? Search and look, for no prophet has arisen out of Galilee." (John 7:50–52)

No prophet comes out of Galilee, and no one of that day had ever heard anyone say that the Christ could come out of Galilee; it was a new thing God was doing, and it confounded their understanding. It is easy to trust our own understanding rather than believe something we sense in our hearts because that takes faith in what we do not see. Faith is the evidence of things not seen (Heb. 11:1). They were trusting in their own understanding, but Nicodemus trusted what he knew in his heart but could not see in scripture yet. Nicodemus said, "We know You are a teacher come from God, for no one can do these signs that You do unless God is with him" (John 3:2). Nicodemus was a learned and well-educated Pharisee, but he was learning to follow what he sensed in his heart. This is what summed it up for Nicodemus—Jesus taught with wisdom greater than Solomon's and the mighty works He did, some of which had been unheard of since the world began, were all the proof he needed. However these things were not sufficient for the leaders of God's people in that day: For it is written, "Although He had done so many signs before them, they did not believe in Him" (John 12:37).

Matthew 3:6, 15, and 23 confirm that the Messiah would come out of Bethlehem, but He would also come out of Egypt, and He would be called a Nazarene. Nazareth was where Jesus had grown up and it was in Galilee. He was called Jesus of Nazareth. But they said, "No prophet has arisen out of Galilee." The scholars of Israel knew only one of the scriptures that said where the Messiah would come from, and they had figured it was the only place where the Messiah could come from. They were trusting in their own understanding instead of accepting that God might have been doing a new thing that required faith. For, without faith, it is impossible to please God (Heb. 11:6).

God "turns wise men backward and makes their knowledge foolishness" (Isa. 44:25), but he who knows God knows Him whom God has sent. It is a connection of the Spirit and not of the letter; the letter kills but the spirit gives life. Was it not according to the letter that the Pharisees sought to kill the author of life? Yes, they were continually trying to catch Him in His words so they might put Him to death.

To fulfill what was written in the prophets, the Messiah had to come out of Bethlehem. He also had to come out of Egypt, and He would be called a Nazarene, indicating He would also come out of Galilee. They were scholars of God's Word, but it was hidden from them. Jesus tells us why.

> In that hour Jesus rejoiced in the Spirit and said, "I thank You, Father, Lord of heaven and earth, that You have hidden these things from the wise and prudent and revealed them to babes. Even so, Father, for so it seemed good in Your sight." (Luke 10:21)

God's plan was hidden yet revealed. Notice that it was good in the Lord's sight to hide what He was doing from one group and reveal it to another. It is the Lord's way to resist the proud but give grace to the humble. One group will see and know while the other will wonder how these things can be so. It should be a warning to all who consider themselves wise and prudent. As it is written, "Woe to those who are wise in their own eyes, and prudent in their own sight!" (Isa. 5:21). Whatever the Lord does before such is a stone of stumbling and a rock of offence.

Notice how those who were babes responded to His appearing.

> Philip found Nathanael and said to him, "We have found Him of whom Moses in the law, and also the prophets, wrote—Jesus of Nazareth, the son of Joseph." And Nathanael said to him, "Can anything good come out of Nazareth?'" (John 1:45–46)

The disciples did not question whether it was according to scripture that He came out of Nazareth. Nathanael asked whether anything good could come out of Nazareth, but they did not stumble over what could be perceived as a lack of support from scripture. The teachings and miracles Jesus had been doing activated something in the early disciples' spirits that caused them to know something in their hearts that could not be explained satisfactorily with the intellect. Faith is of the heart; the scripture says that it is with the heart one believes to righteousness (Rom. 10:10). The Pharisees, however, stumbled over the fact that Jesus came from Nazareth, and He was an offense to them. They had studied the scriptures daily, but the word they knew did not profit them because it was not mixed with faith (Heb. 4:2). The Messiah did in fact come out of Nazareth whether they received it or whether they refused, and the words of the prophets were fulfilled.

They could not have known that the Messiah would come out of all three of those places without divine revelation. The Lord had kept hidden His divine plan until the time appointed. Even His closest disciples did not understand until afterward that the Messiah would fulfill the words of the prophets by coming out of three different places. Flesh and blood did not reveal to Philip and Nicodemus who Jesus was; the Father in heaven did. And so it is today—God is working His plan right before our eyes, but who has believed our report? To whom has the arm of the Lord been revealed?

We see therefore that prophecy may not be fulfilled the way the natural mind may think it should be: "For prophecy never came by the will of man, but holy men of God spoke as they were moved by the Holy Spirit" (2 Peter 1:21). Prophecy did not come to us by the will of man, and it cannot be understood by human reasoning. Prophecy can be fulfilled in a way that uproots all we have previously thought and reasoned out. Revelation comes not from the mind but the heart, the spirit of man: "The spirit of man is the candle of the Lord" (Ps. 20:27 KJV). God will enlighten us through our spirits. It is up to us to read His Word, meditate on it, and speak His Word so that His Word is alive in us and the Holy Spirit can teach us all things and tell us things to come. The Father desires this relationship with all His children.

We can see now how it was hidden from the Pharisees and why it was hidden from them that Jesus was the Messiah. If we are going to learn from the Lord what He is doing in the last days, we must do what He says. He instructs us to abide in His Word while in fellowship with the Holy Spirit so He can open our eyes to His plan. And to know him whom God has sent, we must know God by abiding in, studying, and practicing His Word: "If you abide in My word, you are My disciples indeed. And you shall know the truth, and the truth shall make you free" (John 8:31–32). When we abide in His Word, the Holy Spirit will teach us the truth of all these things.

> But the anointing which you have received from Him abides in you, and you do not need that anyone teach you; but as the same anointing teaches you concerning all things, and is true, and is not a lie, and just as it has taught you, you will abide in Him. (1 John 2:27)

If we abide in His Word, we abide in Him, for He and His Word are one: "In the beginning was the Word, and the Word was with God, and the Word was God" (John 1:1).

In a world full of deceit, arguments, and lies, we can know the truth by abiding in His Word with the fellowship of the Holy Spirit. Jesus is the Word of God in the Spirit, and He was the Word of God made flesh. So that you may know why there are divisions among God's people as far as the end times are concerned, I will point these things out. God works according to His own plan and according to His own will, and according to His Word. The Messiah came out of three different places to fulfill what was written of Him.

The people of those days did not know very much about the Messiah, and most of what they did know was wrong. Some of it was just hearsay. Remember what some in Jerusalem were saying? "However, we know where this Man is from; but when the Christ comes, no one knows where He is from" (John 7:27). We do not need to know every detail of the last days, but we need a general understanding of what should take place. God will do some things we cannot see in scripture until after they happen because that is how He has worked His plan in times past.

He has given us His Word to know and His Spirit to teach us what that Word says, but He has always kept some things hidden until the time is at hand. If we abide in Him and His Word abides in us, we will know the truth concerning His plan for the end times as it unfolds. Jesus did not explain all things to His disciples at the beginning of His ministry, but as the time approached for Him to be taken up, He began explaining things to them. He will not leave us in the dark in these last days but will explain more as the day approaches. We are not in darkness so that this day should overtake us like a thief. We should exhort one another daily as we see the day approaching. We must abide in His Word because He will speak to us through His Word.

We know we will not know everything; some things will be fulfilled right before our eyes, and we will not know that until after the fact when we look back at it and say, "Wow! That is prophecy fulfilled!" It takes time for us to catch up to God when He is moving. Jesus entered Jerusalem on a donkey, but it wasn't until much later that the disciples realized that what they had done to Him had been written by the prophets about Him.

> Then Jesus, when He had found a young donkey, sat on it; as it is written: "Fear not, daughter of Zion; Behold, your King is coming, sitting on a donkey's colt." His disciples did not understand these things at first; but when Jesus was glorified, then they remembered that these things were written about Him and that they had done these things to Him. (John 12:12–16)

We may see something taking place in our world today, and it is not till later that the scriptures explode with revelation and confirmation. Therefore, it is very important in these last days to walk with God, be in His Word daily, and be very vigilant and watchful concerning things taking place in our world. Walk in the Spirit praying with all manner of prayer in the Spirit, worship God in the Spirit, make melodies in your heart to the Lord, and minister to the Lord. Continually offer the sacrifice of praise, the fruit of our lips giving thanks to His name! Those who worship the Father must worship in spirit and in truth, for the Father seeks such to worship Him (John 4:23–24).

We learn how God fulfills His prophecies when we study how He has fulfilled His Word in the past. He said, "I have declared the former things from the beginning, they went forth from My mouth, and I caused them to hear it. Suddenly I did them, and they came to pass" (Isa. 48:3). In many instances in His Word, He spoke a thing, and then when it came to pass, it was observed and recorded.

> "On that day I will raise up the tabernacle of David, which has fallen down, and repair its damages; I will raise up its ruins, and rebuild it as in the days of old; that they may possess the remnant of Edom, and all the Gentiles who are called by My name," says the LORD who does this thing (Amos 9:11–12)

> And after they had become silent, James answered, saying, "Men and brethren, listen to me: Simon has declared how God at the first visited the Gentiles to take out of them a people for His name. And with this the words of the prophets agree, just as it is written: 'After this I will return and will rebuild the tabernacle of David, which has fallen down; I will rebuild its ruins, and I will set it up; so that the rest of mankind may seek the LORD, even all the Gentiles who are called by My name,' says the LORD who does all these things" (Acts 15:13–17)

Though the wording changed a little, the Spirit and the Word agree. Therefore, it is the Spirit's interpretation of the Word that we observe. According to the Spirit, the remnant of Edom is included in all the Gentiles. This is something to note when reading the prophets Obadiah and Ezekiel 35; they speak of Edom first, but in like manner, they have a greater application to the nations as well.

Another interesting prophetic quote of the prophets is in Acts 13:40–41.

> Beware therefore, lest what has been spoken in the prophets come upon you: "'Behold, you despisers, marvel and perish! For I work a work in your days, a work which you will by no means believe, though one were to declare it to you.'"

This is not an exact quote, but it was spoken as revealed by the Holy Spirit through Paul. The writer of Acts did not say to himself *I know that scripture* and then looked it up and write it the way it was first recorded. No, that would have been the letter, and it would have killed the spirit of what was being said. He recorded it just as it was spoken by the Holy Spirit through Paul. It is ministering by the Spirit of the word. Paul wrote, "God has made us sufficient as ministers of the new covenant, not of the letter but of the Spirit; for the letter kills, but the Spirit gives life" (2 Cor. 3:6). The Spirit of the Word speaks to the spirit of man, not to the natural understanding and reasoning of man.

The apostles did not give chapter and verse when they quoted scripture; we do that for the ignorant and uninformed. But those who know God know His Word and know when someone is speaking by the Spirit the words of Him who sent him. Their hearts are full of His Word so that when a word is spoken, their spirit bears witness with the Holy Spirit that though it is not an exact quote, it is the Spirit of the Word from the Lord. They need not chapter and verse to know a Word that comes from the Lord; by the Spirit, they know

His voice. We cannot resist or grieve the Holy Spirit by demanding that the letter be observed if we want to learn from Him. I say to Him, "Holy Spirit, I have knowledge, but without you, I have nothing." Having knowledge without the Holy Spirit is like owning a library but being illiterate.

Peter was filled with the Holy Spirit and moved by Him to quote the prophet Joel with a few changes, and he quoted more than what actually took place on the day of Pentecost.

> But this is what was spoken by the prophet Joel: "And it shall come to pass in the last days, says God, that I will pour out of My Spirit on all flesh, your sons and your daughters shall prophesy, your young men shall see visions, your old men shall dream dreams. And on My menservants and on My maidservants, I will pour out My Spirit in those days; and they shall prophesy. I will show wonders in heaven above and signs in the earth beneath: blood and fire and vapor of smoke. The sun shall be turned into darkness, and the moon into blood, before the coming of the great and awesome day of the LORD." (Acts 2:16–20)

Joel did not use the words *last days*. Peter, by the Holy Spirit, wrote that it would come to pass in the last days. Are there other prophecies of the last days that do not say so in the original text? Only the Holy Spirit can reveal that, but that is the kind of thing He teaches us. This prophecy was only partially fulfilled on the day of Pentecost. This is not how prophecies are normally quoted by New Testament writers; they quote only the scripture that applied to their times or situations. But here, Peter quoted things from Joel that did not take place on the day of Pentecost. He quoted things that are appointed for the last days but we are still in the last das at this time and these things have not taken place yet. The Holy Spirit was poured out, but it did not really fulfill the words *all flesh*.

Since the day of Pentecost, there has been an outpouring of the Holy Spirit here and there that has taken place with God's people, but these could hardly fulfill the words *all flesh*. The Holy Spirit was and is available to all flesh, but to get the experience, you must in a general sense hear about it and believe it. Notice what Paul said to some disciples: "And finding some disciples he said to them, 'Did you receive the Holy Spirit when you believed?' So they said to him, 'We have not so much as heard whether there is a Holy Spirit'" (Acts 19:2). They were believers, but the Holy Spirit did not come upon them automatically. Paul instructed them and laid hands on them to receive the Holy Spirit: "And when Paul had laid hands on them, the Holy Spirit came upon them, and they spoke with tongues and prophesied. Now the men were about twelve in all" (Acts 19:2–7). Does it sound like the Spirit was poured out on all flesh? No. The first fulfillment was only partial. Therefore, not everything Peter quoted from the prophet Joel on the day of Pentecost came to pass.

As we look at all the prophecies related to our target event, we get a confirmation that a much greater outpouring of His Spirit is coming that will cover all flesh and the earth accompanied by the signs. Notice how Peter quoted the part of Joel that did not come to pass: "I will show wonders in heaven above and signs in the earth beneath, blood and fire and vapor of smoke" (Acts 2:19). This prophecy is appointed for the last days; this is God's prophetic Word. He was saying, "I will show wonders in heaven above and signs in the earth beneath blood and fire and pillars of smoke." It sounds like Micah 7:15–16: "As in the days when you came out of the land of Egypt, I will show them wonders. The nations shall see." The Lord said that He would show wonders to Israel in heaven and on earth and that the nations would see it. While the nations are watching His show, it appears He will pour out His Spirit on all flesh. We will investigate prophecies that confirm such a great and awesome event.

All generations of Christians have wondered when Jesus would come back for His church; this supreme topic in scripture has inspired wonder and awe in believers since Jesus was taken up to heaven. Things we see in our world today are fulfilling prophecies written for us, the generation that will be here in the last days. We are seeing prophecies fulfilled that are signs Jesus is coming. The gathering of the children of Israel to the land of their ancestors is fulfilling prophecies spoken more than 2,500 years ago. Just as God did so many times before, He has given His people prophecies of what is to come but reserving them for an appointed time. The angel said to Daniel about his prophecies, "But you, Daniel, shut up the words, and seal the book until the time of the end" (Dan. 12:4). It is the way God has chosen to do things—His plan: "I have declared the former things from the beginning, they went forth from My mouth, and I caused them to hear it. Suddenly I did them, and they came to pass" (Isa. 48:3). But notice that before these things happen, He has told us of them. Shall we see all the signs of His coming and not know it?

The world today is gravitating toward a society that is a mirror image of what existed before the flood—every thought of humanity was evil. Jesus said it would be compared to the days of Noah when everything changed in one day (Luke 17:26). Through the prophetic Word of God, we can see the fulfillment of many prophecies and know everything could change in a day. But it will not be aside from our knowledge because our Lord has said He would do nothing except what He reveals to His servants, the prophets (Amos 3:7): "See, I have told you all things beforehand" (Mark 13:23). "Now I tell you before it comes, that when it does come to pass, you may believe that I am He" (John 13:19). The Lord has always told His people what was to come whether by messengers, prophets, or signs. He has always spoken to those who were walking with Him and had ears that hear.

The Lord said, "There will be signs"; we will see what lies ahead. The Lord Jesus told the Pharisees, "Hypocrites! You know how to discern the face of the sky, but you cannot discern the signs of the times" (Matt. 16:3). The signs were there, and they could have easily discerned them if they had not ignored the obvious. The Lord has not given us words we cannot read, nor has He given us signs we cannot see. We cannot come up with an excuse that will fool Him. The Lord our God has given us signs that are easy to read of what is to come. He has given some to be teachers to teach us how to read the signs. Once you learn what the scriptures say about the signs all around you, you will scratch your head and ask yourself, *Why didn't I see that before?*

There is an appointed time for everything in God's plan, and He reveals some things at appointed times. Generations before us could not know what we know now because it was not the appointed time. We cannot know some things beforehand because they are not revealed by flesh and blood. These things are revealed at the appointed time by the anointing of the Spirit. Yes, there is an appointed time for everything God is doing: "For at the appointed time the end shall be" (Dan. 8:19).

We will know what God is doing by walking in fellowship with the Spirit of truth. The Spirit searches all things, yes, the deep things of God, and no one knows the things of God except the Spirit of God. We have been given the Spirit of God that we may know what God has freely given us. When we pursue His plan and purpose for us, we agree with Him and He can guide us into all truth and tell us things to come. Let he who has ears hear what the Spirit says to the church.

The Lord is taking us places we have never been before because we are in a time we have never been before; we are in the last of the last days, and our Father wants us to be prepared for what lies ahead. He has a grand finale planned for the end of this age, and we have our part to play. We need to pray that we have strength to stand and not be moved while everything around us is being shaken. Yes, there is coming a great shaking.

> See that you do not refuse Him who speaks. For if
> they did not escape who refused Him who spoke
> on earth, much more shall we not escape if we

> turn away from Him who speaks from heaven,
> whose voice then shook the earth; but now He has
> promised, saying, "Yet once more I shake not only
> the earth, but also heaven." Now this, "Yet once
> more," indicates the removal of those things that
> are being shaken, as of things that are made, that
> the things which cannot be shaken may remain.
> (Heb. 12:25–27)

If we are going to be the people of God who cannot be shaken in these last days, we need to be doers of the Word, not hearers only. We will go through some things, so the scriptures may be fulfilled. To remain unshaken, we have to be filled with the Spirit and engaged in fellowship with Him worshiping God in the Spirit because the Father is seeking such. When we know and understand His plan, we can enter true worship. It is extremely powerful when we in one accord worship the Father in Spirit and truth.

When Jesus said, "See, I have told you all things beforehand" (Mark 13:23), He was teaching us that we would know all things pertaining to His plan. Knowing what God is doing does not come by the will of man or the will of the flesh but by the will of God. The Spirit bears witness to these things because the Word and the Spirit agree. Jesus is our example and teacher: "For I have not spoken on My own authority; but the Father who sent Me gave Me a command, what I should say and what I should speak" (John 12:49). Jesus spoke the words of the Father, and that is what He instructed us to speak. Peter instructs us to speak as ambassadors for God.

> If anyone speaks, let him speak as the oracles of
> God. If anyone ministers, let him do it as with the
> ability which God supplies, that in all things God
> may be glorified through Jesus Christ, to whom
> belong the glory and the dominion forever and ever.
> Amen. (1 Peter 4:11)

When the Spirit says; *if anyone speaks, let him speak as the oracles of God*, they must speak what the Father has given them for that hour. Jesus only spoke what the Father said, therefore, when we speak only what the Father says, we are the oracles of God. It is a life in the Spirit, walking in the Spirit, speaking in the Spirit, singing in the Spirit, praying in the Spirit, rejoicing in the Spirit, preparing for the day we step out of the body and into the Spirit.

Jesus's words were not popular among some of the people, and we may not be popular among some people if we speak His words. But the scripture says that blessed are those who suffer persecution for His name's sake because the Spirit of glory and of God rests on them. Those who are doers of His Word and not just hearers will know whether I speak on my own authority or speak the words of Him who sent me. Notice what the Lord says.

> If anyone wills to do His will, he shall know concerning the doctrine, whether it is from God or whether I speak on My own authority. He who speaks from himself seeks his own glory; but He who seeks the glory of the One who sent Him is true, and no unrighteousness is in Him. (John 7:17–18)

He who speaks from himself seeks his own glory. Many have spoken from themselves concerning the end times, but it has been revealed that they were seeking their own glory because the Lord was not in it. Jesus said that if anyone willed to do His will, he would know concerning the doctrine whether it was from God or man. Thus, those who do not will to do His will would not know His doctrine. We cannot know His plan unless we accept His will.

It is the plan and will of God that all His children be conformed into the image of His Son: "For whom He foreknew, He also predestined to be conformed to the image of His Son" (Rom. 8:29).

To be conformed into the image of His Son, we must think, do, and say all His Son did.

> Therefore, Let this mind be in you which was also in Christ Jesus, who, being in the form of God, did not consider it robbery to be equal with God, but made Himself of no reputation, taking the form of a bondservant, and coming in the likeness of men. And being found in appearance as a man, He humbled Himself and became obedient to the point of death, even the death of the cross. Therefore, God also has highly exalted Him. (Phil. 2:5–9)

Paul was saying we should be followers and imitators of Christ. We must exercise the power of our will to do so. It takes a lot of effort on our part to have the mind of Christ. He did not set His mind on earthly things but on heavenly things and emptied Himself of all His privileges as the Son of God. The hardest part is becoming obedient to the point of death, but that is the mind of Christ, and we have been called to this.

Paul instructed us in many places to be followers of Christ, but most Christians do not really know what that means. Just as He set His mind on doing the will of the Father even when it meant obedience to death, all His followers were instructed to have the same mind. Paul instructed us how this could be done.

> If then you were raised with Christ, seek those things which are above, where Christ is sitting at the right hand of God. Set your mind on things above, not on things on the earth. For you died, and your life is hidden with Christ in God. When Christ who is our life appears, then you also will appear with Him in glory. (Col. 3:1–4)

Peter gave instructions on what to do with our mind as well.

> Therefore, since Christ suffered for us in the flesh, arm yourselves also with the same mind, for he who has suffered in the flesh has ceased from sin, that he no longer should live the rest of his time in the flesh for the lusts of men, but for the will of God. (1 Peter 4:1–3)

That brings a whole new understanding to the words of Jesus, "Whoever wills to do His will …." The Word says that if we will to do His will, we must do something with our minds: "Let this mind be in you which was also in Christ Jesus." "Set your mind on things of above." "Arm yourselves also with the same mind." What we do with our minds will have the greatest impact on whether we fulfill the plan of God for our lives. What should we do with the rest of our time in the flesh but do the will of God. When we will to do His will, we will know His doctrine and any false or corrupt doctrine as well.

Let us accept the whole counsel of God and give Him glory. Let us will to do His will so we may know His plan for the end times as revealed in scripture. Let us run with whatever His Word says concerning the last days; let us run with patience the race that is set before us. We are surrounded by a great cloud of witnesses in the heavenly grandstands. They have finished their race and are now cheering us on in ours. They cheer every time they see us receive the Word of God in our hearts and every time we purpose in our hearts to do His will. They cheer whenever they see us choose God's will before our own, and they are cheering all the time.

A body of believers is rising during these last days with the full armor of God and a two-edged sword in their mouths ready to stand and not be shaken by anything they see going on around them. Yes, some will do great exploits by the power of the Spirit and the angels of God, but there will also follow great persecution. However, the

Lord has told us to be of good cheer because it would not be long till we enter our bridal chambers and the door would be shut, while the wrath of God is being poured out on the earth. Yes, God's people will be feasting at the wedding supper of the Lamb while the wicked are being rewarded according to their own works. Lift up your head and rejoice giving glory to God because your redemption draws near. Give all glory and all honor to Him who sits on the throne and to the Lamb forever and ever, amen.

CHAPTER 2

The Last Day

Because our study encompasses many prophecies and events that will take place in the last days, it is very important that we know what the Word of God means by the phrase *last days*. We are in the last of the last days, so it is time we understand what is written in the Word of God about these times. The Word of God teaches that the church will be here on earth until the last day. Therefore, events that are to take place in the last days are things that will come to pass while the church is still on earth.

The Lord has given us last-day prophecies for a reason; there is something to be unlocked in their meaning that will direct us. Last-day prophecies are very closely related to prophecies that speak of the time of the end and the end of the age. We will look at many scriptures that teach us how to recognize when prophecies are speaking about the days in which we live, and these prophecies— God's plan for the last days—will become obvious.

First, let's look at some definitions to understand clearly our subject. The word *last* means following all the rest, the final, the end. *Latter* means more recent, final. Scripture references to the last or latter days are pointing to a day that follows all the rest, the final day. The days that precede the last day are the latter or last days. Many scriptures tell us something about the last days—what they will be like, what people will be like, and events that will take place. These will happen before Jesus comes; the church will be here for them.

Sometimes, the full understanding of a prophecy is hidden until the time calls for it. Peter quoted the prophet Joel on the day of Pentecost, but the wording was changed a little. Joel said, "It shall come to pass afterward" (Joel 2:28), but Peter said after being filled with the Holy Spirit, "And it shall come to pass in the last days, says God" (Acts 2:17). Joel did not use the words *last days*, but he described events that were to take place in the last days. I have to wonder if there could be other prophecies for the last days that are not labeled last days as was this prophecy in Joel. God has a way of hiding things from us until the appointed time. It is His manner of doing things, and it must be considered when studying His Word. The content of a prophecy may tell us more about its appointed time than what the prophets of old may have said.

The whole dispensation we are in right now is called by the New Testament writers or we could say by God the last days; it is a two-thousand-year dispensation that is about to end. Therefore, there is of necessity a last day of this dispensation. The first step to understanding last-day events is knowing what the scriptures say about the last day. Once a good foundation is laid by studying the last day, we can move on to what scriptures teach are last-day events. When we understand events that will happen in the last days, a vision emerges of a grand and awesome work of God that other prophecies do not call last days, but the content is associated by character and nature and will be viewed in a new light.

Jesus began teaching His disciples about the last day in John 6:39–40, 44, and 54.

> This is the will of the Father who sent Me, that of all He has given Me I should lose nothing but should raise it up at the last day. And this is the will of Him who sent Me, that everyone who sees the Son and

believes in Him may have everlasting life; and I will raise him up at the last day.

No one can come to Me unless the Father who sent Me draws him; and I will raise him up at the last day.

Whoever eats My flesh and drinks My blood has eternal life, and I will raise him up at the last day.

Four times in this chapter, Jesus said, "I will raise him up at the last day"; He was making a point. These four scriptures are sufficient to establish that the resurrection will take place on the last day of this age. But we are given even more understanding through the heart of Martha.

Notice at the tomb of Lazarus in John 11:23–26 the words Jesus spoke to Martha about the resurrection of her brother Lazarus and her reply: "Jesus said to her, 'Your brother will rise again.' Martha said to Him, 'I know that he will rise again in the resurrection at the last day.'" Martha had heard Jesus teach in her home while she prepared things and served Him; she had obviously heard Jesus teach about the resurrection on the last day, and His words had sunk deep into her heart. When Jesus said, "Your brother will rise again," she answered from the treasured words of Jesus she had hidden in her heart with a summary of what Jesus had taught in her home. Her perceived understanding was that the resurrection will be on what Jesus refers to as the last day of this age. It began with Jesus's resurrection and will end when He comes again for the resurrection of all the dead on the last day.

Jesus completed His teaching on the last day in John 12:48: "He who rejects Me, and does not receive My words, has that which judges him—the word that I have spoken will judge him in the last day." The last day will see the coming of the Lord Jesus and the rapture of the church but it will also usher in the judgment.

Notice how the Lord Jesus tied the resurrection and the judgment together in the next two verses: "The men of Nineveh will rise up in the judgment with this generation and condemn it … The queen of the South will rise up in the judgment with this generation and condemn it" (Matt. 12:41–42).

The generations in these two passages are hundreds of years apart, but they will rise together at the resurrection. The resurrection appears to be immediately followed by the judgment. The first act of judgment on that day is deciding who will be taken and who will be left; the Lord said, "I tell you, on that night two people will be in one bed; one will be taken and the other left. Two women will be grinding grain together; one will be taken and the other left" (Luke 17:34–35 NIV).

Jesus tells us that the resurrection will be on the last day, and He also indicates in more than one place that it will be followed by the judgment.

> Do not marvel at this; for the hour is coming in which all who are in the graves will hear His voice and come forth—those who have done good, to the resurrection of life, and those who have done evil, to the resurrection of condemnation. (John 5:28–30)

The Greek word translated *condemnation* here is used five times in this chapter and is translated "judge or judgment" in the other four. The flow of meaning with the rest of what Jesus taught about the day of judgment would better serve this passage if it were translated as "judgment." The Amplified translation accurately reads, "Those who have done evil will be raised for judgment." On that day, the bodies of everyone who has lived from Adam and Eve till this day will come forth. All who are in their graves will come forth. Paul said it would be a resurrection of the just and the unjust: "I have hope in God, which they themselves also accept, that there will be a resurrection of the dead, both of the just and the unjust" (Acts 24:15–16). We can conclude that the just will be resurrected to enter life while the unjust will be resurrected for judgment.

Paul indicated that the resurrection would take place when Jesus came.

> But I do not want you to be ignorant, brethren, concerning those who have fallen asleep, lest you sorrow as others who have no hope. For if we believe that Jesus died and rose again, even so God will bring with Him those who sleep in Jesus. For this we say to you by the word of the Lord, that we who are alive and remain until the coming of the Lord will by no means precede those who are asleep. For the Lord Himself will descend from heaven with a shout, with the voice of an archangel, and with the trumpet of God. And the dead in Christ will rise first. Then we who are alive and remain shall be caught up together with them in the clouds to meet the Lord in the air. And thus, we shall always be with the Lord. Therefore comfort one another with these words. (1 Thess. 4:13–18)

This passage is where we get the rapture from. It explains how the resurrection will go; God will bring with Him those who sleep in Jesus. The Lord will descend from heaven with a shout and with the voice of an archangel to deliver His people from the wrath that is to come. The dead in Christ will be raised first, and then those who are alive on earth at that time will be caught up together with them in the clouds to meet the Lord in the air.

Paul was addressing those who were in Christ in this passage, but when the dead are raised, it will be all who are in their graves— the just and the unjust alike. Paul informed us that the resurrection would be the first thing to take place; the dead in Christ would rise, and then those who were alive would be caught up with them to meet the Lord in the air.

We need to pause at this point and take a little side journey so that we can understand this term *fallen asleep*. In scripture, God often referred to the dead as those who have fallen asleep. To Him, our bodies are only asleep when they are buried because He has the power to wake them up. At the voice of His Word, they will come forth. Isaiah also spoke of the resurrection: "Your dead shall live; together with my dead body they shall arise. Awake and sing, you who dwell in dust; for your dew is like the dew of herbs, and the earth shall cast out the dead" (Isa. 26:19). Daniel used similar words referring to the resurrection: "And many of those who sleep in the dust of the earth shall awake, some to everlasting life, some to shame and everlasting contempt" (Dan. 12:2). In the Old Testament, God used the word *sleep* to refer to the dead and the word *awake* to refer to the resurrection of the dead.

In the New Testament, Jesus also used these words when referring to the dead and the resurrection. His disciples did not catch on to what He was saying until He explained it to them. When He used the word *sleep* to refer to the dead, His disciples did not understand what He was saying. Jesus tried to engage them in the prophetic language of scripture, but it went right over their heads. Jesus said concerning Lazarus,

> "Our friend Lazarus sleeps, but I go that I may wake him up." Then His disciples said, "Lord, if he sleeps he will get well." However, Jesus spoke of his death, but they thought that He was speaking about taking rest in sleep. Then Jesus said to them plainly, "Lazarus is dead." (John 11:11–14)

Jesus was using the prophetic language of scripture; He was using a term used by prophets and angels in the Old Testament to refer to Lazarus's death, but the disciples did not get it. He had to speak to them plainly in earthly terms for them to understand what He was saying. When Jesus said, "Our friend Lazarus sleeps, but I go that I may wake him up," the prophetic language meant that Lazarus was dead but that He would go to raise him from the dead. The Lord our God does not see or speak the way we do. He does not see death the way we do. When people die, they go to heaven and are greeted by a host of heavenly beings who are excited and filled with joy to see them. They don't see the death of the natural body here on earth the way we do. The Lord does not see the death of the physical body the way we do because He has the power to wake them up or call them forth from the dead if He so chooses. When people die, it is not the end of life, and whether we believe it or not, it is the truth.

Now we can understand more clearly what Paul was saying when he explained how the resurrection will take place in 1 Thessalonians 4.

> I do not want you to be ignorant, brethren, concerning those who have fallen asleep, lest you sorrow as others who have no hope. For if we believe that Jesus died and rose again, even so God will bring with Him those who sleep in Jesus.

Remember that Paul said, "This we say to you by the word of the Lord," these things came to him by revelation, it is a word that came from God how these things shall take place. It was not Paul's opinion, it was not what he concluded through much study, it was not persuasive words of human wisdom, it was divine revelation that had been kept secret from the foundation of the world, that God revealed to him.

Therefore, when Paul says, "God will bring with Him those who sleep in Jesus," he is saying that the spirits of those who have died and gone to be with the Lord will be coming with Him in that day. Their physical bodies are dead and in the dust of the earth: "For dust you are, and to dust you shall return" (Gen. 3:19). But their spirits are alive and with God. As Paul says in another place, "We are confident, yes, well pleased rather to be absent from the body and to be present with the Lord" (2 Cor. 5:8). The spirits of all His saints who are absent from the body, because it is dead and buried in the ground, are with the Lord and will be coming with Him! Family members, loved ones, all of them!

It is not until we are absent from the body that we will truly know what eternal life is. You will not know the person you truly are until you enter eternal life. We are eternal living spirits just as is God our Father. A great multitude of saints, a great cloud of witnesses, all those who are dead in Christ will be coming with Him to receive their new, resurrected, immortal bodies. Remember what Paul said about the resurrection in his letter to the Corinthians?

> Behold, I tell you a mystery: We shall not all sleep, but we shall all be changed—in a moment, in the twinkling of an eye, at the last trumpet. For the trumpet will sound, and the dead will be raised incorruptible, and we shall be changed. For this corruptible must put on incorruption, and this mortal must put on immortality. (1 Cor. 15:51–54)

In the twinkling of and eye. It will be in a flash, as when lightning flashes from one end of heaven to the other! That moment will come as a surprise to all those on the earth who do not know God. Jesus said, "For as the lightning comes from the east and flashes to the west, so also will the coming of the Son of Man be" (Matt. 24:27).

Those who are alive on earth will be mortals one second and immortals the next. Those whose bodies are buried in the earth will witness the resurrection of their bodies as it puts on incorruption and immortality. The earth shall cast out the dead because it no longer has a hold on them. The spirits of just men made perfect, as it says in

Hebrews 12:22–23, who come with Christ will be united with their new bodies. Then they will be caught up together with those who are alive on earth at that time to be with the Lord forever. What an awesome event God has revealed to us! The end of this age of death and the grave is coming!

When the church is taken out of the earth, the day of judgment will begin. Jesus said in John 5 that the hour was coming when all who were in the graves would hear His voice and come forth. Those who have done good will be resurrected to eternal life, and those who have done evil will be resurrected to enter the judgment. It appears that the resurrection of the unjust will be followed by judgment as quickly as the resurrection of the righteous will be followed by the rapture. A paraphrased translation of Isaiah 61:2 reads, "He has sent me to tell those who mourn that the time of the LORD's favor has come, and with it, the day of God's anger against their enemies." This agrees with what Isaiah says in another place as well. Notice how Isaiah 26 describes the resurrection and the hiding of God's people while the day of judgment and wrath is accomplished.

> Your dead shall live; Together with my dead body they shall arise. Awake and sing, you who dwell in dust; For your dew is like the dew of herbs, and the earth shall cast out the dead. Come, My people, enter your chambers, and shut your doors behind you; Hide yourself, as it were, for a little moment, until the indignation is past. For behold, the LORD comes out of His place to punish the inhabitants of the earth for their iniquity. (Isa. 26:19–21)

The earth casts out the dead; that's the resurrection. Then, His people enter their bridal chambers and shut the doors behind them while the Lord in His indignation punishes the world for its iniquity. The Day of Judgment follows the resurrection and rapture. In Isaiah 35:4, we find similar words: "Behold, your God will come with vengeance, with the recompense of God; He will come and save you." In 2 Thessalonians, we read,

> Since it is a righteous thing with God to repay with tribulation those who trouble you, and to give you who are troubled rest with us when the Lord Jesus is revealed from heaven with His mighty angels, in flaming fire taking vengeance on those who do not know God, and on those who do not obey the gospel of our Lord Jesus Christ. (2 Thess. 1:6–8)

God is going to give His people rest in their safe chambers while He deals with the wicked on His terms. It becomes obvious that: as soon as the Lord removes His people from the earth the Day of Judgment begins. Woe, woe, woe to the inhabitants of the earth! Peter in his epistle agrees that deliverance for the righteous comes at the same time as judgment for the wicked.

> Later, he turned the cities of Sodom and Gomorrah into heaps of ashes and swept them off the face of the earth. He made them an example of what will happen to ungodly people. But at the same time, God rescued Lot out of Sodom because he was a good man who was sick of all the immorality and wickedness around him. (2 Peter 2:6–7 NLT)

These scriptures make it clear that when Jesus comes to deliver His people from their troubles, or tribulation, the day of judgment has come and those who are left behind will enter it: "For He is coming, for He is coming to judge the earth. He shall judge the world with righteousness and the peoples with His truth" (Ps. 96:13).

God's people are delivered from wrath through Jesus having their conscience purged from guilt. Having been washed in the blood of the Lamb, they shall stand without fault and blameless on that day: "Much more then, having now been justified by His blood, we shall be saved from wrath through Him" (Rom. 5:9). "And to wait for His Son from heaven, whom He raised from the dead, even Jesus who delivers us from the wrath to come" (1 Thess. 1:10).

The church is delivered from the wrath to come and shall not come into judgment: "Most assuredly, I say to you, he who hears My word and believes in Him who sent Me has everlasting life and shall not come into judgment" (John 5:24). The day of wrath and judgment will follow the last day. Those left behind are those who have not been delivered from the wrath to come and are deserving of God's judgment of punishment.

Paul informed us in Romans 2 that the day of wrath and revelation of the righteous judgment of God will be a rendering to each one according to his or her works: "Indignation and wrath, tribulation and anguish on every soul of man who does evil." It is a rendering to all who do evil according to their deeds, works, and ways. That is justice equal to that which we seek in our own courts of law. We do not execute undo punishment and neither does God. He judges according to each ones own deeds and so do we.

In Daniel and the teachings of Jesus in Matthew 24, Mark 13, and Luke 21, events are explained that should take place in the last days and the time of the end. These passages do not address the day of wrath and judgment. It is a time of the Devil's wrath, not God's. However, in Revelation, the day of wrath and judgment of God is explained in great detail: "For the great day of His wrath has come" (Revelation 6:17). "Fear God and give glory to Him, for the hour of His judgment has come" (Revelation 14:7).

Therefore, the last day of this age is the last day that the church will be on earth. It will be a time of trouble like no other, but it is clearly a time they will never see again. It is the last day of trouble and tribulation the church will ever know. Yes, God's people will have to endure a time of great tribulation and trouble like there has never been before, but they will never have to endure such a time again, because they will be removed from the earth.

It will be a time of great trouble, but it will be a time of great glory as well! When Stephen gazed into heaven he saw the glory of God and Jesus standing at His right hand (Acts 7:55–56). After the stoning of Stephen, it says, "At that time a great persecution arose against the church which is at Jerusalem" (Acts 8:1). There is coming a time of great glory for God's people, but it will follow afterwards that great persecution or *tribulation* will arise against them. Daniel says, "The people who know their God shall be strong and carry out great exploits" (Dan 11:32). Because of the glory of God, the church will see a time of persecution like they have never seen before but be of good cheer; there will never come a time like it again.

Just as when Jesus came the first time, everything timewise had been dated as either before or after His coming; so also everything concerning end-time prophecies can be dated as either before or after the last day. God's judgment and wrath are to follow the last day, but while we are in the world, we will have tribulation. "These things I have spoken to you, that in Me you may have peace. In the world you will have tribulation; but be of good cheer, I have overcome the world" (John 16:33). Be of good cheer and let the joy of the Lord be your strength! If the devil cannot kill your joy, he cannot steal your strength.

The Lord is coming for a glorious church without spot or blemish; He will clothe His bride with beautiful white garments that we may attend the wedding supper of the Lamb. When she comes out of her chambers, she will be rejoicing with joy unspeakable and full of glory. The banqueting tables will be set for the wedding supper, and angels will minister to His bride. We will sit at the banqueting tables before the heavenly city, the New Jerusalem, which comes down out of heaven from God. It will be a time of great rejoicing and worshiping our Lord Jesus because the power of death has been destroyed forever.

Another term scripture uses to refer to the last of the last days is *the time of the end*. According to scripture, there is coming and end of this age. As far back as Daniel, the Lord began to reveal that there was an end to this age. Notice what the angel said to Daniel concerning the vision He had shown him: "Understand, son of man that the vision refers to the time of the end" (Dan. 8:17). The vision tells us things that will happen at the time of the end. The time of the end refers to the last of the last days. Some of the things that will occur in the latter days will happen at the time of the end. Daniel 10–12 covers Daniel's encounter with an angel, who explained the reason for his visit: "Now I have come to make you understand what will happen to your people in the latter days, for the vision refers to many days yet to come" (Dan. 10:14). He said, "many days yet to come," and we know there is coming a last day. The angel was revealing what would happen in the latter days or at the time of the end. Daniel received details about the time of the end: "The end will still be at the appointed time" (Dan. 11:27). "And some of those of understanding shall fall, to refine them, purify them, and make them white, until the time of the end; because it is still for the appointed time" (Dan. 11:35). There is an anticipation of what is coming, the time appointed in which the end shall be.

The angel assured Daniel that the end is not yet; there are still some things that are to come first. Similar words are found in Daniel 8:19: "For at the appointed time the end shall be." When the appointed time for the end has finally arrived, the angel says, "At the time of the end ..." and describes a time of trouble. Events in this passage will take place at the time of the end just before the resurrection on the last day. The events Daniel described culminate with the resurrection indicating the last day: "And many of those who sleep in the dust of the earth shall awake" (Dan. 12:2). Jesus said all those who sleep in the dust of the earth shall hear His voice and come forth or awake (John 5:28–29). This is talking about the last day or the end of days. We know the angel was not speaking to Daniel about the time of God's judgment and wrath in this visit because neither the time nor the description agree with what is said about the great and terrible day of the Lord's wrath. Neither Daniel nor Jesus addressed the day of judgment or God's wrath in their end-time prophecies. The time of trouble Daniel spoke of is what Jesus called a time of tribulation and persecution.

Daniel 12:1–2 describes what shall take place at the time of the end as seen from a place in the Spirit.

> At that time Michael shall stand up, the great prince who stands watch over the sons of your people; and there shall be a time of trouble, such as never was since there was a nation, even to that time. And at that time your people shall be delivered, everyone who is found written in the book. And many of those who sleep in the dust of the earth shall awake, some to everlasting life, some to shame and everlasting contempt.

It is a time when nation will rise against nation in the natural realm and kingdom against kingdom in the spirit realm. It is a time of trouble and tribulation, persecution and distress like there has never been before, and at that time, God's people will be delivered. We see a time of trouble or tribulation followed by the resurrection and deliverance of God's people in the same order as Jesus explained in Matthew 24. These things in Daniel 11–12 appear to be describing events that take place just before the last day when the resurrection takes place.

Then finally, the end that scriptures allude to in so many places is revealed to Daniel: "But you, (Daniel) go your way till the end; for you shall rest, and will arise to your inheritance at *the end of the days*" (Dan. 12:13). The angel told Daniel that he would die and be buried for many years after which he would rise or be resurrected to receive his inheritance at the end of days. We already know the resurrection is on the last day, the end of a long procession of days that has covered many generations from the beginning. It all comes together here in Daniel, where we see that many who sleep in the dust of the earth shall awake or rise at the end of days. Daniel agrees that the resurrection is on the last day.

What Jesus taught about the time of the end gives us a little more insight about what will take place at the time of the end; see Matthew 24, Mark 13, and Luke 21. The information we are given is drawn out of the Lord by the disciples asking Him some questions. It Matthew, the disciples showed Jesus the beautiful stones of the temple. Jesus said, "Do you not see all these things? Assuredly, I say to you, not one stone shall be left here upon another, that shall not be thrown down" (Matt. 24:2). They must have marveled at His answer, because they came to Him privately and asked, "Tell us, when will these things be? And what will be the sign of Your coming, and of the end of the age?" (Matt. 24:3).

The destruction of the temple does not concern us but the disciples and the Jews who would be in Jerusalem when the temple would be destroyed. The question: What will be the sign of Your coming and of the end of the age, does concern us. Because Jesus answered all in one discourse, His answers are not separated very well. He answers partly about the destruction of the temple that was coming and partly about the end of the age. We know His coming signifies the end of the age, so what may appear to be two questions: What will be the sign of Your coming? And what will be the sign of the end of the age? May in fact be one question that could be worded like this: What will be the sign of Your coming at the end of the age?

The latter question was based on what they had heard Jesus teach about His coming at the end of the age. In the parable of the tares and the wheat, Jesus said, "So it will be at the end of this age. The Son of Man will send out His angels, and they will gather out of His kingdom all things that offend and those who practice lawlessness" (Matt. 13:40–41). In this parable, the angels are the reapers who are gathering the wicked. Then in Matthew 24 Jesus also says that the angels are the reapers who would gather together His elect. Jesus says the harvest would be at the end of the age and the angels would be the reapers in two places. (Matt. 13:39

and Matt. 24) Notice what Jesus said here about His coming at the end of the age.

> They will see the Son of Man coming on the clouds of heaven with power and great glory. And He will send His angels with a great sound of a trumpet, and they will gather together His elect from the four winds, from one end of heaven to the other. (Matt. 24:30–31)

In Matthew 13 Jesus is speaking to the multitudes and describes His coming to gather the wicked and send them into the judgment. In Matthew 24 He is speaking privately about His coming to His disciples, therefore, this view is about His gathering the elect. When He comes at the end of the age, He will send His angels to gather the wicked and the elect and send them each to their reward. We have already seen that a trumpet will signal the resurrection of the dead, of both the just and the unjust, and in this passage Jesus says He will send His angels with a great sound of a trumpet. Paul said the dead would be raised incorruptible (1 Cor. 15:52), and again, it is with the sound of a trumpet that the dead in Christ would rise. (1 Thess. 4:16) And remember what Jesus said,

> The time is coming when all those who are in the tombs shall hear His voice, and they shall come out—those who have practiced doing good [will come out] to the resurrection of [new] life, and those who have done evil will be raised for judgment [raised to meet their sentence]. (John 5:28–29 AMP)

Jesus's coming, and the resurrection are at the end of the age and will take place on the last day. According to scripture, the day of judgment and wrath will immediately follow the departure of God's people.

Therefore, we see that in Jesus's end-time discourse, some of what He said pertained to the destruction of the temple, while some refers to His coming at the end of the age. In Jesus's end-time discourse in Luke 21, He addressed more acutely the destruction of Jerusalem. Some of what He wrote was not for us but for those who saw the destruction of the temple in AD 70.

> Then let those who are in Judea flee to the mountains, let those who are in the midst of her depart, and let not those who are in the country enter her. For these are the days of vengeance, that all things which are written may be fulfilled. But woe to those who are pregnant and to those who are nursing babies in those days! For there will be great distress in the land and wrath upon this people. (Luke 21:21–23)

It was God's day of vengeance and wrath on His people, Israel, for putting His Messiah to death. Some of the wording in this passage refers to the time of the destruction of the temple that the disciples had asked about and can also be found in Matthew.

> Then let those who are in Judea flee to the mountains. Let him who is on the housetop not go down to take anything out of his house. And let him who is in the field not go back to get his clothes. But woe to those who are pregnant and to those who are nursing babies in those days! And pray that your flight may not be in winter or on the Sabbath. (Matt. 24:16–20)

He is addressing their question about the destruction of the temple in AD 70. You can see the similarities between the two passages, but in Luke, His answer is more clearly made. Luke ends with the words; there will be wrath upon this people. While Matthew ends with; pray that your flight is not in the winter or on a Sabbath. Both are referring to the Jews. If they fled on a Sabbath the Jews would stone them, if they did not flee the Romans would kill them.

Some of the words can refer to both events, like: "Let him who is on the housetop not go down to take anything out of his house. And let him who is in the field not go back to get his clothes." When Jesus speaks of His coming in Luke 17 He uses similar words: "Even so will it be in the day when the Son of Man is revealed. "In that day, he who is on the housetop, and his goods are in the house, let him not come down to take them away. And likewise, the one who is in the field, let him not turn back. Remember Lot's wife" (Luke 17:30-32). When the angel of the Lord led Lot and his family out of Sodom; so they would not be destroyed with the city, they were told not to look back; but Lot's wife didn't listen. She looked back and was turned into a pillar of salt. (Gen. 19:17-26) Some will not take heed to the warnings the Lord gives them. "Remember Lot's wife," is a warning.

However, when Jesus answered the question concerning the sign of His coming at the end of the age we see similar words to what we read in Daniel; they both have the same anticipation of the end. Daniel described wars one after the other in 11:21–44 and said the end was still for the time appointed. Jesus said, "And you will hear of wars and rumors of wars. See that you are not troubled; for all these things must come to pass, but the end is not yet" (Matt. 24:6). Jesus described the same anticipation of the end that we see in Daniel. The end of the age is the goal of what both Jesus and Daniel are teaching us in these passages. The end they both spoke of was the last day or the end of days, the day of the resurrection and rapture.

Notice what the angel said in Daniel as his prophecy reached its end.

> And at that time your people shall be delivered, everyone who is found written in the book. And

many of those who sleep in the dust of the earth
shall awake, some to everlasting life, some to shame
and everlasting contempt. (Dan. 12:1–2)

It is a day when God's people are delivered from the wrath
of God that is about to come upon an evil and wicked world.
"Those who sleep in the dust of the earth shall awake" refers to
the resurrection. God's people are delivered from this world in the
rapture and translated into the glorious kingdom of His dear Son.
They will be taken up into the great cloud of glory Jesus comes on.

Jesus spoke to His disciples after His resurrection and: "While
they watched, He was taken up, and a cloud received Him out of
their sight" (Acts 1:9); that great cloud of witnesses that is mentioned
in Hebrews 12:1 received Him. In Hebrews 11 many of the great
saints that have gone before us are acknowledged and referred to in
the following chapter: "Therefore we also, since we are surrounded
by so great a cloud of witnesses." All the saints that have gone before
us are in that great cloud of glory. When we die we are caught up
into that cloud, it is the glory of God's presence. When Moses
and Elijah appeared to Jesus and the disciples on the Mount of
Transfiguration, a bright cloud overshadowed them, and God spoke
from the cloud (Matt. 17:5).

God's people will be raised up into the clouds of glory to be
with the Lord forever: "They will see the Son of Man coming on
the clouds of heaven with power and great glory" (Matt. 24:30). The
Lord will bring with Him those who sleep in Jesus (1 Thess. 4:14),
they are that great cloud of witnesses (Heb. 12:1). Clouds in scripture
refer to the glory God's presence.

> And it came to pass, when the priests came out of the
> holy place, that the cloud filled the house of the LORD,
> so that the priests could not continue ministering
> because of the cloud; for the glory of the LORD filled
> the house of the LORD. (1 Kings 8:10–11)

Jesus is coming on the clouds of heaven with power and great glory to raise us up to be with Him and all our loved ones in the glory! Glory to God!

Daniel was instructed to seal these things up for a time appointed: "But you, Daniel, shut up the words, and seal the book until the time of the end; many shall run to and fro, and knowledge shall increase" (Dan. 12:4). This means that understanding of the vision would not come to God's people until the time of the end. Other translations of this passage describe days not unlike the days in which we live.

> But you, O Daniel, shut up the words and seal the Book until the time of the end. [Then] *many shall run to and fro and search anxiously* [through the Book], and knowledge [of God's purposes as revealed by His prophets] shall be increased and become great. (Dan. 12:4 AMP)

> But Daniel, keep this prophecy a secret; seal it up so that it will not be understood until the end times, when *travel and education shall be vastly increased.* (Dan. 12:4 TLB)

These translations give us some amazing signs of the time of the end: Many shall run to and fro; some travel great distances going back and forth every day, commute, it is like no other time in history. Travel shall be vastly increased; never before have so many people, up to 600, been able to get on an airplane and fly nearly halfway around the world in less than a day. Travel has increased tremendously. Many are searching anxiously through the Bible in these times and with the aid of the computer can do it faster and more efficiently than any time in history. As a result, knowledge of God's plan as revealed through His prophets has increased like never before. We are the generation that has seen all these things, and we are in the last of the last days.

The angel told Daniel, "Go your way, Daniel, for the words are closed up and sealed till the time of the end" (Dan. 12:9). We are in the last of the last days; we are very near the time of the end. The scriptures are being fulfilled before our eyes. The words are not a mystery any longer; they are no longer sealed up. Our days of mortality shall soon end: "So when this corruptible has put on incorruption, and this mortal has put on immortality, then shall be brought to pass the saying that is written: 'Death is swallowed up in victory'" (1 Cor. 15:54–55). Death will be no more; our mortal bodies will be clothed with immortality. An end is coming to this age of death, hell, and the grave; an end is coming to this evil and adulterous generation. We have a living hope in the truth of God's Word. Heaven and earth will pass away, but His powerful Word lives, and abides forever. Every word God has spoken shall be fulfilled.

Many scriptures refer to the last or latter days; it is very important that we understand what the Word of God means when it refers to the last or latter days. There is a gathering of Israel back to their land in the last days, and we are watching it take place on the news nearly every day. The main fulfillment of the prophet Joel's prophecy of the outpouring of God's Spirit on all flesh is in the last days is about to be fulfilled. The prophecy tells us that the Lord will show wonders in heaven and on earth and that blood and fire, and pillars of smoke will be part of His show that will take place in the last days. Jeremiah said the whirlwind of the Lord will go forth in fury, and we will understand perfectly what that means in the latter days.

Now that we have an understanding of what God means when He uses the words last days, we can move on to Ezekiel 38 in a new light. Notice when the Lord said he would bring the forces of Gog against His people, Israel.

> In the latter years you will come into the land of those brought back from the sword and gathered from many people on the mountains of Israel …You

will come up against My people Israel like a cloud,
to cover the land. It will be in the latter days that I
will bring you against My land, so that the nations
may know Me. (Ezek. 38:8, 16)

Who has understood the counsel of the Lord? Who has perceived
and heard His word? Who has marked His Word and heard it?
The whirlwind of the Lord has gone forth in fury, a continuing
whirlwind, it will not turn back until it has spent its energy on His
enemies. Who understands the plan in His heart? Who is the wise
man who understands what the Spirit is saying to the church? Who
is he to whom the mouth of the Lord has spoken that he may declare
it? In the latter days they will understand perfectly.

Now, having greater insight into what the Word of God says
and means about the last days or the latter days, it becomes obvious
that the end of all things is at hand. All things that are appointed
to take place in the last days have either happened or are about to
happen. The great event we see in Ezekiel 38–39 has not taken place
yet, but it has been appointed for the last days. This event in Ezekiel
is the epicenter of God's grand finale, it is the pinnacle of the great
and high mountain from which we see by the prophetic Word of
God all that is about to come. With this foundation, we may now
move forward into God's Word and see more of His plan as revealed
through His servants, the prophets.

CHAPTER 3

The Messianic Cycle

This chapter covers the plan of God for the coming of His Messiah. It is how He fixed the time and started the countdown for the first coming of the Messiah. This cycle of events reveals to us where we are on God's clock. God has done this before, and He is doing it again right before our eyes.

The Messianic cycle has ignited me on the inside more than anything else and has kept me burning in my walk with God in these last days. When this revelation came to me, I was hit with the reality of the living Word of God. What God said thousands of years ago is taking place all around us. History became very interesting to me; I wanted to know what God had done before I was born. The more I studied God's Word, the more I saw Him in everything— what is going on among nations, what is happening in my country, and the transformation in my life. I became intoxicated with the Word of God, and it became the center of my life.

I began to talk to God and ask Him questions, and I was shocked to find He would answer! Many years ago as a young man, I asked Him, "When are you coming? I have heard older and wiser ministers say, 'They have been saying Jesus is coming soon for hundreds of years,' and it seemed to me they didn't have a clue as to when You are coming. If I am to bear witness to Your coming, I would like to know what you say about it." I knew that the Lord had said, "Ask and you shall receive," so I asked; I figured it couldn't hurt. To my surprise, He said, "Look at My first coming" in a small, still voice inside.

I began to study all the prophecies about Christ's first coming. What details did God reveal to Israel beforehand? What should they have been looking for? I believed He would reveal to us what He had revealed to them. I read all the prophecies fulfilling the Messiah's first coming in the New and Old Testaments to see how God did things. It was interesting to see how prophecies were first spoken and how they were fulfilled.

When I came across Daniel 9, something lit up in me. This chapter was framed in a time when Israel had been in captivity in Babylon for seventy years. Jerusalem had been destroyed seventy years earlier and lay desolate the whole time Israel was in captivity just as God had said in Jeremiah. When the time had been fulfilled, Daniel knew it by his reading the book of Jeremiah the prophet. He began to petition the Lord knowing it was time for them to go home and rebuild the holy city of Jerusalem. Although he knew the time had been fulfilled, he still took it to the Lord and prayed that he might know His plan.

In Daniel 9, Daniel observed the seventy years of desolation that had been announced by the Lord through Jeremiah: "I, Daniel, understood by the books the number of the years specified by the word of the LORD through Jeremiah the prophet, that He would accomplish seventy years in the desolations of Jerusalem" (Dan. 9:2). Understanding the time had been fulfilled, Daniel began to petition the Lord concerning His promise to cause them to return to their land. As it is written in Jeremiah, "For thus says the LORD: After seventy years are completed at Babylon, I will visit you and perform My good word toward you and cause you to return to this place" (Jer. 29:10).

Daniel petitioned the Lord regarding what God has planned next: "O my God, incline Your ear and hear; open Your eyes and see our desolations, and the city which is called by Your name" (Dan. 9:18). "O Lord, hear! O Lord, forgive! O Lord, listen and act! Do not delay for Your own sake, my God, for Your city and Your people are called by Your name" (Dan. 9:19). God heard Daniel's petition and sent Gabriel with more than Daniel had asked for; His message covered not only the time in which Daniel lived but extended all the way to the end of the age. Daniel was told that there would be a decree permitting the Jews to return and rebuild Jerusalem and the cities of Judah and that the time from the going forth of the decree to rebuild Jerusalem until the Messiah came would be seven weeks and sixty-two weeks. One week was seven years, so it was saying seven sevens, or 49 years, and sixty-two sevens, 434 years.

What lit me up inside was that God was establishing the coming of the Messiah by the rebuilding of Jerusalem. Does that have any significance for us today? After around two thousand years of being desolate and trampled by the Gentiles, has Jerusalem been rebuilt? Notice that the angel gave two divisions of time in his decree for the rebuilding of Jerusalem and the coming of the Messiah—seven weeks and sixty-two weeks. We know there are two prophetic destructions of Jerusalem, one by Nebuchadnezzar before Christ came and the second by Titus in AD 70. That means that after Christ came, there would be another desolation and rebuilding of Jerusalem that would precede the coming of the Messiah. Many are saying, "The temple of the Lord, the temple of the Lord," but these prophecies in Daniel 9 are not addressing the temple of the Lord but His holy people and Jerusalem as far as the coming of the Messiah is concerned. There are two gatherings of the Jews to the land God promised their fathers, and there are two prophetic rebuildings of Jerusalem that usher in two comings of the Messiah. The same cycle of events that ushered in the first coming of the Messiah is ushering in the second coming of the Messiah right before our eyes.

We will journey through scripture and the history of Israel and Jerusalem to see how God's plan has worked through Israel to usher in His Messiah. There are many similarities between what God did with Israel to bring in His Messiah and what He is doing with Israel today. There is a pattern in scripture for how He fixed the time of His coming two thousand years ago, and the timing of His second coming appears to be set by the same series of events. The Messianic cycle is God's clock for the coming of the Messiah done through His people, Israel—the fig tree. Jesus told us in a parable to watch the fig tree. Once we understand this cycle and its wording, we can recognize when God is speaking to us prophetically in scripture about the last days and His coming.

We will look at the whole cycle of events in scripture that ushered in the first coming of the Messiah. Then we will look at what the Messiah said concerning another cycle that would begin after He was taken up to heaven and all that was prophesied in scripture about His second coming.

When Jesus came the first time, the Jews were looking for a conquering king to deliver them from those who hated them, the Roman Empire, the Gentiles. They were right that there would be a coming in this manner, but it was not at that time. Many prophecies of His coming in this manner are about to be fulfilled, and we will visit them later.

To understand how this cycle begins, we need to go back to the early days of Israel, to the book of Leviticus, in which God outlined what would happen if Israel obeyed Him and what would happen if it did not. Before the Lord brought the children of Israel into the Promised Land, He gave them laws and statutes to live by to be blessed in the good land He gave them that was flowing with milk and honey. It seems the Lord knew that once the children of Israel had come into the Promised Land and had filled their bellies with good things, had built beautiful houses, and had multiplied their herds and flocks and their silver and gold, they would forget the Lord and become corrupt (Deut. 8:12–14). He made it clear, even calling heaven and earth to witness against them, that to enjoy His blessings in the land, they had to obey His commandments, laws, and statutes as a condition of the blessings of His covenant. In Deuteronomy 28:1–14 and Leviticus 26:3–13, the Lord instituted the blessings for collective obedience. If Israel would have diligently obeyed the voice of the Lord, He would have set them above all nations. They would have been a kingdom of priests, a holy nation, a special treasure to the Lord on earth. And all His blessings would be poured out on them. People from all the nations who passed by would say, "This is the people whom the Lord has blessed."

On the other hand, if Israel did not obey the voice of the Lord, curses and punishments would come upon them. In Deuteronomy 4:15–39, 28:15–68 and Leviticus 26:14–39, the Lord described the curses. Soon after receiving the living oracles from their God, they began to act corrupt and kindle His anger. The Lord is not quick to anger; He is patient and long-suffering. Only after He punished Israel seven times for its sins to correct the people in measure did He say He would bring upon them what Daniel called "the curse and the oath written in the Law of Moses" (Dan. 9:11). It is found in Leviticus 26:27–28: "And after all this, if you do not obey me, but walk contrary to me, then I also will walk contrary to you in fury. And I, even I, will chastise you seven times for your sins."

Then in verses 32–33, after the Lord had exhausted all means of turning them from their evil ways, He described the fullness of the curse that was declared to them under oath: "I will bring the land to desolation, and your enemies who dwell in it shall be astonished at it. I will scatter you among the nations and draw out a sword after you; your land shall be desolate and your cities waste." Repeatedly, the Lord chastised them for their sins, and they cried out to Him; He had mercy on them and delivered them from their afflictions. This went on through the days of the judges.

Something else the Lord said to Israel in its bridal days is very important to us today because of the consequences; it was an instruction they were to follow as He brought them into the Promised Land—they were to drive out all the inhabitants of the land. Israel was to be a pure people who were near to God in holiness and sanctification without spot or blemish. To let any of the Canaanites remain among them would be like giving a glass of pure water tainted by mud to a beloved spouse. The corruption of the Canaanites was not just the immorality of the flesh but also spiritual adultery; they worshiped idols, images that they had made and called gods. For the nation of Israel to remain pure, it could not let any of these people and their wicked ways remain in the land.

The Lord gave them this warning two times, once through Moses and once through Joshua. Notice what God instructed them to do when they got into the Promised Land.

> You shall dispossess the inhabitants of the land and dwell in it, for I have given you the land to possess ... But if you do not drive out the inhabitants of the land from before you, then it shall be that those whom you let remain shall be irritants in your eyes and thorns in your sides, and they shall harass you in the land where you dwell. (Numbers 33:53–55)

The Canaanites were corrupt; they had filled up to the full measure their sins, and God did not want Israel to be influenced by them and their immoral ways.

However, Moses did not lead the children of Israel into the Promised Land because he had sinned at the waters of Meribah. Joshua led Israel into the Promised Land and gave them this very important instruction.

> Therefore, take careful heed to yourselves, that you love the LORD your God. Or else, if indeed you do go back, and cling to the remnant of these nations—these that remain among you—and make marriages with them, and go into them and they into you, know for certain that the LORD your God will no longer drive out these nations from before you. But they shall be snares and traps to you, and scourges on your sides and thorns in your eyes, until you perish from this good land which the LORD your God has given you. (Joshua 23:11–13)

Joshua told them to love the Lord their God. We wrestle today with this. We know that our love for the things of the world has always contended with our love for God. In the case of Israel, the love for the world won.

Israel did not drive out all the inhabitants of the land as the Lord had instructed.

> But the children of Benjamin did not drive out the Jebusites who inhabited Jerusalem; so the Jebusites dwell with the children of Benjamin in Jerusalem to this day. (Judg. 1:21)

> However, Manasseh did not drive out the inhabitants of Beth Shean and its villages. (Judg. 1:27)

> Nor did Ephraim drive out the Canaanites who dwelt in Gezer; so the Canaanites dwelt in Gezer among them. (Judg. 1:29)

> Nor did Zebulun drive out the inhabitants of Kitron or the inhabitants of Nahalol; so the Canaanites dwelt among them and were put under tribute. (Judg. 1:30)

> Nor did Asher drive out the inhabitants of Acco or the inhabitants of Sidon. (Judg. 1:31)

> Nor did Naphtali drive out the inhabitants of Beth Shemesh or the inhabitants of Beth Anath; but they dwelt among the Canaanites. (Judg. 1:33)

In Judges 2, the Lord sent an angel to Israel.

> Then the Angel of the LORD came up from Gilgal to Bochim and said: "I led you up from

Egypt and brought you to the land of which I swore to your fathers; and I said, 'I will never break My covenant with you. And you shall make no covenant with the inhabitants of this land; you shall tear down their altars.' But you have not obeyed My voice. Why have you done this? Therefore, I also said, 'I will not drive them out before you; but they shall be thorns in your side, and their gods shall be a snare to you.'" So it was, when the Angel of the LORD spoke these words to all the children of Israel that the people lifted up their voices and wept. (Judg. 2:1–4)

The people who lived among the children of Israel have been a thorn in their side from that day to this day. But there is a prophecy we will look at later in which God removes the thorn in their side, the thorn we see in the side of Israel today.

The pinnacle of Israel's blessings came in the days of King David and his son, Solomon. Afterward there was a steady decline in morality because of idol worship. Although the Lord was patient for years with Israel, the fullness of the curse was coming. The Lord said,

They have committed adultery, and blood is on their hands. They have committed adultery with their idols, and even sacrificed their sons whom they bore to Me, passing them through the fire, to devour them. Moreover, they have done this to Me: They have defiled My sanctuary on the same day and profaned My Sabbaths. For after they had slain their children for their idols, on the same day they came into My sanctuary to profane it; and indeed, thus they have done in the midst of My house. (Ezek. 23:37–39)

The Lord compassionately brought their iniquity to their attention many times, but they stopped their ears, shut their eyes, hardened their hearts, and refused to receive His instruction or rebuke, which led to the fullness of the curse. The Lord instructed them how to avoid the disaster, but they responded in arrogance and received their sentence.

> "Behold, I am fashioning a disaster and devising a plan against you. Return now everyone from his evil way and make your ways and your doings good." And they said, "That is hopeless! So we will walk according to our own plans, and we will everyone do the imagination of his evil heart." Therefore, thus says the Lord ... "Because My people have forgotten me ... They have caused themselves to stumble in their way ... To make their land desolate and a perpetual hissing. Everyone who passes by it will be astonished and shake his head. I will scatter them as with an east wind before the enemy. I will show them the back and not the face in the day of their calamity." (Jer. 18:15–17)

"To make their land desolate, I will scatter them"—that was the fullness of the curse. When the Lord gave them into the hands of their enemies, He showed them the back and not the face. Later in Ezekiel 39:28 after they had borne their shame the curse is reversed and the Lord says: "I will not hide My face from them anymore."

The Lord went into a prophetic mode; He issued a decree and set the number of years they would go into exile and the land would lay desolate.

> Therefore, thus says the Lord of hosts, because you have not heard My words. Behold, I will send and take all the families of the north, says the Lord, and

> Nebuchadnezzar the king of Babylon, My servant,
> and will bring them against this land, against its
> inhabitants, and against these nations all around,
> and will utterly destroy them, and make them an
> astonishment. And these nations shall serve the
> king of Babylon *seventy years.* (Jer. 25:8–11)

When the Lord caused them to be led away captive to Babylon,
He gave them a future and a hope; that was how the Lord dealt with
His people. When the Israelites went into captivity, they knew how
long they would be there and that they would come back to their
own land afterward. Their punishment was to be under the yoke of
the king of Babylon and do his will for seventy years.

In 2 Chronicles 36:11–23, we see the judgment fulfilled.

> And the LORD God of their fathers sent warnings
> to them by His messengers, rising up early and
> sending them, because He had compassion on His
> people and on His dwelling place. But they mocked
> the messengers of God, despised His words, and
> scoffed at His prophets, until the wrath of the
> LORD arose against His people, till there was no
> remedy. Therefore, He brought against them the
> king of the Chaldeans, who killed their young men
> with the sword in the house of their sanctuary, and
> had no compassion on young man or virgin, on the
> aged or the weak; He gave them all into his hand.
> And all the articles from the house of God, great
> and small, the treasures of the house of the LORD,
> and the treasures of the king and of his leaders, all
> these he took to Babylon. They burned the house
> of the Lord, broke down the wall of Jerusalem,
> burned all its palaces with fire, and destroyed all its

precious possessions. And those who escaped from the sword he carried to Babylon, where they became servants to him and his sons until the reign of the kingdom of Persia, to fulfill the word of the Lord by the mouth of Jeremiah, until the land had enjoyed her Sabbaths. As long as she lay desolate she kept Sabbath, to fulfill *seventy years*.

The desolation of Jerusalem and the scattering of the Jews to all nations was the first step in a cycle of events that would usher in the Messiah. Not all the Jews went into captivity in Babylon; others were scattered into all nations to be a reproach, a byword, a taunt, and a curse in every land where He drove them. Many of them were there for 2,500 years and have come back to their land only now at the end of the age.

The word scatter is best illustrated with the visual picture of a farmer scattering seed in his field. In Jesus's parable, "a sower went out to sow"; the seed was the Word of God. The scattered Israelites took the Word wherever they went; the scattering for them was punishment, but for the nations a blessing.

As we learn more about the Messianic cycle, the terms and phrases the Lord used for the scattering will help us to recognize when the Lord was giving us a prophecy for our times. Remember these terms and phrases that describe their punishment because the Lord used them when referring to their return and regathering to their land in the prophets.

The Lord spoke of those who refused to go into captivity in Babylon.

> I will deliver them to trouble into all the kingdoms of the earth, for their harm, to be a reproach and a byword, a taunt and a curse, in all places where I shall drive them. (Jer. 24:9)

> I will bring an everlasting reproach upon you, and
> a perpetual shame, which shall not be forgotten.
> (Jer. 23:40)

> I will deliver them to trouble among all the kingdoms
> of the earth—to be a curse, an astonishment, a
> hissing, and a reproach among all the nations where
> I have driven them. (Jer. 29:18–19)

> They shall be consumed by the sword and by
> famine. They shall die, from the least to the
> greatest, by the sword and by famine; and they
> shall be an oath, an astonishment, a curse and a
> reproach! (Jer. 44:12–13)

We are viewing these things now at the end of the age; all these things have come to pass. We have the prophetic Word confirmed in history. The Jews have been a curse in every land where they have gone, not because they were bad people, but because the curse of the law was on them. They were despised because of the curse. They were accused of things, tortured, and put to death. Wherever they went, the people there ruled over them, and they had no power to stand against their enemies. The Lord said,

> And as for those of you who are left, I will send
> faintness into their hearts in the lands of their
> enemies; the sound of a shaken leaf shall cause
> them to flee; they shall flee as though fleeing
> from a sword, and they shall fall when no one
> pursues. They shall stumble over one another,
> as it were before a sword, when no one pursues;
> and you shall have no power to stand before your
> enemies. You shall perish among the nations,
> and the land of your enemies shall eat you up.

And those of you who are left shall waste away in
their iniquity in your enemies' lands; also in their
fathers' iniquities, which are with them, they shall
waste away. (Lev. 26:36–39)

Though their punishment and burdens were severe, the Lord
had always told them the end from the beginning so they were never
without hope. The Lord had always had a plan for them after they
had borne their shame. He sent a letter through Jeremiah to those
who were carried away captive to Babylon that gave the Israelites
a future and hope—something to look forward to at the end of
seventy years.

After seventy years are completed at Babylon, I
will visit you and perform My good word toward
you and cause you to return to this place. For I
know the thoughts that I think toward you, says
the LORD, thoughts of peace and not of evil, to
give you a future and a hope ... I will bring you
back from your captivity; I will gather you from
all the nations and from all the places where I have
driven you, says the LORD, and I will bring you
to the place from which I caused you to be carried
away captive. (Jer. 29:10–11, 14)

In Isaiah, about 150 years before the captivity in Babylon, the
Lord had told Hezekiah, the king of Judah, through Isaiah the
prophet that the captivity was coming.

Isaiah said to Hezekiah, "Hear the word of the
LORD of hosts: Behold, the days are coming when
all that is in your house, and what your fathers
have accumulated until this day, shall be carried
to Babylon; nothing shall be left," says the LORD.

"And they shall take away some of your sons who
will descend from you, whom you will beget; and
they shall be eunuchs in the palace of the king of
Babylon." (Isa. 39:5–7)

The Lord knew the precise time needed for the seed of the
wicked one, which was flourishing in His good soil, to mature; at
which time the ax would be laid to the root of the tree. For: "Every
tree which does not bear good fruit is cut down and thrown into
the fire" (Matt 3:10). As a stump remains when a tree is cut down;
so the holy seed shall be the stump. (Is. 6:13)

Jeremiah began his ministry to Israel about twenty years before
the desolation of Jerusalem and the captivity in Babylon. He gave
them warnings right up until it happened. So Israel, or you could
say the elect, those who believed God, knew that they would be
going into captivity, how long it would last, and that they would be
brought back to their land at the end of seventy years. The Lord had
told them all things beforehand, so that when it came to pass, they
would believe. That is how the Lord dealt with that generation, and
it is how He is dealing with this generation: "See! I have told you all
things beforehand!" (Mark 13:23).

The book of Daniel begins with Daniel being carried away
captive to Babylon as a young man and being chosen with his three
friends, Hananiah, Mishael, and Azariah, to serve Nebuchadnezzar.
The Lord had told Hezekiah, "They shall take away some of your
sons who will descend from you, whom you will beget; and they shall
be eunuchs in the palace of the king of Babylon". In Daniel 1:3–4,
Nebuchadnezzar instructed Ashpenaz, the master of his eunuchs, to
bring some of the children of Israel, some of the king's descendants,
and some of the nobles to serve in the king's palace. "Now from
among those of the sons of Judah were Daniel, Hananiah, Mishael
and Azariah" (Dan. 1:6).

It seems Daniel and his three companions were made eunuchs to
serve in the palace of the king of Babylon just as the Lord had spoken

to Hezekiah many years before. Daniel was among the first carried away to Babylon and continued there until the reign of the kingdom of Persia. Through Daniel and his three friends, the Lord made a name for himself in the eyes of the kings and the people of Babylon.

Daniel recorded some important things that happened to the kings of Babylon that brought about the reign of the kingdom of Persia. To understand the Messianic cycle more completely, we need to look at the events and information in Daniel. In 2 Chronicles 36, we read that the children of Judah served the king of Babylon until the reign of the kingdom of Persia to fulfill the Word of the Lord by the mouth of Jeremiah to fulfill seventy years.

In Daniel 5, we see how the reign of the kingdom of Persia came about and ended the seventy years of captivity and desolation's according to 2 Chronicles 36:20–23. Belshazzar, the son of Nebuchadnezzar, was the last king of Babylon. Daniel 5 tells us that Belshazzar and the people in his court had drunk from some of the gold and silver vessels his father had brought from the house of the Lord in Jerusalem and praised the gods of gold and silver, bronze and iron, wood and stone. Then Belshazzar saw the fingers of a man's hand writing on the wall of the palace "Mene, Mene, Tekel, Upharsin."

> This is the interpretation of each word. MENE: God has numbered your kingdom and finished it. TEKEL: You have been weighed in the balances and found wanting. PERES: *Your kingdom has been divided and given to the Medes and Persians.*" That very night Belshazzar, king of the Chaldeans, was slain." And *Darius the Mede received the kingdom,* being about sixty-two years old. (Dan. 5:25–31)

It is important here to note the changing of the kingdom because 2 Chronicles 36:20 says the desolations of Jerusalem lasted till the reign of the kingdom of Persia. Here in Daniel we have a record of the kingdom of Babylon being divided and given to the Medes and Persians. Darius the Mede receives the kingdom at age sixty-two years old.

In the next chapter we have the story of Daniel in the lions' den and how king Darius the Mede was so astonished that the lions did not eat Daniel; he made a proclamation throughout all his kingdom.

> To all peoples, nations, and languages that dwell in all the earth. Peace be multiplied to you. I make a decree that in every dominion of my kingdom men must tremble and fear before the God of Daniel. For He is the living God, and steadfast forever; His kingdom is the one which shall not be destroyed, and His dominion shall endure to the end. He delivers and rescues, and He works signs and wonders in heaven and on earth, who has delivered Daniel from the power of the lions. (Dan. 6:25)

Then the scripture says, "So this Daniel prospered in the reign of *Darius* and in the reign of *Cyrus the Persian*." These two kingdoms began at the same time. According to Daniel 6, these two kingdoms had the same governing law, "The law of the Medes and Persians, which does not alter." These two kingdoms were tied together politically. So when one of the ruling kings made a decree as Darius did, "To all people, nations, and languages that dwell in all the earth," you can be sure Cyrus also heard the story of Daniel in the lions' den and was influenced by it and the decree honoring the true God of Daniel. All that had happened to Nebuchadnezzar and Belshazzar was made known throughout the kingdom.

The Lord made an everlasting name for Himself in Babylon in those days. I'm sure Darius and Cyrus feared and trembled at the Word of the Lord knowing He would hold them accountable also for all they knew. They saw Belshazzar find that out the hard way.

When Daniel knew the seventy years of captivity were complete, he sought the Lord concerning His bringing Israel back to their land.

> In the *first year of Darius* the son of Ahasuerus, *of the lineage of the Medes*, who was made king over the realm of the Chaldeans—in the first year of his reign I, Daniel, understood by the books the number of the years specified by the word of the LORD through Jeremiah the prophet, that He would accomplish seventy years in the desolation's of Jerusalem. Then I set my face toward the Lord God to make request by prayer and supplications, with fasting, sackcloth, and ashes ... O Lord, to us belongs shame of face, to our kings, our princes, and our fathers, because we have sinned against You. Yes, all Israel has transgressed Your law, and has departed so as not to obey Your voice; therefore, *the curse and the oath written in the Law of Moses* the servant of God has been poured out on us, because we have sinned against You. (Dan. 9:1–3, 8, 11)

> I pray, let Your anger and Your fury be turned away from Your city Jerusalem, Your holy mountain; because for our sins, and for the iniquities of our fathers, *Jerusalem and Your people* are a reproach to all those around us. (Dan. 9:16)

God heard that prayer!

Daniel prayed this prayer in the first year of Darius's reign in Media. That was also the first year of Cyrus's reign in Persia during which he decreed that the Jews were to return and rebuild the house of the Lord in Jerusalem.

Now in the *first year* of Cyrus king of Persia, that
the word of the LORD by the mouth of Jeremiah
might be fulfilled, the LORD stirred up the spirit of
Cyrus king of Persia, so that he made a proclamation
throughout all his kingdom, and also put it in
writing, saying, Thus says Cyrus king of Persia:
All the kingdoms of the earth the LORD God of
heaven has given me. And He has commanded
me to build Him a house at Jerusalem which is in
Judah. Who is among you of all His people? May
the LORD his God be with him and let him go up!
(2 Chron. 36:22–23)

The Lord had inspired that decree. The historian Josephus
recorded some interesting details about what happened in the first
year of Cyrus's reign in Persia.

In the first year of the reign of Cyrus which was
the seventieth from the day that our people were
removed out of their own land into Babylon, God
commiserated the captivity and calamity of these
poor people, according as he had foretold to them
by Jeremiah the prophet, before the destruction of
the city, that after they had served Nebuchadnezzar
and his posterity, and after they had undergone
that servitude seventy years, he would restore
them again to the land of their fathers, and they
should build their temple, and enjoy their ancient
prosperity. And these things God did afford them;
for he stirred up the mind of Cyrus, and made him
write this throughout all Asia: "Thus saith Cyrus
the king: Since God Almighty hath appointed me
to be king of the habitable earth, I believe that he is
that God which the nation of the Israelites worship;

for indeed he foretold my name by the prophets, and that I should build him a house at Jerusalem, in the country of Judea. "This was known to Cyrus by his reading the book which Isaiah left behind him of his prophecies; for this prophet said that God had spoken thus to him in a secret vision: "My will is, that Cyrus, whom I have appointed to be king over many and great nations, send back my people to their own land, and build my temple." This was foretold by Isaiah one hundred and forty years before the temple was demolished. Accordingly, when Cyrus read this, and admired the Divine power, an earnest desire and ambition seized upon him to fulfill what was so written; so he called for the most eminent Jews that were in Babylon, and said to them, that he gave them leave to go back to their own country, and to rebuild their city Jerusalem, and the temple of God. (Antiquities of the Jews: Book 11, Chapter 1)

We see how the Lord stirred up Cyrus's spirit when he read the prophecy in Isaiah in which God called him by name before he had been born! The Lord knew Cyrus would read these things; notice the whole message the Lord was sending to Cyrus and his kingdom.

I am the LORD, who makes all things, who stretches out the heavens all alone, who spreads abroad the earth by Myself; who frustrates the signs of the babblers, and drives diviners mad; who turns wise men backward, and makes their knowledge foolishness; who confirms the word of His servant, and performs the counsel of His messengers, who says of Cyrus, "He is My shepherd, and he shall perform all My pleasure, saying to Jerusalem, 'You

shall be built,' and to the temple, 'Your foundation
shall be laid.' Thus says the LORD to His anointed,
to Cyrus, whose right hand I have held to subdue
nations before him and loose the armor of kings I
will give you the treasures of darkness and hidden
riches of secret places that you may know that I, the
LORD, who calls you by your name, am the God
of Israel. For Jacob My servant's sake, and Israel
My elect, I have even called you by your name; I
have named you, though you have not known Me.
I am the Lord and there is no other, there is no God
besides Me. (Isa. 44:24–28, 45:1–5)

In this passage, God made Himself known to the Medes and
Persians by His divine power; He declared to the inhabited world
that He was and is the Creator of the heavens and earth and that
He was and is God—there is no other. He called their king Cyrus
more than a hundred years before he was born. How awesome are
the works of the Lord; how mighty are His deeds! How inspiring it
must have been to the kingdoms of the Medes and Persians to see
God revealing Himself to their kingdoms through their kings as
the god who is God. Cyrus made a decree and sent it throughout all
the kingdom of Persia. Darius made a decree and sent it throughout
all the kingdom of Media. God made Himself an everlasting name
once again in those days!

Through Cyrus, God gave liberty to His people to return to the
land of their ancestors and rebuild the waste and desolate cities in the
land of Judah before the eyes of all nations. Though many nations
have counseled against giving the Holy Land to His people, the Lord
has made that counsel have no effect. It is the hand of the Lord at
work: "The LORD brings the counsel of the nations to nothing; He
makes the plans of the peoples of no effect" (Ps 33:10).

At first, Cyrus oversaw the return of the Jews to their land and
the rebuilding of the house of God in Jerusalem. It sounded like all

was going well for the Jews having the favor of the king and a decree in their hands, but there was trouble ahead for them.

The people who inhabited their land while they were gone were angry that the Jews were returning. In the seventh month after they returned, the Jews gathered in Jerusalem to offer sacrifices to the Lord. However, fear came upon them because of the people of those countries (Ezra 3:1–3); that is very similar to what we see today. Later on: "The people of the land tried to discourage the people of Judah. They troubled them in building and hired counselors against them to frustrate their purpose all the days of Cyrus king of Persia" (Ezra 4:4–5). The people who had taken over their land did not consider the decree of King Cyrus or regard the God of the Jews. They considered the land theirs, but that was not how God saw it. For He says:

> Thus says the Lord: "Against all My evil neighbors who touch the inheritance which I have caused My people Israel to inherit—behold, I will pluck them out of their land and pluck out the house of Judah from among them. Then it shall be, after I have plucked them out, that I will return and have compassion on them and bring them back, everyone to his heritage and everyone to his land. (Jer. 12:14–15)

Anyone can see that the Holy Land belongs to the people of the Lord, the people whom God calls: "My people Israel." The Lord is here addressing His evil neighbors, those who lay hands on their land to take it from them.

Artaxerxes king of Persia reigned about seventy-five years after Cyrus. In his days the people of the land sent a letter to king Artaxerxes and brought accusation against the Jews and said: "The Jews who came up from you have come to us at Jerusalem and are building the rebellious and evil city" (Ezra 4:12). So the king commanded a search of his records and found that this city had revolted against kings. Therefore, he sent a letter commanding the people of the land to make the Jews cease from building this city, and by force of arms they made them cease. Many years after the reign of Cyrus; we can see how the people of the land took counsel among themselves to accuse the Jews of evil and frustrate their purpose.

Some years later during the reign of the Persian King Darius, The Jews under the prophets Haggai and Zechariah began to build the house of the Lord and the wall of Jerusalem. Again, the people of the land; namely, Tattenai the governor of the region; sent a letter to Darius king of Persia, and a record of the decree of Cyrus king of Persia was found, not in the kingdom of Persia, but in the palace in the province of Media, and it was read before Darius. What happened to the decree that was in the archives of the Persian kingdom? There must have been enemies of the Jews there who made it disappear. When the decree of Cyrus was read, it must have stirred Darius in spirit as Cyrus was stirred, he also issued a decree that they were to let the Jews alone; "Let the house be rebuilt, the place where they offered sacrifices; and let the foundations of it be firmly laid… Let the expenses be paid from the king's treasury" (Ezra 6:3-4).

Darius's decree commanded Tattenai the governor of the region to provide whatever the Jews needed to offer sacrifices to God, that they may pray for the king and his sons. (Ezra 6:10) It goes on to say: "Also I issue a decree that whoever alters this edict, let a timber be pulled from his house and erected, and let him be hanged on it" Ezra 6:11). It seems the king realized the people of the land were hindering the Jews from building and added a death penalty to anyone who would hinder the Jews. Thus, the temple was built and dedicated in the days of Zerubbabel and the prophets Haggai and Zechariah.

Then, years later, Nehemiah, the cupbearer to king Darius of Persia at the time, heard that the wall of Jerusalem was broken down and its gates were burned, and the Jews who had gone back from the captivity were in great trouble in the land. The people of the land clearly did not want the Jews to have their land back even though the kings of Persia decreed that the Jews should be left alone. Nehemiah was so stirred in spirit that he asked of king Darius permission to go back to the city of his fathers, Jerusalem, and rebuild it; Darius then gave him leave to go and rebuild Jerusalem. Nehemiah led more Jews back to their land, but again, the people of the land became very angry that they had come back: "But it so happened, when Sanballat heard that we were rebuilding the wall, that he was furious and very indignant, and mocked the Jews" (Neh. 4:1). As Nehemiah and the Jews began to finish the wall, the anger of those peoples again became stirred up against them:

> Now it happened, when Sanballat, Tobiah, the Arabs, the Ammonites, and the Ashdodites heard that the walls of Jerusalem were being restored and the gaps were beginning to be closed, that they became very angry, and all of them conspired together to come and attack Jerusalem and create confusion. (Neh. 4:7–8)

However, Nehemiah encouraged the Jews: "Do not be afraid of them. Remember the Lord, great and awesome, and fight for your brethren, your sons, your daughters, your wives, and your houses" (Neh. 4:14). "Those who built on the wall, and those who carried burdens, loaded themselves so that with one hand they worked at construction, and with the other held a weapon" (Neh. 4:17).

What we see happening to the Jews today has happened before when the Lord brought His people back to their land. The people of the land today, also being Arabs, have troubled them for building on the land and have attacked them numerous times to create confusion and frustrate their purpose. The Arabs bring accusations against the Jews at the United Nations, which in turn issues decrees against the Jews for building settlements in the West Bank; which are the mountains of Israel; the Promised Land.

Years before, the angel of the Lord had prophesied to Daniel that there would be trouble for them when they returned to build: "The street shall be built again, and the wall even in troublesome times" (Dan. 9:25). There was trouble for them then just as there is trouble for them now. The Arab nations around Israel today have resisted their return and trouble them in building the cities of Judea and their holy city, Jerusalem; but they cannot stop the plan of God.

Notice that the rebuilding of Jerusalem in those days was in preparation for the first coming of the Messiah, and that Jerusalem has been raised up and restored recently in our times; wouldn't it also be in preparation for the coming of Messiah? When the time appointed expires Messiah comes! When the time appointed for the first coming had been fulfilled, an angel of the Lord gave a clear proclamation of the Messiah's arrival to shepherds: "Do not be afraid, for behold, I bring you good tidings of great joy which will be to all people. For there is born to you this day in the city of David a Savior, who is Christ the Lord" (Luke 2:10–11). Andrew was one of the first to bear witness that Jesus was the Messiah.

> One of the two who heard John speak, and followed Him, was Andrew, Simon Peter's brother. He first found his own brother Simon, and said to him, "We have found the Messiah" (which is translated, the Christ). And he brought him to Jesus. (John 1:40–42)

This coming of the Messiah completed the first Messianic cycle; it fulfilled Isaiah 53—how Christ would bear the sins of many and be cut off from the land of the living. But that was not what the Jews were looking for; they had not seen this coming of the Messiah in scripture, and it caught them completely off guard. The Jews were looking for a Messiah who would gloriously deliver them from Roman oppression and restore the kingdom to Israel. They had put God in their box, and that is where they wanted Him to meet them.

Jesus, knowing all things concerning Himself, began to prophesy that after His death, the fullness of the curse would come again— the Jews would be scattered, and Jerusalem would be made desolate as the Messianic cycle begins again. In His end-time discourse, Jesus said: "When you see Jerusalem surrounded by armies, then know that its desolation is near" (Luke 21:20). Compare that with what the angel said in Daniel 9:26 should take place after the Messiah was cut off from the land of the living: "The people of the prince who is to come shall destroy the city and the sanctuary. The end of it shall be with a flood."

These things were fulfilled in AD 70. Titus and his legions were the children of the prince who is to come, he fulfilled the prophecies of Daniel and Jesus when he destroyed Jerusalem and scattered the Jews into all nations. Jesus said, "And they will fall by the edge of the sword and be led away captive into all nations. And Jerusalem will be trampled by Gentiles until the times of the Gentiles are fulfilled" (Luke 21:20, 24). The Jews were again carried away captive to be a byword, a taunt, and a curse to the four corners of the earth.

It takes a little more studying to find the length of this captivity or scattering in scripture, but it is there. The reason for the much longer desolation and captivity was the level of sin that had been committed. Jesus said that eternal condemning sin was blasphemy against the Holy Spirit. Until Christ came, this sin was not possible. This sin is supernatural in nature because the consequences are supernatural and eternal. The murderers of Christ committed this sin when they hated Him without a cause and put the author of life to death. They filled up to the full measure the sin of their fathers. It was the pinnacle of sin.

Jesus told Pilate, "You could have no power at all against Me unless it had been given you from above. Therefore, the one who delivered Me to you has the greater sin" (John 19:11). Jesus taught that there is sin that can be forgiven and there is a greater sin that cannot be forgiven:

> Assuredly, I say to you, all sins will be forgiven
> the sons of men, and whatever blasphemies they
> may utter; but he who blasphemes against the Holy
> Spirit never has forgiveness but is subject to eternal
> condemnation. (Mark 3:28–29)

We have been told that all sin is the same, sin is sin. But all sin is not the same: Jesus said there are two levels of sin, there is sin that can be forgiven and there is sin that cannot be forgiven. Forgivable sin is carnal sin, the works of the flesh. The apostle Paul describes these works in Galatians: "Now the works of the flesh are evident, which are: adultery, fornication, uncleanness, lewdness, idolatry, sorcery, hatred, contentions, jealousies, outbursts of wrath, selfish ambitions, dissensions, heresies, envy, murders, drunkenness, revelries, and the like" (Gal 5:19-21). These are all natural sin, the sins of the flesh; Jesus said all these sins shall be forgiven. But His forgiveness is not automatic, one must renounce and forsake these sins to enter the kingdom.

Jesus said; every sin and whatever blasphemies one may utter shall be forgiven. No one may enter the kingdom of heaven while in sin, but we know that the state of a man in sin can be changed in an instant through the forgiveness of Christ. However, the state of a man who has committed eternal condemning sin cannot be changed. Without an understanding of eternal sin, and its place in the Day of Judgment, end time doctrine can be erroneous.

When the angel gave Daniel the decree of seventy weeks for his people and holy city in chapter 9, it covered the time line from his day to the end of the age. The decree was divided into three parts: "Seventy weeks are determined for your people and for your holy city, (1) to finish the transgression, to make an end of sins, (2) to make reconciliation for iniquity, to bring in everlasting righteousness, (3) to seal up vision and prophecy, and to anoint the Most Holy" (Dan 9:24).

The first division is for the first coming of Christ; when He came to bear the sins of many as He was cut off from the land of the living. The work of Christ in this season was twofold; on one hand He put an end to the power of sin over men, its dominion over His people; on the other the Jews completed their transgression, they filled up to the full measure the sin of their fathers. They finished the transgression while Christ put an end to sin. Some Jews accepted and loved Jesus, while others hated Him without a cause and sought to put Him to death. For the Jews who hated Him; this time was appointed to usher in eternal condemning sin, permanently sealing the fate of those who commit it.

The sixty-two weeks are explained as specifically for the first coming of Messiah: "And after the sixty-two weeks Messiah shall be cut off, but not for Himself" (Dan 9:26). This agrees with what Isaiah spoke concerning Christ: "But He was wounded for our transgressions, He was bruised for our iniquities; The chastisement for our peace was upon Him" (Isa. 53:5). All He went through was not for Himself, it was for us! And what the angel said in Daniel 9:26 agrees with what Isaiah said: "He was cut off from the land of the living" (Isa 53:8).

Unpardonable sin was committed by the elders and leaders of God's people by speaking blasphemy against the Holy Spirit and putting the author of life to death. It was a new level of sin that had not been before Christ. Jesus explains that this is so:

> Fill up, then, the measure of your fathers' guilt. Serpents, brood of vipers! How can you escape the condemnation of hell? Therefore, indeed, I send you prophets, wise men, and scribes: some of them you will kill and crucify, and some of them you will scourge in your synagogues and persecute from city to city, that on you may come all the righteous blood shed on the earth, from the blood of righteous Abel to the blood of Zechariah, son of Berechiah, whom you murdered between the temple and the altar. Assuredly, I say to you, all these things will come upon this generation. (Matt 23:32-36)

No generation before them could fill to the full measure the level of sin they had. It is the greatest sin there is. The men who committed this sin are guilty of all the righteous blood shed on earth, from Abel to Zechariah, as well as the innocent blood of Christ. Their eternal destiny is sealed, they cannot escape eternal damnation. This is supernatural sin because the punishment is supernatural and eternal.

Israel went into captivity in Babylon for seventy years because of their evil and wicked deeds of which all were natural and carnal sin, the same level of sin Jesus came to forgive. But those who commit unpardonable sin never have forgiveness but are subject to eternal condemnation. It was this level of sin that sent Israel into captivity for two-thousand years. The time appointed was long for them to endure the curse and the oath written in the law of Moses. However, their punishment ended with the establishing of the state of Israel. Their King-Messiah is now coming to save them and deliver them from all those who afflict them. It is the coming of their King-Messiah that Israel expected when He came the first time.

The second division of the seventy weeks is the time in which we live today and will be complete when all Israel is saved. The angel says it is appointed to make reconciliation for iniquity, to bring in everlasting righteousness. It is when Israel will be reconciled to God; they get saved and everlasting righteousness will be theirs through Christ. (Rom. 5:17,21)

The last and final division of the seventy weeks is appointed to close this age. All prophecy for the last days and the time of the end will be fulfilled at the arrival of the last day. The church, when she enters her glory on that day is anointed most holy, she is the bride of Christ and has made herself ready for the wedding. At the marriage of the Lamb, the two, Christ and His bride, shall become one. The three divisions appear to define the purpose of the three time periods given in the prophecy; seven weeks (49yrs.), sixty-two weeks (434yrs.), and one week (7yrs.). The seven and sixty-two weeks establish two restorations of Jerusalem and two comings of Messiah, while the one week establishes the time appointed when the end shall be.

The second scattering is much longer than the first for the reason we just covered. To find the length of it we must first turn to the words of Peter. Written in his later years before he had to put-off his tent (die) as the Lord had shown him (2 Peter 1:14), Peter had to address the coming of the Lord because some of that time believed that the day of Christ had either come already or was not coming. Paul also addresses this issue. (See: 2 Thess. 2:1-2) Peter, however, gives us instruction and a clue directing us to the answer we seek.

> Beloved, I now write to you this second epistle (in both of which I stir up your pure minds by way of reminder), that you may be mindful of the words which were spoken before by the holy prophets and of the commandment of us, the apostles of the Lord and Savior, knowing this first, that scoffers will come in the last days walking according to their own lusts and saying, "Where is the promise of His coming? For since the fathers fell asleep all things continue as they were from the beginning of creation." (2 Peter 3:1–4)

Peter was near the time of his exodus when he had to deal with a specific problem in the church. People had heard that Jesus was coming soon, but now, Peter and the other apostles were getting old and dying, and some were beginning to speculate and mock them, because Jesus hadn't come. On that note, Peter instructed God's people to be mindful of the words of the holy prophets; because the answer to when Jesus should come again is in their writings.

Peter directs us to the prophets, but he also gives us this clue to remember when we read their words: "But beloved, do not forget this one thing, that with the Lord one day is as a thousand years and a thousand years as one day. The Lord is not slack concerning His promise" (2 Peter 3:8–9). This clue is something we need to keep in mind when we read the prophets.

Now we turn to the prophet that immediately follows Daniel, Hosea, to put this clue to use. These are the words I believe Peter was directing us to. The words of Hosea the prophet for the nation of Israel.

> Come, and let us return to the LORD; For He has torn, but He will heal us; He has stricken, but He will bind us up. After two days He will revive us; On the third day He will raise us up, that we may live in His sight. Let us know, let us pursue the knowledge of the LORD. His going forth is established as the morning, He will come to us. (Hos. 6:1–3)

Can you see the wisdom in the words of Peter? Be mindful of the words of the holy prophets and don't forget this one thing, that with the Lord one day is as a thousand years, and a thousand years are as one day. Here in the prophet Hosea, we find that the Lord has stricken them, but He will bandage their wounds, He has torn them, but He will heal them; after two days (two thousand years), He will revive them. Revive means to bring back to life from a dead state.

Hebrew was a dead language for two thousand years; it was not spoken or taught as an official language in any nation. When Israel became a nation in 1948, the people revived the language and made it the official language of the state of Israel. Along with the Hebrew language, the nation of Israel has been revived. After two thousand years of captivity among the nations, Jews from all over the world are returning to a revived country and a rebuilt holy city, Jerusalem. Jesus is coming soon. Hosea said, "He will come to us!" To understand these things, we must pursue the knowledge of the Lord. Everything we need to know about His coming is all in His Word.

Jesus also confirms that the time frame would be two thousand years or two prophetic days.

> On that very day some Pharisees came, saying to Him, "Get out and depart from here, for Herod wants to kill You." And He said to them, "Go, tell that fox, 'Behold, I cast out demons and perform cures today and tomorrow, and the third day I shall be perfected.' Nevertheless, I must journey today, tomorrow, and the day following; for it cannot be that a prophet should perish outside of Jerusalem." (Luke 13:31–33)

This prophetic passage agrees with Hosea. God's plan is that Jesus casts out demons and performed cures through His body of believers, the church. He said His ministry would be for two days, prophetically—two thousand years. Jesus confirms that this is His plan for the church, "As the Father sent Me, I also send you" (John 20:21). As the Father sent Jesus to cast out demons and perform cures; Jesus commissions His church to do the same, "As you go, preach, saying, 'The kingdom of heaven is at hand.' Heal the sick, cleanse the lepers, raise the dead, cast out demons. Freely you have received, freely give" (Matt 10:7-8). Jesus commissioned His body of believers to continue His work for two days, or two-thousand years.

He confirms the delegation of His ministry to the church in several places, "Most assuredly, I say to you, he who believes in Me, the works that I do he will do also; and greater works than these he will do, because I go to My Father" (John 14:12). It is how He sent His church two-thousand years ago, and it continues till this day. "And they went out and preached everywhere, the Lord working with them and confirming the word through the accompanying signs. Amen" (Mark 16:20). The Lord goes with them and works for them; and so it will be until the last day of this age.

Hosea said the Lord would revive them after two days—two thousand years; that referred to the nation of Israel coming back to life—the rebirth of a nation, a culture, and a language. The people of the Lord have been revived! The Lord indicates that what follows the rebirth in the natural is a rebirth of the spiritual, that the nation of Israel would be born again and saved as Paul said: "And so all Israel will be saved, as it is written: 'The Deliverer will come out of Zion, and He will turn away ungodliness from Jacob; for this is My covenant with them, when I take away their sins'" (Rom. 11:26–27). We are in the third day now and the state of Israel has been revived in the natural; but the Lord is about to roar out of Zion and revive them in the spiritual, all Israel will be saved.

At the same time, there will come a great revival to the whole world, the likes of which has never been before, nor shall there be again. Paul goes on to say: "If their being cast away is the reconciling of the world, what will their acceptance be but life from the dead?" (Rom. 11:15). Life from the dead is the definition of revival! When all Israel is saved, they will accept Jesus as Lord and Savior and the world will experience the greatest revival ever. We are after the two days and are now in the third day, revival is coming!

Not long after the revival, the Lord will raise us up that we may live in His sight. I believe that refers to the rapture. Jesus said He would be perfected on the third day; that refers to the wedding supper of the Lamb—Jesus will marry His bride, the church, and the two will become intimately one. We will know as we are known, and we will see as we are seen. It is a state of perfection for Him and His bride, the goal of this age, a time of perfection and restoration of all things. So we clearly see what Peter meant when he said to be mindful of the prophets. The Lord is not slack concerning His promise, and He promised to return.

> In My Father's house are many mansions; if it were not so, I would have told you. I go to prepare a place for you. And if I go and prepare a place for you, I will come again and receive you to Myself; that where I am, there you may be also. (John 14:2–3)

Let's look again at a prophetic word the Lord gave us that brings us to the same conclusion, for in the mouth of two or more, every word may be established. It is concerning Jerusalem. Jesus gave us an undisputable sign to look for when the time of Israel's captivity had ended: "And Jerusalem will be trampled by Gentiles until the times of the Gentiles are fulfilled" (Luke 21:24). After the destruction of Jerusalem by Titus in AD 70, Jerusalem was trampled by Gentiles and remained under Gentile rule for around two thousand years. In AD 130, after crushing the final Jewish revolt, The Roman emperor Hadrian changed the name of the Holy Land from Judea to Syria-Palestina and declared the province to be a Jew-free zone in an attempt to disconnect the Jewish people from their land. The British, after World War I, took control of the Holy Land; but they named it Palestine rather than Judah, so as not to anger the Arabs.

Israel became a state in 1948 but it did not take physical possession of Jerusalem, they did not begin to build Jerusalem until they took possession of it in the 1967 Six-Day War. As soon as they took possession, they began to rebuild Jerusalem; the Jewish captivity effectively ended. The angel told Daniel that from the going forth of the command to restore and build Jerusalem until the Messiah, there would be a certain number of years. In the unseen world the command went forth to restore and build Jerusalem. In the world we see, Israel captured Jerusalem and began to rebuild and raise up the holy city from the former desolations, the desolations of many generations. The rebuilding of Jerusalem was what began the countdown till the Messiah before, and it has also begun the countdown till Messiah now.

Daniel said nothing about the temple in connection with the coming of the Messiah, probably because the temple of the Lord in the New Testament is a building not made with hands (Heb. 9:11). According to scripture, the rebuilding of Jerusalem, not the rebuilding of the temple, started the countdown till the Messiah (Dan. 9:25). Jerusalem could not be rebuilt unless the Jews were given liberty by the Lord to return to their land and rebuild it.

The Lord scattered Israel and brought Jerusalem to desolation; and only the Lord could reverse that. They have been given permission; the Lord has issued the command, and the children of Israel have returned to the land of promise and have rebuilt Jerusalem and the cities of Judah. Messiah is coming!

According to prophecies of scripture, Jerusalem was made desolate and Israel was carried away captive two times. The first was when they were carried away captive to Babylon, and the second was when Jesus said Jerusalem would be made desolate and the Jews would fall by the edge of the sword and be led away captive into all nations (Luke 21:20, 24). Both of these scatterings and desolations of Jerusalem are followed by a return to the land and a rebuilding of Jerusalem. And each of these returns and rebuildings of Jerusalem are followed by a coming of the Messiah. God's plan is unfolding before our eyes, it is unfolding before the eyes of the nations.

The captivity that ended in 1948 was under different rules than those of the first captivity because of the upgrade in sin the nation had committed. The Lord said of this captivity, "Therefore I will cast you out of this land into a land that you do not know … where I will not show you favor" (Jer. 16:13). When the Jews were carried into captivity in Babylon, they had favor with the Lord and the king of Babylon. (See Jer. 24:5–7) Then there was also the great deliverance we see in the story of Esther. But in the second captivity, the Lord said He would not show them favor, and there was no deliverance from the Nazis in World War II because they were to receive from the Lord's hand double for all their sins. They were a byword, a taunt, and a curse in the days of Hitler. Their punishment was not over. The holocaust was a terrible thing to bear just like the deaths of all the children in Bethlehem when Jesus was born, but there was a reason—that the scriptures might be fulfilled.

> Then was fulfilled what was spoken by Jeremiah the prophet, saying: "A voice was heard in Ramah, lamentation, weeping, and great mourning, Rachel

weeping for her children, refusing to be comforted, because they are no more." (Matt. 2:17–18)

It has come to pass once again preceding the second coming. Rachel is weeping again for her children and refusing to be comforted due to the great loss of loved ones—because they were no more. But that is behind us now, and the time of favor is at hand; it shall come with the destruction and a great slaughter of their enemies. The new season for Israel begins with the return of the Jews to Israel.

The Lord said He would not show them favor, but He also said in this same passage of scripture that He would bring them back to their land.

> "For I will bring them back into their land which I gave to their fathers. Behold, I will send for many fishermen," says the LORD, "and they shall fish them; and afterward I will send for many hunters, and they shall hunt them from every mountain and every hill, and out of the holes of the rocks … And first I will repay double for their iniquity and their sin." (Jer. 16:15–16, 18)

> Speak comfort to Jerusalem, and cry out to her, that her warfare is ended, that her iniquity is pardoned; for she has received from the LORD's hand double for all her sins. (Isa. 40:2)

Israel had sinned and was in a state of war or controversy with the Lord for two thousand years. The Jews had rejected the Messiah because He had not come to them on their terms. Therefore, they received of the Lord's hand double for their sins; and the words of the prophets have been fulfilled.

The Jews have received from the Lord's hand double for all their sins, but the Lord has also promised them a double-portion blessing. Now is the time to speak comfort to Jerusalem; now is the time to cry out to her, that her warfare has ended and her iniquity is pardoned. Everywhere the Jews went, there was always someone or some group persecuting them because of the curse. But when their punishment was over, their iniquity was pardoned.

Another translation says, "Encourage the people of Jerusalem. Tell them they have suffered long enough, and their sins are now forgiven. I have punished them in full for all their sins" (Isa. 40:2 GNT). Because of the level of sin that was committed, their punishment was to continue for two thousand years, and they had no favor with the Lord. After they had received in full the punishment for their tremendous sin, reconciliation is made and their iniquity is pardoned. "In those days and at that time I will cause to grow up to David a Branch of righteousness; He shall execute judgment and righteousness in the earth. In those days Judah will be saved, and Jerusalem will dwell safely. And this is the name by which she will be called: THE LORD OUR RIGHTEOUSNESS" (Jer. 33:16). All Israel shall be saved and receive from the Lord everlasting righteousness.

They will enter a new season; it is a time of restoration and blessing. The seventy weeks are determined for the Jews and for their holy city Jerusalem; after all Israel is saved, they are in the church and bride of Christ from that point on. The last week (7 years) are a time when the church and Israel are joined together as one body in Christ. It is His plan and there is a purpose: "That He would gather together in one the children of God who were scattered abroad" (John 11:52).

In Isaiah, the Lord spoke of rebuilding Jerusalem and mentioned the double-portion blessing that the Jews would possess in their land—they would feed on the riches of the Gentiles, and the Lord would lavish them with honor. Nothing could come until they had been gathered to their land. Jerusalem has been raised up after the desolations of many generations, the prophecies of scripture have been fulfilled: "And they shall rebuild the old ruins, they shall raise up the former desolations, and they shall repair the ruined cities, the desolations of many generations" (Isa. 61:4).

The desolation of Jerusalem, when the Jews went into captivity in Babylon, was for seventy years, about one generation, but here, they are raising up the desolations of many generations. This prophecy is referring to the rebuilding of Jerusalem and the cities of Judah after nearly two thousand years of desolation; and it is taking place in Israel today.

Notice what the Lord says should take place next.

> But you shall be named the priests of the LORD, they shall call you the servants of our God. You shall eat the riches of the Gentiles, and in their glory, you shall boast. Instead of your shame you shall have double honor, and instead of confusion they shall rejoice in their portion. Therefore, in their land they shall possess double. Everlasting joy shall be theirs. (Isa. 61:6–7)

The Lord mentions the return to their land and the double portion blessing again in Zechariah: "Because of the blood of your covenant, I will set your prisoners free from the waterless pit. Return to the stronghold, you prisoners of hope. Even today I declare that I will restore double to you" (Zech. 9:11–12). Another translation says: "Return, you exiles who now have hope; return to your place of safety. Now I tell you that I will repay you twice over with blessing for all you have suffered" (Zech. 9:12 GNT). There is a double portion blessing for Israel that is about to come.

Zechariah, in this chapter, reveals more of what the Lord is about to do for His people: "Then the LORD will be seen over them, and His arrow will go forth like lightning. The Lord GOD will blow the trumpet and go with whirlwinds from the south. The LORD of hosts will defend them" (Zech. 9:14–15). When the Lord defends His people from their enemies, it will be like a whirlwind!

Remember in Jeremiah, how it says that the whirlwind of the Lord has gone forth in fury, and in the latter days you will understand it perfectly? (Jer. 23:19–20) We are in the latter days; the prophets are referring to the same event. The nations will see the Lord over His people. Israel will look upon Him, whom they pierced. He will plead His case with them face to face, and all Israel will be saved! Their Messiah will do great things for them!

Just as the Jews have received from the Lord's hand double for all their sins, it is time that He should bestow upon them the double-portion blessing.

> "Nor will I let you hear the taunts of the nations anymore, nor bear the reproach of the peoples anymore, nor shall you cause your nation to stumble anymore," says the Lord GOD. (Ezek. 36:15)

> For in My wrath I struck you, but in My favor, I have had mercy on you. (Isa. 60:10)

> "Surely it is coming, and it shall be done," says the Lord GOD. "This is the day of which I have spoken." (Ezek. 39:8)

As we go further into what is written in the prophets, all these things will be understood.

Many in the church have a negative view of the Jewish people because the Jews do not believe in their Messiah. This was a problem in the early church as well, and Paul addresses it. Notice what he says in Romans 11. Consider that the Holy Spirit was speaking these things through Paul to the church when he wrote,

> For I do not desire, brethren, that you should be ignorant of this mystery, lest you should be wise in your own opinion, that blindness in part has

happened to Israel until the fullness of the Gentiles has come in. And so, all Israel will be saved. The Deliverer will come out of Zion, and He will turn away ungodliness from Jacob; for this is My covenant with them, when I take away their sins. (Rom. 11:25–27)

Jesus is coming, glorious in His apparel, traveling in the greatness of His strength! He who speaks in righteousness, mighty to save! Behold, He is coming!! The psalmist said, "Oh, that the salvation of Israel would come out of Zion! When the LORD brings back the captivity of His people, let Jacob rejoice and Israel be glad" (Ps. 14:7). When the Lord brings back the captivity of His people, the salvation of Israel is at hand. All Israel shall be saved! The salvation of Israel will come out of Zion, the deliverer will come out of Zion, the Lord will roar out of Zion, and utter His voice from Jerusalem, the heavens and earth will shake! It is going to be a SHOW! Let Israel rejoice, and Jacob be glad because their King-Messiah is coming to do great things for His people and the whole world!

The Jews have received from the Lord's hand double for their greater sin, but the Lord did not say the whole nation was condemned for eternity because of the sin of a few but only those who had committed this sin.

> The soul who sins shall die ... His blood shall be upon him ... The son shall not bear the guilt of the father, nor the father bear the guilt of the son. The righteousness of the righteous shall be upon himself and the wickedness of the wicked shall be upon himself. (Ezek. 18:4, 13, 19)

The Jews of that day had ushered in this new level of eternal condemning sin, and it caused the whole nation to see no favor from God when they were scattered into all the earth. They bore their shame among the nations wherever they went, and the fullness of the curse was upon them for two-thousand years. However, whenever the Lord spoke of sending Israel into captivity, He always promises them that He would bring them back to their land.

The nations around Israel today are still eager to punish them as they have been doing for so many years. But the time of their punishment has ended, and their iniquity has been pardoned. However, the nations around them do not take notice of what God says to their own destruction. The Lord has declared that He will show His mighty power in the day that He destroys the enemies of Israel. It is going to be a great show! It is God's grand finale. The Lord said He would lift His hand in an oath to the nations and they would gather His scattered ones because He has glorified them with His presence.

> Behold, I will lift My hand in an oath to the nations, And set up My standard for the peoples; They shall bring your sons in their arms, And your daughters shall be carried on their shoulders; Kings shall be your foster fathers, And their queens your nursing mothers; They shall bow down to you with their faces to the earth, And lick up the dust of your feet. Then you will know that I am the LORD, for they shall not be ashamed who wait for Me. (Isa. 49:22–23)

The Lord does not raise His hand in an oath very often in scripture, but here, we see Him do so to demonstrate His firm resolve. It appears that the very thing that will cause Israel to be honored by the nations will be something He again; raises His hand in an oath to do. His resolve against His enemies is just and firm.

> Thus says the Lord GOD: "Behold, I have spoken in My jealousy and My fury, because you have borne the shame of the nations." Therefore, thus says the

Lord GOD: "I have raised My hand in an oath that surely the nations that are around you shall bear their own shame." (Ezek. 36:6–7)

Israel has borne the shame of the nations for two thousand years; now it is these nations' turn to bear their own shame. We see that His anger is against the nations around Israel that despise them. Once the rest of the nations see the destruction of His enemies, the people of the Lord will be garnished with praise and double honor.

Sing, O daughter of Zion! Shout, O Israel! Be glad and rejoice with all your heart, O daughter of Jerusalem! The LORD has taken away your judgments, He has cast out your enemy. The King of Israel, the LORD, is in your midst; You shall see disaster no more. In that day it shall be said to Jerusalem: "Do not fear Zion, let not your hands be weak. The LORD your God in your midst, the Mighty One, will save; He will rejoice over you with gladness, He will quiet you with His love, He will rejoice over you with singing. (Zeph. 3:14–17)

The Lord will save Israel and quiet His people with His love and rejoice over them with singing after He has gathered them back and demonstrated His mighty hand and outstretched arm against His enemies.

"I will gather those who sorrow over the appointed assembly, who are among you, to whom its reproach is a burden. Behold, at that time I will deal with all who afflict you; I will save the lame and gather those who were driven out; I will appoint them for praise and fame in every land where they were put to shame. At that time, I will bring you back, even

at the time I gather you; for I will give you fame
and praise among all the peoples of the earth, when
I return your captives before your eyes," says the
LORD. (Zeph. 3:18–20)

The Lord will give Israel fame and praise among all the nations
where they were put to shame: "But the LORD will arise over you,
And His glory will be seen upon you. The Gentiles shall come to
your light, And kings to the brightness of your rising" (Isa. 60:2–3).

Isaiah described this time of favor and blessing more so than
any other prophet.

Then you shall see and become radiant, and your
heart shall swell with joy; because the abundance
of the sea shall be turned to you, the wealth of the
Gentiles shall come to you. (Isa. 60:5)

They shall bring gold and incense, and they shall
proclaim the praises of the LORD ... And I will
glorify the house of My glory ... Therefore, your
gates shall be open continually; they shall not be shut
day or night that men may bring to you the wealth
of the Gentiles and their kings in procession ... I
will make you an eternal excellence, a joy of many
generations. You shall drink the milk of the Gentiles
and milk the breast of kings; you shall know that
I, the LORD, am your Savior and your Redeemer,
the Mighty One of Jacob. (Isa. 60:6, 7, 11, 15–16)

Their hearts will swell with joy when they see the leaders of
nations bringing their gold and wealth with incense as they proclaim
praises to the Lord; because they have seen the wonders the Lord does
for His people. The Lord will make bare His holy arm in the eyes of
all nations, and all the ends of the earth shall see the salvation of the

Lord our God, the Mighty One of Jacob. By their enemy's destruction, the Lord will be magnified and glorified; all the nations who observe these things will honor and adorn the people of the Lord.

> Thus says the LORD of hosts: "In those days ten men from every language of the nations shall grasp the sleeve of a Jewish man, saying, 'Let us go with you, for we have heard that God is with you.'" (Zech. 8:23)

> The LORD their God will save them on that day as the flock of his people. They will sparkle in his land like jewels in a crown. How attractive and beautiful they will be! (Zech. 9:16–17 NIV)

Their reproach and shame will be remembered perpetually, but the time of favor He has promised them is now at hand: "For thus says the LORD: 'Just as I have brought all this great calamity on this people, so I will bring on them all the good that I have promised them'" (Jer. 32:42). They have borne their shame; the time of their promised blessing is at hand.

> Therefore, thus says the Lord GOD: "Now I will bring back the captives of Jacob and have mercy on the whole house of Israel; and I will be jealous for My holy name, after they have borne their shame, and all their unfaithfulness in which they were unfaithful to Me." (Ezek. 39:25–26)

The Lord has gathered Israel back to their land and established the state of Israel to signify that the time of their punishment and exile has ended. Now He is about to perform all the great and marvelous things He promised them. Their King-Messiah is coming to deliver them, He is coming to save them, and He is coming to fulfill all His promises to them. Jesus their King-Messiah is coming to do great things for His people.

More prophecies refer to the gathering and restoration of Israel than any other event in scripture. Many prophecies about God's grand finale can be understood only when we know the Messianic cycle. After two thousand years in captivity, the sign of the coming of the Messiah is the gathering of the Jewish people to the land of their fathers. The gathering of Israel is the budding of the fig tree in Jesus' parable. "Then He spoke to them a parable: "Look at the fig tree, and all the trees. When they are already budding, you see and know for yourselves that summer is now near" (Luke 21:29-32).

All the nations of prophecy were not on the map in the 1800's. But after World War I all the nations of prophecy began to appear on the world stage as they took root down and began budding upward; preparing to bloom into what the Lord has prophesied about them. But of Israel He says: "Those who come He shall cause to take root in Jacob; Israel shall blossom and bud and fill the face of the world with fruit" (Isa. 27:6) The harvest is coming!

CHAPTER 4

God's Blessing to the Nations

The Biblical history of Israel will help us understand God's plan for His people today. God created Israel not just to bless Abraham and his descendants but also to bless all nations. The Lord promised Abraham in Genesis 12:3, "I will bless those who bless you and curse those who curse you, and in you all the families of the earth shall be blessed." This is one of several blessings God gave Abraham that would come upon him and his descendants and then upon the Gentiles or the nations.

Another blessing and a promise God made to Abraham, that applies only to his descendants, shines a light on why we have come to the place we are today in the Middle East. This promise has had a tremendous effect on our world today; it is the promise of the land God gave Abraham and his descendants forever.

> And the LORD said to Abram ... "Lift your eyes now and look from the place where you are northward, southward, eastward, and westward; for all the land which you see I give to you and your descendants forever." (Gen. 13:14–15)

> He remembers His covenant forever, the word which He commanded for a thousand generations,

> the covenant which He made with Abraham, and
> His oath to Isaac, and confirmed it to Jacob for a
> statute, to Israel as an everlasting covenant, saying;
> "To you I will give the land of Canaan as the
> allotment of your inheritance." (Ps. 105:8–11)

That should end all dispute over the land. God gave Abraham and his descendants that land forever! And the Bible says, "The earth is the Lord's and the fullness thereof" (1 Cor. 10:26). If God owns the world and has given a small piece of land to His chosen people, Israel, who can overcome God? What are the nations that they can make war with Him? "The nations raged, the kingdoms were moved, He uttered His voice, the earth melted" (Ps. 46:6). There is no place in God's Word where He said He would ever take the land back or give it to another people; that idea came from the mind of man.

There has been a dispute over the Promised Land for nearly a hundred years that continues to this day. When God gives a land to a people and another nation or people say, "The land is given to us as a possession," there will be war between that people and the Lord God almighty. However, this conflict and coming battle are a part of God's plan that began to come to light in Genesis. God said to Abram,

> Know certainly that your descendants will be
> strangers in a land that is not theirs, and will serve
> them, and they will afflict them four hundred
> years. And also, the nation whom they serve I will
> judge; afterward they shall come out with great
> possessions. Now as for you, you shall go to your
> fathers in peace; you shall be buried at a good old
> age. But in the fourth generation they shall return
> here, for the iniquity of the Amorites is not yet
> complete. (Gen. 15:13–16)

God told Abraham that He gave Canaan to his descendants forever, but first, they would be strangers in another land and be afflicted for four hundred years. Abraham must have thought, *Four hundred years! Does it have to be that long? That is an awful long time to be afflicted, and we're talking about my children here! What is God thinking?* If God told us our children would be afflicted all their lives and die as slaves in affliction, we would contend with God because that would not be fair. But God had a plan that was beyond human reasoning.

God was establishing the prophetic ministry and the prophetic word. He prophesied to Abraham what would happen in the next five hundred years so that when his descendants went to Egypt, they would know how long they would be there and when to look for their deliverer. The plan was passed down from generation to generation—God would bring them out of Egypt and into the land He had promised them. Joseph bore witness to what his great-grandfather had spoken; when he was dying, he made mention of the departure of the children of Israel from Egypt and gave instructions concerning his bones. He wanted to be buried in the Promised Land (Gen. 50:25).

By the time the prophetic word was to be fulfilled, it was probably considered almost a myth. They saw the power of the Egyptian army; it looked impossible for them to be freed of slavery by human means. And besides, the promise was an ancient word that was nothing more than a hope for the future for the children of Israel—not too much different from the promise of Christ's second coming for most people today. However, the people who know their God are fully persuaded that what He has promised will come to pass.

God had a purpose for all He did. Yes, Abraham's descendants would be afflicted for four hundred years, but afterward, God would judge that nation and the Israelites would come out with great possessions. God planned to bring Abraham's descendants into the Holy Land and establish them as His chosen people in the midst of the nations; but first He wanted to display His mighty power in such a way that it would be talked about for thousands of years. By this opening show, God would reveal Himself to all nations and every generation that would come afterward, as the God of Israel, the everlasting God. From that event on, all nations would be blessed with a written record of all God had done in Egypt, so there would be no question that the Lord God of Israel is God in heaven above and on the earth beneath there is no other.

When the time arrived for the Lord to bring the children of Israel out of Egypt, He announced the purpose for this great and awesome event in Exodus. God said to Pharaoh,

> Thus says the LORD God of the Hebrews: "Let My people go, that they may serve Me, for at this time I will send all My plagues to your very heart, and on your servants and on your people, that you may know that there is none like Me in all the earth. Now if I had stretched out My hand and struck you and your people with pestilence, then you would have been cut off from the earth. But indeed, for this purpose I have raised you up, that I may SHOW My power in you, and that MY NAME may be declared in all the earth."
> (Ex. 9:13–16)

Notice that God pointed out that He could have sent pestilence and killed all the Egyptians in a single blow, but that would not have been much of a show. God wanted to make a great and mighty show of His power, so His name would be declared in all the earth. God planned this opening show to take place in the largest kingdom and commerce center in the world in that day; news of whatever happened in Egypt would be carried home by tradesmen and merchants to the four corners of the earth; Joseph had been sold to traveling merchants on their way to Egypt.

> And they sat down to eat a meal. Then they lifted
> their eyes and looked, and there was a company of
> Ishmaelites, coming from Gilead with their camels,
> bearing spices, balm, and myrrh, on their way to
> carry them down to Egypt. (Gen. 37:25)

Traveling merchants from all over the world came to Egypt to buy and sell goods. Those who were in Egypt at that time, saw the plagues of frogs, lice, flies, boils, locusts, and hail mingled with fire rain down on Egypt. They saw that Pharaoh's wise men asked him, "Do you not yet know that Egypt is destroyed?" (Ex. 10:7) Traveling merchants saw that the crops and cattle of Egypt were destroyed, that their firstborn were dead. They saw that none of these plagues had affected the children of Israel. It was evident to them that God had sanctified Israel, so that they were untouched by all that was going on around them. But though Egypt was destroyed, it was not over for Pharaoh; the greatest show of God's power was yet to come.

Pharaoh finally let the children of Israel go; they left Egypt for the land God had promised them. But when the Israelites came to the Red Sea, they stopped. We can see Pharaoh's pride; he was on top of the world. He was the king of Egypt with an army so great that no one could withstand his will. He was praised for his greatness, splendor, power, and might, but he had been humbled by Hebrew slaves. His counselors and all the ambassadors from other nations were looking at him in astonishment; how he had fallen from his greatness and was found to be just a man. His whole kingdom was destroyed; his greatness and glory had left him. The horde of slaves who had made his kingdom great had left him. Then Pharaoh and his men asked, "Why have we let Israel go?"

Pharaoh made ready all the chariots of Egypt and pursued the children of Israel to bring them back. I imagine many tradesmen followed them curious to see what the end of these things would be. They watched Pharaoh's army approach the children of Israel. They saw the sea at their backs and Pharaoh charging before them. They saw the pillar of fire the Lord put between the children of Israel and the Egyptians. They saw the waters of the sea part and a mighty wind dry the floor of the sea so the Israelites could walk between the walls of water on dry ground. They saw that after Israel had crossed through the Red Sea, when the Egyptians tried to follow them the sea came crashing down on all of Pharaoh's chariots. They saw God destroy Pharaoh's army in an instant with his mighty hand and outstretched arm. The news of what God did to the Egyptians spread like wildfire blown by a mighty wind in all directions. The testimony of the merchants was powerful; the people who heard them probably had to calm them down, so they could understand what they were saying.

As a result of this great and mighty show of God's power His name was and is declared in all the earth to this day. He chose Israel to reveal Himself and make His mighty power known in the eyes of all nations, His intended audience in all His dealings with Israel. It was not just His power that He wanted the nations to know, but His righteous judgments, laws and statutes. God knew a great show of His mighty power would put the nations in awe and tingle the ears of all who heard of His awesome power. The show was not just for Israel, there was an audience God was wooing.

> I will remember the covenant of their ancestors, whom I brought out of the land of Egypt in the sight of the nations, that I might be their God. (Lev. 26:45)

> But I acted for My name's sake, that it should not be profaned before the nations among whom they were, in whose sight I had made Myself known to them, to bring them out of the land of Egypt. (Ezek. 20:9)

God could have cut off all the people of Egypt with a single blow, but He wanted to demonstrate His great and awesome power so all peoples of the earth would know He alone is God.

Even forty years after the parting of the Red Sea, we see the effects of His show when Joshua sent two spies to Jericho; the harlot Rahab testified of what the people of Jericho had heard from some traumatized witness of the great acts of the God of Israel.

> I know that the Lord has given you the land, that the terror of you has fallen on us, and that all the inhabitants of the land are fainthearted because of you. For we have heard how the Lord dried up the water of the Red Sea for you when you came out of Egypt, and what you did to the two kings of the Amorites who were on the other side of the Jordan, Sihon and Og, whom you utterly destroyed. And as soon as we heard these things, our hearts melted; neither did there remain any courage in anyone because of you, for the Lord your God, He is God in heaven above and on the earth beneath. (Josh. 2:10–11)

The inhabitants of the land were fainthearted because of what they had heard of the mighty God of Israel. The nations feared and trembled at the mention of His name.

More than four hundred years later, the Philistines remembered what God had done. In 1 Samuel, we read that the Philistines had captured the Ark of the Covenant and a destruction came upon them; many died, the rest were stricken with tumors, and rats plagued their land. So they decided to send the Ark of the Covenant back to Israel. In case anyone objected they said, "Why then do you harden your hearts as the Egyptians and Pharaoh hardened their hearts? When He did mighty things among them, did they not let the people go, that they might depart?" (1 Sam. 6:6).

The testimony of what God had done was still doing its work in the hearts of the nations hundreds of years later though, at that time, it had been carried only by word of mouth. No one could say the God of Israel was a worthless carved image as were the gods of other nations. Because of the testimony, many were drawn to visit the house of God in Jerusalem according to what was written: "For My house shall be called a house of prayer for all nations" (Isa. 56:7). Solomon prayed at the dedication of the house of God in Jerusalem for foreigners who would hear of the great name of the God of Israel and come to pray before Him in Jerusalem.

> Moreover, concerning a foreigner, who is not of Your people Israel, but has come from a far country (from the nations) for Your name's sake, for they will hear of Your great name and Your strong hand and Your outstretched arm, when he comes and prays toward this temple, hear in heaven Your dwelling place, and do according to all for which the foreigner calls to You, that all peoples of the earth may know Your name and fear You, as do Your people Israel. (1 Kings 8:41–43)

It is still His aim that all nations fear His awesome name and walk in His ways. The fear of the Lord is the beginning of wisdom! God wanted all nations to know Him.

> "Let not the wise man glory in his wisdom, Let not the mighty man glory in his might, Nor let the rich man glory in his riches; But let him who glories glory in this, That he understands and knows Me, That I am the Lord, exercising lovingkindness, judgment, and righteousness in the earth. For in these I delight," says the Lord. (Jer. 9:23–24)

Not only was God's name and power made known to all nations through His people but also His ways and wisdom and the things in which He delights—loving-kindness, judgment, and righteousness. The Egyptians were shedding the innocent blood of the Hebrew slaves, and that demanded judgment after the time had been fulfilled. God's judgment is righteous; He is known by His judgments. Let he who glories glory in this, that he knows and understands the Lord.

In their latter end, Israel began to worship false gods, and that was their downfall. People who turn from the true and living God to worship idols set aside their moral and godly character. Idols have no godly rules; those who worship them cast off restraint and run wild. It seems that murder, rape, stealing, lying, and cheating are on their to-do list. Those who make their own rules can be wicked, brutal creatures without God.

To punish Israel, God sent them into captivity in Babylon and told them through Jeremiah that they would be there for seventy years. While many in the kingdom of Judah went into captivity, most of them resisted His will and were scattered into all nations. The story of Esther takes place after the seventy-year captivity and the Jews had returned to Israel; many others were still scattered, but with them was the story of God's might.

> It was written, according to all that Mordecai commanded, to the Jews, the satraps, the governors, and the princes of the provinces from India to Ethiopia, one hundred and twenty-seven provinces in all, to every province in its own script, to every people in their own language, and to the Jews in their own script and language. (Est. 8:9)

It would not have made sense for Mordecai to send his letter to all these 127 provinces to save the Jews if there were no Jews there. And if there were Jews in every province, the story of Moses leading the children of Israel out of Egypt was preached in every city in the synagogues: "For Moses has had throughout many generations those who preach him in every city, being read in the synagogues every

Sabbath" (Acts 15:21). The Jews carried into every nation where ever they went the written account of the show of God's power!

In Acts 2, we see that on the day of Pentecost, there were dwelling in Jerusalem; Jews from every nation under heaven. (Acts 2:5–11) Even in the days of Jesus, Jews were still dwelling in every nation. If Jews were in every nation, there were synagogues in every nation. And if there were synagogues, they were preaching Moses to all people throughout every generation in every city every Sabbath. The story of what God did in Egypt by His mighty hand and outstretched arm had no equal; it has captured the attention of nations and moved people deeply throughout many generations.

It was God's way of making Himself and the truth known because there had always been many man-made gods and idols, so there were always questions in people's hearts: Is this really God? Is there really a God? How can I know God? The questions were answered when the story of Moses and the parting of the Red Sea was told. There is no other story like it in all the earth because there is no other God in all the earth; there is no god who acts for His people as the God of Israel does. Notice how God pointed these things out.

> For ask now concerning the days that are past, which were before you, since the day that God created man on the earth and ask from one end of heaven to the other, whether any great thing like this has happened, or anything like it has been heard. Did any people ever hear the voice of God speaking out of the midst of the fire, as you have heard, and live? Or did God ever try to go and take for Himself a nation from the midst of another nation, by trials, by signs, by wonders, by war, by a mighty hand and an outstretched arm, and by great terrors, according to all that the LORD your God did for you in Egypt before your eyes? To you it was shown, that you might know that the LORD

Himself is God; there is none other besides Him …
Therefore, know this day, and consider it in your
heart, that the LORD Himself is God in heaven
above and on the earth beneath; there is no other.
(Deut. 4:32–35, 39)

The servants of God preached to every generation in every
synagogue in every nation under heaven that the Lord is God in
heaven and on earth and that there was no other god. That was
confirmed by God's mighty hand. Even before Christ, this message
was prospering among Jews and Gentiles; notice what Acts 17:17 says
about Paul's audience: "Therefore he reasoned in the synagogue with
the Jews and with the Gentile worshipers." Jew and Gentile alike
were in synagogues listening as Moses was read and preached every
Sabbath. God put synagogues in every nation so He could reveal
Himself to every generation in every nation.

Now we can understand what the Lord meant and planned
when He said to Pharaoh, "For this purpose I have raised you up,
that I might show My power in you and that My name might be
declared in all the earth!" (Ex. 9:16) The Lord made known to all
nations His power and His great and awesome name through His
people. Israel was and is God's witness to the nations that the Lord
is God: "You are My witnesses, Says the Lord, that I am God" (Isa.
43:12). Israel was a witness of the blessings that would come upon a
people if they obeyed God's judgments and statutes and His anger if
they did not. Israel was a witness of all these things in the synagogue
every Sabbath in every city of every nation.

We can be certain the testimony did not turn the hearts of
everyone from evil, but many generations heard the stories of the
God of Israel, and it changed their lives. The testimony of what God
had done produced Gentile believers such as Cornelius in Acts 10.

There was a certain man in Caesarea called
Cornelius, a centurion of what was called the Italian

Regiment, a devout man and one who feared God
with all his household, who gave alms generously to
the people, and prayed to God always.

This was the fruit of God's message. Consider how many
people were blessed through Cornelius when many Jews were not
as generous. Through this one man, the blessing extended to his
household, neighbors, and community. And others like Cornelius
were produced in every generation in every nation by what they
heard in the synagogues.

Yes, there is the plan of salvation, but the nations were prepared
and cultivated with the Word of God even before Christ so that
when Christ came, they would believe even when many Jews did
not. We see the proof of this all through Acts. It has been God's
plan from the days of old to bless the nations through Abraham
and his descendants, and now we know His plan in its fullness. As
Cornelius's household was, many Gentile households were blessed
because they heard how God had shown His might when He brought
the children of Israel out of Egypt and how He made a great and
awesome name for Himself.

Another person worth mentioning is the eunuch from Ethiopia
in Acts 8. All we know of this brother is what was written about
him in Acts. He was in charge of the treasury of Queen Candace of
Ethiopia; and had come to Jerusalem to worship. He had everything
a man could want as far as wealth goes, but the treasure he sought
was not silver and gold. He had traveled for many days because he
had heard of the great and awesome name of the Lord. He came to
Jerusalem to worship the living God and had probably purchased
a copy of the book of Isaiah at great price. He was eagerly reading
through it when Philip overtook his chariot. He was one of those of
whom Solomon prayed for where he said,

"Moreover, concerning a foreigner, who is not of
Your people Israel, but has come from a far country

for Your name's sake (for they will hear of Your great
name and Your strong hand and Your outstretched
arm), when he comes and prays toward this temple,
hear in heaven Your dwelling place, and do according
to all for which the foreigner calls to You, that all
peoples of the earth may know Your name and fear
You, as do Your people Israel." (1 Kings 8:41-43)

This man of Ethiopia was rewarded because he sought God with
all his heart; the scripture says God rewards those who diligently
seek Him.

The first evangelist in the New Testament was sent by an angel
to preach Christ to this man. He got the gospel fresh of the press as
we would say today. The whole and full gospel was preached to this
man, so when they came upon some water, the first thing that came
to his mind was obedience to the faith—he wanted to be baptized.
The impact of that moment was so tremendous that a nation was
blessed by what one man brought back from the Holy Land.

This man had heard way down in Ethiopia about God's great
name and power and was deeply moved to travel all the way to
Jerusalem to seek the Lord and worship Him. After his return to
Ethiopia with the gospel, his household, neighbors, community, and
country were blessed. Remember what Solomon said would be the
result of the foreigner who would encounter God at the temple in
Jerusalem: "That all peoples of the earth may know Your name and
fear You!" This is a perfect picture of how the nations were blessed
through Abraham and his descendants. This was God's plan, and
this happened in generation after generation in all nations, but we
will not hear the testimony of them all till we get to heaven.

Abraham, the father of Israel, did not have the whole picture of
how God would bless all nations through his descendants or how
He would make a great show of His might to all nations. He did not
know how God would make His great name declared in all the earth.
He did not have any prophetic word describing how God would

divide the Red Sea or destroy Pharaoh's great and mighty army. He did not know a lot of things, but what he did know, all came to pass. We may not know a lot of things concerning the end times, but we can believe and know that His prophetic word will come to pass.

We can now look back at God's plan for those days and see that Abraham did not know a lot of things that we know. We understand why God permitted Abraham's descendants to be afflicted by the Egyptians and how God in His righteousness at the appointed time judged those who afflicted them. We know that though the time appointed was long, all God prophesied over Abraham came to pass. We know it took about five hundred years to set the stage for what He did in the days of Moses. It was not what the children of Israel would have planned or how they would have done it; God's plan was much greater than what they expected, because when they saw it they couldn't believe it.

Do we know everything there is to know about God's plan for the last days? Did Abraham know everything about God's plan because he was a prophet? (Gen. 20:7) No. We have more knowledge of God today than any other generation before us; we have the prophetic word confirmed to us in all the stories in the Bible, and we have the prophetic word confirmed to us in what is happening in our world today. If we want to know what God's plan is for the last days, we must first consider all He has already done in the sight of the nations; He will not act out of character.

If any man should boast, let him boast in this, that he knows and understands the Lord. The most important thing we can glean from these things today is how God has revealed Himself to all the nations of the world through what He has done with His people Israel. Because He is speaking to all nations today through what He is doing with His people. He is telling us what time it is. He is revealing the work of His hands in Israel and watching to see whether the nations are for or against Him. The Lord has given Israel and their land a place in His plan that none can take away though they may try.

We have an unshakeable foundation for all that is said in the prophets concerning the last days. All God did in the days of Moses was a type and a foreshadowing of what was to come. There is confirmation after confirmation that a similar, but much greater show of His mighty power will come to pass in the last days. As in the days of old, it will be accomplished through His people Israel in the sight of the nations.

All God's dealings with Israel have been in the sight of the nations, and they tell us what is to come. God is still fulfilling His promise to Abraham. He is still blessing the nations today by what He is doing with Israel and they do not even know it. All nations have seen how God gathered His people back to their land, they see that their evil neighbors have an "ancient hatred and have shed the blood of the children of Israel." They hear them say, "Aha! The ancient heights (mountains of Israel which they call the West Bank today), have become our possession!" And how all the enemies of Israel have said; "Come, let us cut them off from being a nation, that the name of Israel may be remembered no more!" The nations have seen how the enemies of the Lord, have divided up His land. (Ezek. 35:5, 36:2, Ps. 83:4, Joel 3:2) But God has a plan.

Many have asked, "Why doesn't God demonstrate His great and mighty power today like He did in the days of Moses? Where are the great and mighty works of the Lord God of Israel today? If God is with Israel today, why doesn't He do something about all the affliction that His people Israel are suffering from all those around them who despise them?"

He permitted His chosen people to be afflicted before for a reason and a purpose, and now we know the reason and the purpose. However, the iniquity of His enemies must be complete before He will judge those who afflict His people. When the time has been fulfilled, He will execute judgment on those around them who afflict them; it will be a great and awesome show in the eyes of all the nations. If God will do an awesome work before all nations will He not tell His people beforehand? As it is written: "Surely the Lord

God does nothing, unless He reveals His secret to His servants the prophets" (Amos 3:7). The Lord said,

> As in the days when you came out of the land of Egypt I will SHOW them wonders. The nations shall see and be ashamed of all their might, they shall put their hand over their mouth, their ears shall be deaf ... They shall be afraid of the LORD our God and shall fear because of You. (Mic. 7:15–17)

This act of God will be so great and awesome that He compared it to the days when He brought Israel out of Egypt. It will be a show of God's mighty power that all the nations shall see; they will be ashamed of all their useless military might. All the nations will fear the Lord God of Israel; their knees will knock against each other because of what they see. They will be filled with disbelief and dismay as they watch His SHOW. God has prepared a great and awesome show for us and the world in the last days.

> Awake, awake, put on strength, O arm of the LORD! Awake as in the ancient days, in the generations of old ... Are You not the One who dried up the sea, the waters of the great deep, that made the depths of the sea a road for the redeemed to cross over? (Isa. 51:9–10)

That is a call to arms for the Lord as in the ancient days. It is a call to Him who dried up the Red Sea so His redeemed could cross over. Where is the great and awesome arm of the Lord we have heard about in ancient times? This is the cry of Israel and the nations today. Where is the great and awesome God of Israel we have heard about for hundreds of years? Wake up, O arm of the Lord, as in the ancient days.

In Isaiah 52, the Lord recounted the show He put on when He brought Israel out of Egypt and then spoke of bringing back Zion to its land and how He would bare His holy arm in the eyes of all nations. He has spoken of making His great power known in the past by His servants the prophets, and then brought it to pass in the eyes of the nations. And He has done the same again. The Lord said,

> "My people went down at first Into Egypt to dwell there; then the Assyrian oppressed them without cause. Now therefore, what have I here," says the LORD, "That My people are taken away for nothing? Those who rule over them Make them wail," says the LORD, "And My name is blasphemed continually every day. Therefore, My people shall know My name; therefore, they shall know in that day that I am He who speaks: 'Behold, it is I.'" (Isa. 52:4-6)

His people are being afflicted and killed without cause; those who are around them, and in their midst, make them wail by suicide bombings and knife attacks whereby they kill the unsuspecting and shed innocent blood. The families of the innocent wail and grieve for their loss and His name is blasphemed continually as they ask, "Where is our God?" But His people shall know in that day that it is He who has spoken these things. The Lord said,

> Break forth into joy sing together you waste places of Jerusalem! For the LORD has comforted His people, He has redeemed Jerusalem. The LORD has made bare His holy arm in the eyes of all the nations, and all the ends of the earth shall see the salvation of our God. (Isa. 52:9–10)

> The LORD their God will save them in that day, as the flock of His people. (Zech. 9:16)

The Messiah Israel has been waiting for, for thousands of years will suddenly come and not keep silent; He will appear in these

last days with a mighty hand and outstretched arm to deliver them
from those who hate them, and their enemies will have no power to
stand against Him. It will be a time of great glory for His people:
"The glory of the LORD shall be revealed, and all flesh shall see
it together, for the mouth of the LORD has spoken" (Isa. 40:5).
The glory of God shall be revealed to the nations through His
people Israel. The blessing the Lord spoke about to Abraham will
be fulfilled through his descendants: "In you all the nations of the
earth shall be blessed" (Gen. 12:3). For they shall know that the Lord
is God in heaven above and on the earth beneath there is no other.

> Arise, shine, for your light has come! And the glory
> of the LORD is risen upon you. For behold, the
> darkness shall cover the earth and deep darkness the
> people, but the LORD will arise over you and His
> glory will be seen upon you. (Isa. 60:1–2)

This agrees with what the Lord says in Ezekiel: "I will set My
glory among the nations; all the nations shall see My judgment
which I have executed, and My hand which I have laid on them"
(Ezek. 39:21). The Lord will be exalted in the eyes of all nations
when they see His judgment on His enemies, a great and mighty
show! "Be still and know that I am God; I will be exalted among the
nations, I will be exalted in the earth!" (Ps 46:10).

The epicenter of all the prophecies referring to this event is in
Ezekiel; the prophecies in Micah and Isaiah are a few of the many
satellite prophecies that speak of the same event. They are different
views from the same great and high prophetic mountain. Several of
the characteristics of the acts of God we see in the days of Moses
parallel this massive event for the last days. Because it will be a great
and awesome show of His power, a grand finale culminating the age,
we can expect to find many references to it in the prophetic Word
of God. And as in so many events in the days of old, Israel will be
center stage of this world-changing event!

CHAPTER 5

The Judgment of the Gods

There are several things God did in the days of Moses that parallel what we see lining up in our days. Another thing God did in the days of Moses that gives us more insight to what we see today is the judgment of the gods of Egypt. In Exodus, God's judgment not only came upon the Egyptians as He spoke to Abraham saying, "Afterwards the nation whom they serve I will judge," but it also came upon all the gods of Egypt as well: "I will pass through the land of Egypt on that night and will strike all the firstborn in the land of Egypt, both man and beast; and against all the gods of Egypt I will execute judgment: I am the LORD" (Ex. 12:12–13).

How did God execute judgment on all the gods of Egypt? How do you judge gods? There isn't anything to them; they are nothing. As we can see in scripture, flesh and blood cannot judge a god even though it is a false god. It takes an intervention of the Lord God almighty to execute judgment on the gods men have created in their own minds. False gods have been around for a long time. They have been found in excavation sites in the oldest civilizations of mankind. Who decided to carve images and call them gods? Where did the idea come from?

The first thing that comes to my mind is 1 Timothy 4:1: "Now the Spirit expressly says that in latter times some will depart from the faith, giving heed to deceiving spirits and doctrines of demons." How do people give heed or attention to deceiving spirits and doctrines or teachings of demons? Ancient people got the idea of making gods from deceiving spirits who taught them these lies. Just as the Holy Spirit teaches us the things of the Spirit of God, evil spirits teach things of the kingdom of darkness to those who will listen to them. People have thought that these evil doctrines came from God, but they did not. The apostle Paul said we must cast down imaginations that are against God and bring every thought into subjection to the words of Christ or we too can be deceived (2 Cor. 10:5). Notice what Revelation says about Satan: "He laid hold of the dragon, that serpent of old, who is the Devil and Satan, and bound him … so that he should deceive the nations no more" (Rev. 20:2–3).

Just as Satan deceived Adam and Eve, he is deceiving the nations today. He has not yet been locked up. Wars and destruction are the work of his hands, and they have been taking place all through history and are taking place today. Lies and deception are the root of every strange religion. Here in Revelation, we see why there are so many religions and where all false gods have come from. There is only one true God, but there are many false gods. Jesus said, "I am the way, the truth, and the life. No one comes to the Father except through Me" (John 14:6). There is only one God and Father of all spirits, but many through the ages have been led into error by fallen angels, deceiving spirits, or lying spirits. When we know and believe the truth, we find it hard to understand how people can be led away by dumb idols. God, long ago established who He is, that the truth may be known.

> I am the First and I am the Last; besides Me there is no God. Who can proclaim as I do? Then let him declare it and set it in order for Me, since I appointed the ancient people. And the things that are coming and shall come, let them show these. (Isa. 44:6)

He indicates that this is the test—can idols tell us things to come? No.

The Lord has always proclaimed to His people what was to come. He told Abraham what would happen to his descendants over a time span of more than five hundred years, that when it all came to pass, the world would know that there is a true and living God. Around one hundred years before king Cyrus was born God called him by name and said that He would send His captives back to the land of their inheritance. He proclaimed to Daniel the time and season, about four hundred years beforehand, when the Messiah should come, and it happened just as the Lord had prophesied. He declares in His Word, "I am God, and there is no other; I am God, and there is none like Me, declaring the end from the beginning, and from ancient times things that are not yet done" (Isa. 46:9–10). Idols and false gods have never proclaimed what is to come; can anything be expected from a god that is deaf, dumb, and blind?

In His Word the Lord pleads His case, not only to Israel but to all who worshiped idols.

> Who would form a god or mold an image that profits him nothing?
>
> The blacksmith with the tongs works one in the coals, fashions it with hammers and works it with the strength of his arms. Even so, he is hungry, and his strength fails; he drinks no water and is faint.
>
> The workman molds an image, the goldsmith overspreads it with gold, and the silversmith casts silver chains. Whoever is too impoverished for such a contribution chooses a tree that will not rot; he seeks for himself a skillful workman to prepare a carved image that will not totter.
>
> And no one considers in his heart, nor is there knowledge nor understanding to say, "I have burned

> half of it in the fire, Yes, I have also baked bread on its
> coals; I have roasted meat and eaten it; and shall I make
> the rest of it an abomination? Shall I fall down before a
> block of wood?" (Isa. 40:19, 44:6–7, 10, 12, 19)

God points out the flawed thought process of one who worships idols, he is lacking common sense. How can an idol have more to give than the man who labors and sweats and grows faint and weary making it? If he has no gold or silver, he must choose a wood that will not rot and burn well to cook his food on. Then he makes an image with the leftover pieces of wood to fall down before and call upon to deliver him in times of trouble, to give health and prosperity, or rain in its season. But the Lord says, they can neither see, nor hear, nor speak, they that worship them are like them, so is everyone who trusts in them. (Ps. 135:15-18)

The history of idols goes back to the beginning of civilization. The patriarchs of the Bible were descendants of idol worshipers. Terah, the father of Abram, and Abram's brother Nahor started out in Ur of the Chaldeans and worshiped idols. What do we know about Ur of the Chaldeans and the house of Terah? Why did God instruct Abraham to leave his relatives and his father's house? Excavations of Ur in the early part of the last century revealed that in its day, Ur was a center of industry and worship of the moon god Nanna and the Babylonian equivalent, Sin. There were devotees of many idols at Ur, but the moon god was chief of them all. Abraham was steeped in idolatry in Ur and in his father's house; Joshua 24:2 reads, "Your fathers, including Terah, the father of Abraham and the father of Nahor, dwelt on the other side of the River in old times; and they served other gods." Terah worshiped the moon god, and it seems to have deep roots in the house of Terah generations later.

The Lord instructed Abraham to leave his father's house, but there was a family bond that was not easy to break: "Now the LORD had said to Abram: 'Get out of your country, from your family and from your father's house, to a land that I will show you'" (Gen. 12:1).

Upon hearing Abraham's commission Terah seems to have taken over and led them on their journey to Canaan. Terah was a normal dad who didn't like his son talking about leaving the family and going to Canaan, where he had no family.

> Terah took his son Abram and his grandson Lot, the son of Haran, and his daughter-in-law Sarai, his son Abram's wife, and they went out with them from Ur of the Chaldeans to go to the land of Canaan; and they came to Haran and dwelt there. (Gen. 11:31)

Terah led them out of Ur to go to Canaan, but they went to Haran and dwelt there. The delay was probably because there was family in Haran. Later in scripture, we find that the descendants of Nahor, Abram's brother, dwelt there. When Abram sent his servant to find a wife for Isaac, he was sent to Abraham's family in the city of Nahor (Gen. 24:4, 10). Haran and Nahor were the names of the brothers of Abraham, and this city was called both Haran and Nahor. Nahor had eight sons by his wife, Milcah, one of which was Bethuel, the father of Rebekah and Laban. So, there could have been quite a clan of relatives in Haran.

Isaac and Rebekah had two sons, Esau and Jacob. When Jacob stole the birthright from Esau, his mother instructed him to go to her brother Laban in Haran (Gen. 27:43). While in Haran, Jacob married Leah and Rachel, the daughters of Laban, and went back to Canaan. When they left the house of Laban, Rachel stole her father's idols: "Now Laban had gone to shear his sheep, and Rachel had stolen the household idols that were her father's" (Gen. 31:19–20). This city was where most of Abraham's family dwelt. A temple to the moon god was found in Haran. The household idols of Laban may have included the moon god as well seeing it was chief among the gods of Ur.

After the death of Sarah, Abraham took another wife, her name was Keturah. Besides Ishmael and Isaac, there were born to Abraham

six more sons by Keturah, one of them was named Midian. Abraham
gave gifts to his sons by Keturah, and sent them away from his son,
Isaac, eastward toward Ur (Gen. 25:1–6). The Midianites were of
the sons of Abraham, but also served the gods of their fathers. Notice
that in Judges, Gideon killed the two Midianite kings and took the
crescent ornaments from their camels' necks. (Judg. 8:5, 21) The
crescent ornament indicates that hundreds of years later, many of the
family of Abraham still worshiped the moon god. It is important to
note that the Ishmaelites were closely knit to their half-brothers the
Midianites (Gen. 37:25–28). They were both children of Abraham,
but they were not included in God's promise of the inheritance, and
they worshiped other gods.

It is also very important to note here that Muhammad and
his followers were referred to as Ishmaelites and Hagarites in their
early years. Abraham had had Ishmael by Hagar, Sarah's Egyptian
maid, but God said Ishmael would not be Abraham's heir (Gen.
16). Muhammad claimed to be a descendant of Abraham through
Ishmael. The patriarchs in the Koran are listed as Abraham, Ishmael,
Isaac, and Jacob. Ishmael was Abraham's firstborn, so Muslims
believe they are the true heirs of God's promises and blessings. But
the moon god seems to be behind the revelations of Muhammad;
the symbol chosen for Islam was the crescent moon.

There were hundreds of idols in Mecca in Muhammad's day.
His revelation instructed him to create a monotheistic religion, so
he needed a name for his god. The name he chose was the name of
an existing idol in Mecca that happened to be the same one his
father's house worshiped. It was a small stone idol known as
the moon god Allah. This moon god must be a chief prince in
the Middle East. We can see through scripture and excavations
that it has been at work there for thousands of years and is still
present today. It is curious how the scriptures say that in the
last days, some will depart from the true faith and give heed to
deceiving spirits and doctrines of devils. Muhammad and the
bloody conquest of Islam has taken place in a dispensation known

in scripture as the last days. Could this all be according to what God has spoken in His Word?

While in his father's house, Abraham was surrounded on every side by idolatry. Idols were worshiped in Ur of the Chaldeans, where Abraham and his father Terah came from; it was in his father's house in Haran, where the wives of the patriarchs came from, and it was in the land of Canaan all around him. For Abraham to hear and follow the true God went against the world he lived in. It took a lot of faith to put God above his father and his brothers in Haran and go to a land he had never seen and knew nothing about. By his acts Abraham became a great father of faith.

> By faith he [Abraham] dwelt in the land of promise
> as in a foreign country, dwelling in tents with Isaac
> and Jacob, the heirs with him of the same promise;
> for he waited for the city which has foundations,
> whose builder and maker is God. (Heb. 11:9–10)

Through God's words and promises, Abraham overcame the idols all around him. These spirits of idolatry have been around for many generations, and their desire is to invade God's chosen people and lead them away through lies and deceit.

When the time came to lead the children of Israel into the Promised Land, the Lord instructed them to drive out all the inhabitants of the land because they were idol worshipers. He charged them with driving out all the inhabitants of the Promised Land. He said that if they did not, "They shall be thorns in your side, and their gods shall be a snare to you" (Num. 33:50-55, Josh. 23:4-13)). However, Judges 1–2 says that the children of Israel did not drive out the inhabitants of the land as they had been told, and their gods became a stumbling block for Israel. With all the idolatry of the people of the land mingling with the children of Israel, they eventually fell into idolatry and the wickedness the Canaanites practiced. Notice what is recorded of Israel's idolatry.

> So they left all the commandments of the LORD their God, made for themselves a molded image and two calves, made a wooden image and worshiped all the host of heaven, and served Baal. And they caused their sons and daughters to pass through the fire, practiced witchcraft and soothsaying, and sold themselves to do evil in the sight of the LORD. (2 Kings 17:16–17)

> They even sacrificed their sons and their daughters to demons and shed innocent blood, the blood of their sons and daughters, whom they sacrificed to the idols of Canaan. (Ps. 106:37–38)

> For they have committed adultery, and blood is on their hands. They have committed adultery with their idols, and even sacrificed their sons whom they bore to Me, passing them through the fire, to devour them. (Ezek. 23:37)

Demons teach their worshipers to sacrifice their children to them to separate them from the good and holy God. This practice is very much alive today and is being practiced in the Middle East. Children are being trained and conditioned to be suicide bombers for the greatness of their god. Palestinians are training their children to be martyrs for Allah. They are told that they should chant before they blow themselves up, "Great is Allah!" Go to YouTube and search for "Palestinian children taught hatred." Many videos show children being taught to sacrifice themselves as martyrs for Allah. The terrorists are the only ones in the world today beside devil worshipers who believe sacrificing children is desired and good in their god's eyes, and they teach this openly today.

The training and brainwashing come from older Palestinians who are cowards and do not wish to be martyrs themselves. It is evil when leaders encourage others, including children, to be martyrs for the greatness of Allah while they sit back and take the glory for it. And it is all in the name of a god who does not hear their prayers and cannot deliver Israel into their hands. They sacrifice to demons, not to God (1 Cor. 10:20).

Now that we understand some of the history of idols and how these demon spirits recruit generation after generation to do the devil's will, it is easy to see why it will take an act of God almighty to reveal the truth. God judged the gods of Egypt by proving they could neither see, nor hear, nor speak, nor deliver. All who called upon them did so in vain.

There was at first a contest between the gods of Egypt and the God of Moses. The contest was a sign that Pharaoh's wise men could see, and they even brought it to Pharaoh's attention, but his pride forced him to ignore it. When Aaron threw down Moses's rod and it turned into a serpent, Pharaoh called his wise men, the sorcerers, and the magicians of Egypt, those who were the priests of their gods, and they each threw down their rods and they also became serpents (Ex. 7:10–11).

The devil gives his people power to do some magical tricks, but his power is very limited. Pharaoh at first believed that his gods could do whatever Moses's God could do, and his heart grew hard. The God of Moses was being challenged by the gods of Pharaoh. The first contest ended in victory for the God of Moses when Moses's serpent swallowed the magicians' serpents. But Pharaoh's heart was hardened.

The next challenge was when Aaron struck the waters of Egypt with his rod, and all the rivers, ponds, pools, and even buckets of water became blood; there was no water to drink in all of Egypt! Then the magicians of Egypt did so with their enchantments, and Pharaoh's heart grew hard, and he did not heed the word of the Lord.

Afterward, the Lord smote the land of Egypt with frogs— so that in their houses, bedrooms, beds, ovens, kneading bowls, and on their servants, there were frogs! Then the magicians also brought up frogs with their enchantments (Ex. 8:7). So far, the magicians could do anything Moses's God could do, and the contest was gaining attention. Pharaoh, however, did not consider that the weakness of his magicians was being manifest in that they could counterfeit what the God of Moses was doing, but they could not reverse it.

Next, the Lord God had Moses and Aaron stretch out their rod and strike the dust of the land so that it became lice. The magicians worked their enchantments to do so, but they could not. When they saw that their powers had reached their limits, they admitted that a superior power had won the contest: "Then the magicians said; 'This is the finger of God!'" (Ex. 8:19).

The contest was over. Pharaoh had seen the finger of God, but because of his hard heart, he was about to see a mighty hand and an outstretched arm! The truth about Pharaoh's gods was becoming evident to all. After all the plagues came on Egypt and culminated with the death of the firstborn of all Egypt, they called upon their gods for protection and deliverance, but nothing happened; no god heard their cry. It was revealed that they were not gods at all, they could neither hear, nor see, nor speak, nor deliver. Jethro, the father-in-law of Moses, put it well.

> Jethro, the priest of Midian, Moses' father-in-law, heard of all that God had done for Moses and for Israel His people, that the LORD had brought Israel out of Egypt. (Ex 18:1)

> Moses told his father-in-law all that the LORD had done to Pharaoh and to the Egyptians for Israel's sake, all the hardship that had come upon them on the way, and how the LORD had delivered them. Then Jethro rejoiced for all the good which the LORD had done for Israel, whom He had delivered out of the hand of the Egyptians. And Jethro said, "Blessed be the LORD, who has delivered you out

of the hand of the Egyptians and out of the hand
of Pharaoh, and who has delivered the people from
under the hand of the Egyptians. Now I know that
the LORD is greater than all the gods; for in the
very thing in which they behaved proudly, He was
above them." (Ex. 18:8–11)

The Egyptians were proud of their gods. They had built huge
temples to them, carved large images of them, and overlaid parts of
them with gold. They adorned all their priests with royal garments
to perform enchanting ceremonies and burn incense to them. All
the nations would look at them in awe and marvel at the beauty
and greatness of their appearance. Surely, they looked magnificent!
Surely, they were great gods! But when the Egyptians prayed to
their gods, nothing happened—no one heard. The God of Moses
delivered the children of Israel from the hand of Pharaoh, but the
gods of Egypt could not deliver their people from all the plagues
or the death that took their firstborn. I like the way the Amplified
Bible says the words of Jethro: "Now I know that the Lord is
greater than all gods. Yes, in the [very] thing in which they dealt
proudly [He showed Himself infinitely superior to all their gods]"
(Ex. 18:11 AMP).

The Lord executed judgment on all the gods of Egypt and
showed all the nations that He was greater than all the gods of the
nations. Everyone who had idols in Egypt and all the nations who
heard what God had done in Egypt would look at their idols with
contempt and see them as the worthless objects they were. If the
magnificent images of all the gods of Egypt could not deliver the
Egyptians, what could their little idols do for them?

God's plan was to prove that all the magnificent gods of Egypt
were nothing and that He alone was God. This was done in the
sight of the nations so they would know that idols of gold and silver,
wood and stone, were nothing. Having heard of the awesome power
and deliverance of the Lord God Almighty the nations would say,

"Surely our fathers have inherited lies, and things in which there is no profit. Shall a man make gods for himself which are not gods?" But note that it took a mighty work of God to prove to the nations that false gods were nothing.

We should consider another awesome show the Lord did for Israel along this line; it is in 1 Kings 18:17–40 and took place in the days of Elijah. It was a contest to prove that God alone was God and that false gods could do nothing and were nothing. The children of Israel had been faltering between two gods, the Lord and Baal. Elijah instructed Ahab, the king of Israel, to gather the children of Israel along with the prophets of Baal to Mount Carmel. Then he asked the people how long they would falter between the two gods. He said that if the Lord is God, follow Him, but if Baal is god, follow him. Elijah knew the odds against him were overwhelming, that he alone was facing them a prophet of God; and the prophets of Baal were 450. However, we know that the odds were perfect in the eyes of the Lord. So Elijah had the prophets of Baal prepare two altars and lay a bull as a sacrifice on each.

Elijah instructed the prophets of Baal to call on the name of their god and he would call on the name of the Lord God of Israel; and the god who answered by fire would be God. The 450 prophets called on Baal from morning till noon saying, "O Baal, hear us!" And they danced around their altar, but no one answered. Then Elijah began to mock them.

> "Cry aloud, for he is a god; either he is meditating, or he is busy, or he is on a journey, or perhaps he is sleeping and must be awakened." So they cried aloud, and cut themselves, as was their custom, with knives and lances, until the blood gushed out on them. And when midday was past, they prophesied until the time of the offering of the evening sacrifice. (1 Kings 18:27–28)

The prophets of Baal prophesied? What would they have prophesied? The only thing I can imagine is they were prophesying that they were all going to die soon, a fate worshipers of what is not God have in common when the true and living God is on the scene. And they were right on; it came to pass.

After the prophets of Baal gave up on their god, Elijah called all the people to himself and said,

> LORD God of Abraham, Isaac, and Israel, let it be known this day that You are God in Israel and I am Your servant and I have done all these things at Your word! Hear me, O Lord that this people may know that You are God. And that You have turned their hearts back to You again. (1 Kings 18:37)

Then the fire of the Lord fell from heaven and consumed the sacrifice in a flaming fiery whirlwind! When all the people saw it, they fell on their faces and said with a loud voice, "The Lord! He is God! The Lord! He is God!" What a show!

Elijah ordered that all the prophets of Baal be seized, and he took them down to the brook Kishon and executed them there. This was written so that a generation yet to be created may praise the name of the Lord. God can put on quite a show when the time calls for it.

It took God to judge Baal; humans could not do it. It took a demonstration of God's awesome supernatural power to judge a god that humans had created in their own minds. This needs to be done today! Many false gods are among the nations today. Could it be in God's plan to do something very similar now at the end of the age to prove that false gods are nothing? That all who put their trust in strange gods and not the Lord God Almighty, who has done great things, will be put to shame. If now, at the end of the age, the Lord God almighty were to put on a show of His awesome power in the eyes of all the nations, would it turn the hearts of many nations back to Him? Would they also fall with their faces to the ground and shout, "The Lord! He is God!?" Remember that it is written in God's Word, "Every knee shall bow, and every tongue confess that Jesus Christ is Lord!" (Phil. 2:10-11) What would make people do that? We shall see.

We now have a vision of God's plan for the last days through the prophets. We can see an event that is well able to turn the hearts of many peoples back to Him by His mighty hand and out-stretched arm. We can see through the words of the prophets how a demonstration of His mighty power can convince people they have inherited lies.

> The nations shall come to You from the ends of the earth and say, "Surely our fathers have inherited lies, worthlessness and unprofitable things. Will a man make gods for himself, which are not gods?" Therefore behold, I will this once cause them to know, I will cause them to know My hand and My might; and they shall know that My name is the LORD. (Jer. 16:19–21)

When the Lord God almighty puts on a SHOW of His power, those who trust in what is not God will know that they inherited lies—worthless and unprofitable beliefs and religions. After they have seen the awesome power of the living God, this generation will wonder why their fathers would have made gods that are not gods. What God has planned for the nations will cause them to know that the works of men's hands are worthless and unprofitable things, and that the Lord is God in heaven above and on earth beneath, there is no other.

All through the prophets and the psalms, the Lord spoke of such a tremendous event that would turn all people back to Him. Think of these two scriptures in a prophetic setting. They prophesy of something that turns all nations to righteousness and the Lord, the righteous King. "When Your judgments are in the earth the inhabitants of the world will learn righteousness" (Isa. 26:9). It will take something like seeing God's awesome power manifested in judgment against His enemies to turn the hearts of man. Such a demonstration would make men stagger with fear and reverence and become like intoxicated people who fall to the ground because there is no strength to stand.

The Lord said that the wicked did not learn righteousness when He was good to them for He has sent His rain on the just and the unjust alike. But it is not His blessings that turn the hearts of most men. His goodness may lead men to repentance, but some refuse to be led by His goodness. Therefore, He said,

> Let grace be shown the wicked yet he will not learn righteousness, in the land of uprightness (upright people) he will deal unjustly (take advantage of good and trusting people) and will not behold the majesty of the LORD. (Isa. 26:10)

The Lord is saying the wicked will not learn righteousness though God has shown them grace and goodness, but when they see His righteous judgments on a great scale, they will learn righteousness: "For as the earth brings forth its bud, as the garden causes the things that are sown in it to spring forth, so the Lord GOD will cause righteousness and praise to spring forth before all the nations" (Isa. 61:11). God turned the hearts of Israel back to Himself with a great demonstration of His power; now it appears He intends to turn the hearts of many peoples and great nations back to Himself with a great demonstration of His mighty power. And the harvest will be gathered at the end of the age!

Something else we must take note of that identifies false gods, that also pertains to our times, is how they have always been advanced with glory by the chanting of their followers. A false god must be advanced in glory by their followers because they have no glory of their own. No matter how magnificent they make them, no matter how loud they chant the greatness of their gods, no matter how much gold they adorn them with, false gods can do nothing. Notice how the Ephesian followers of the goddess Diana reacted when someone spoke against their idol.

> Now when they heard this, they were full of wrath and cried out, saying, Great is Diana of the Ephesians! ... Some therefore cried one thing and some another, for the assembly was confused, and most of them did not know why they had come together ... But when they found out that he [Paul] was a Jew, all with one voice cried out for about two hours, "Great is Diana of the Ephesians!" (Acts 19:28, 32, 34)

Does that sound familiar? Is there any god today that is advanced in glory with similar words chanted? How about, "Great is Allah!"? Is he really great? What has he done? What had Diana done? Probably the same thing—nothing. After all the chanting of these many followers and their devotion to Diana, we find that the great image of Diana and her temple are nothing but ruins and rubble today. The Ephesians had inherited lies from their fathers, things in which there was no profit. Has chanting the greatness of any god done its followers any good? Not that we are aware of.

After the state of Israel was established in 1948, five surrounding Muslim nations spoke boastful words of how they would wipe the new state off the map and chanted as they attacked, "Great is Allah!" The conflict could have been compared to the battle between David and Goliath; though Israel was greatly outnumbered and outgunned, the Arab nations lost that war and several others afterward, and Israel is still there to this day. Though Allah is great in the eyes of his followers, he has come up against a God who is greater, a God who acts for His people. For LORD says:

> Behold, I will gather them out of all countries where
> I have driven them in My anger ... I will bring them
> back to this place ... They shall be My people and
> I will be their God. Yes, I will rejoice over them to
> do them good and I will assuredly plant them in
> this land with all My heart and with all My soul.
> (Jer. 32:37–41)

Who can uproot what God has planted? When He works, who will reverse it? Who among all the gods of the nations are greater than He?

We know all too well that if someone speaks against Muhammad, the Muslims are filled with wrath and chant as they riot and murder in pockets all throughout the nations, "Great is Allah." If he really was great and the Muslims do his will, I don't believe there would be a nation of Israel today. And if they do not do his will, why do they kill people because they do not do his will? Hypocrites! Israel celebrated its sixtieth year of independence in 2008, and all the Muslims can do is be humbled. Chanting loudly for hours and days how great Allah was did not help the Muslims defeat the God of Israel. Allah has proclaimed nothing and has done nothing, but the Lord created the heavens.

Satan threatens to kill anyone who will not believe and worship him through lies or images of gold and silver, wood and stone. According to Revelation, he will cause the deaths of all those who will not bow down and worship the image he sets up (Rev. 13:15). Later in Revelation we see the souls of those who refused to worship his image. "Then I saw the souls of those who had been beheaded for their witness to Jesus and for the Word of God, who had not worshiped the beast or his image" (Rev. 20:4). You will submit to Satan or be killed. Satan's chosen means of killing is beheading. It is the preferred method radical Islamists today choose for putting people to death when they do not bow down and worship Allah, and it is satanic. Satan was a murderer from the beginning. John 10:10

tells us he comes not, but to steal, kill, and destroy, and John 8:44 tells us his children do likewise.

The great and powerful Islamic nations, which are many, are unable to destroy the tiny state of Israel because the true and living God has declared long ago that He would bring His people back to their land and shepherd them. By doing so He has shown all nations that He acts for His people and performs His Word. He has spoken prophetic words thousands of years ago that are now being fulfilled before our eyes. Israel is His witness to the nations that He is God. The Lord God has declared to the nations long ago that He would scatter Israel, and that He would gather them back to their land: "Hear the word of the LORD, O nations, And declare it in the isles afar off, and say, 'He who scattered Israel will gather him, And keep him as a shepherd does his flock'" (Jer. 31:10). "Surely, I will take the children of Israel from among the nations, wherever they have gone, and will gather them from every side and bring them into their own land" (Ezek. 37:22).

Proclaim it among the nations—The Lord God of Israel has gathered His people back to their own land in our sight! The Lord has demonstrated in the sight of the nations that He is God, and there is no other, He is God and there is none like Him in all the earth! The Islamic nations cannot destroy the state of Israel because the Lord is their shepherd. If God is for Israel, who can be against them?

The nations around Israel are resisting what God has spoken thousands of years ago concerning His people; the stage is set for a great showdown! Israel's adversaries have set themselves against the LORD. A contest has been arranged between the God of Israel and the god of these people? They gather together against Israel and chant, "Allah Akbar!" [Great is Allah] But the LORD says, "Have you not known? Have you not heard? Has it not been told you from the beginning? Have you not understood from the foundations of the earth? It is He who sits above the circle of the earth, and its inhabitants are like grasshoppers... He will also blow on them, and they will wither, and the whirlwind will take them away like stubble" (Isa 40:21-22, 24).

Zephaniah also said some powerful things about this event. In chapter 2, he spoke of a judgment against the Philistines as well as Moab and Ammon, the peoples around Israel today. Why the burden is uttered against them is the key to the prophecy. Note the peoples involved: Gaza, Ashkelon, Ekron, and Ashdod, these are the ancient cities of the Philistines. The word *Palestine* is the Greek form of the Hebrew word *Philistia*, which means, "land of the Philistines." Whenever prophecy speaks of the Philistines there may be a prophetic utterance against the Palestinians today. The purpose of the prophecy is to issue judgment against the peoples mentioned who are resisting the return of the captives of God's people to their land. The chief of these are the Philistines, those whom we call the Palestinians. God says He will intervene for His people, so that they can return to their land. And He says of those who resist His plan, "I will destroy you!"

Whenever God speaks in the prophets of returning, recovering, or bringing back His people, it is a prophetic passage and holds information about the gathering and returning of Israel we see today. Today we see not only the resisting of the return of God's people to the land, but they are being resisted by, among others, the Philistines, the Palestinians. The people around Israel today, as in times past, are making arrogant threats against them and are resisting God's plan. They are contending against the Lord God Almighty when they contend with those whom He calls "My people." Notice what Zephaniah says in this passage,

> For Gaza shall be forsaken, and Ashkelon desolate;
> They shall drive out Ashdod at noonday, and Ekron
> shall be uprooted. Woe to the inhabitants of the
> seacoast, the nation of the Cherethites! The word
> of the LORD is against you, O Canaan, land of
> the Philistines: "I will destroy you; so there shall

be no inhabitant. The seacoast shall be pastures, with shelters for shepherds and folds for flocks. The coast shall be for the remnant of the house of Judah; They shall feed their flocks there; In the houses of Ashkelon they shall lie down at evening. For the LORD their God will intervene for them and return their captives.

I have heard the reproach of Moab, and the insults of the people of Ammon, with which they have reproached My people, and made arrogant threats against their borders. Therefore, as I live," says the LORD of hosts, the God of Israel, "Surely Moab shall be like Sodom, and the people of Ammon like Gomorrah—Overrun with weeds and salt pits and a perpetual desolation. The residue of My people shall plunder them, and the remnant of My people shall possess them."

This they shall have for their pride, because they have reproached and made arrogant threats against the people of the LORD of hosts. The LORD will be awesome to them, for He will reduce to nothing all the gods of the earth; People shall worship Him, each one from his place, indeed all the shores of the nations. (Zeph. 2:4–11)

The Palestinians as well as the descendants of Moab and Ammon, Lot's grandsons, are mixed into the Arab nation. Moab and Ammon were cities and peoples that existed on the other side of the Jordan River from Israel in ancient times. Amman is the capital of Jordan today. Edom, also called, Mount Seir, is across the Dead Sea from Israel in Jordan, that in ancient times belonged to Esau, the brother of Jacob. Ishmael was the son of Hagar by Abraham and has been closely associated with these peoples because they are all of the house of Abraham and now days of the Islamic faith.

Because of religious pride the Muslims cannot except Israel having the Promised Land. When the suicide bombers attack, they shout, "Great is Allah!" All they do against the people of the Lord is in the name of their god. It is time for their god to be judged. The stage is set for a contest between the God of Israel and the god of Islam. This prophecy is uttered against those of the house of Abraham and their gods. Notice it ends with God reducing to nothing all the gods of the earth. We know how that should be accomplished! God is going to judge them and their gods, just as He did in the days of Moses!

All the forces of the Arab nations around Israel today appear to be very great like Goliath; while the little state of Israel is like David. Goliath made arrogant threats against David and cursed David by his gods and said: "Come to me and I will give your flesh to the birds of the air and the beasts of the field!" (1 Sam. 17:42–44). In like manner, the Arab nations have made arrogant threats against the people of the Lord and said, "What Hitler did to the Jews is nothing compared to what we are going to do." But their words returned upon their own heads.

There was no such thing as a Palestinian people or nation that possessed the land before Jordan moved in and took it in the war of Israel's independence in 1948. None of the Arabs who had settled in the land complained about Jordan occupying the land because there were no Arab people who called themselves Palestinians at that time; they were all one people, the Arab nation.

Most of the Arabs who were already in the land when Jordan occupied the West Bank were immigrants from Arab nations. It was not until after the 1967 Six-Day war, when Israel was attacked by Jordan and several other Arab nations, that Israel drove the Jordanian armies out and took possession of the West Bank and Jerusalem. It was at that time that the Jews began to rebuild Jerusalem and the Arabs created the Palestinian identity where there had not been one previously. By taking on the name of the ancient enemies of Israel, the Palestinians have become in every way a modern-day incarnation of Israel's ancient enemies, the Philistines.

The Lord utters a judgment against the Philistines and their confederacy in Zephaniah and here in Psalm 83, both of which speak of a fiery judgment like that which is noted in Ezekiel 38,

> For behold, Your enemies make a tumult; and those who hate You have lifted up their head. They have taken crafty counsel against Your people and consulted together against Your sheltered ones. They have said, "Come, and let us cut them off from being a nation, that the name of Israel may be remembered no more." For they have consulted together with one consent; They form a confederacy against You: The tents of Edom and the Ishmaelites; Moab and the Hagarites; Gebal, Ammon, and Amalek; Philistia with the inhabitants of Tyre; Assyria also has joined with them; They have helped the children of Lot...
>
> O my God, make them like the whirling dust, Like the chaff before the wind! As the fire burns the woods, and as the flame sets the mountains on fire, so pursue them with Your tempest, and frighten them with Your storm...
>
> That they may know that You, whose name alone is the LORD, are the Most High over all the earth. (Ps. 83:2–8, 13–15, 18)

This is a very prophetic passage. The peoples listed in this psalm are the same ones in Zephaniah's prophecy, and they are still around Israel today; they still make arrogant threats against their borders, they are still a confederacy with a common goal—to destroy Israel. They are children of Abraham and cousins of the children of Israel; but they serve other gods, the gods of their fathers, the spiritual prince that is still at work deceiving the Arab nations today.

The Lord's plan is to demonstrate His great power by a fiery judgment against all His enemies and their gods in the last days. None of them will be delivered by their gods, none will hear a peep from their gods. Their gods will hide themselves when the LORD God Almighty arises to make Himself known. There is a phase of God's great show of power that is like the fiery destruction of Sodom and Gomorrah. In this SHOW the LORD speaks of reducing to nothing all the gods of the earth, that means He will judge their gods! Then all nations will know that the LORD, He is God! Then they shall know that the LORD is the Most High over all the earth!

This judgment can be compared to the days of Elijah. Remember how Elijah had the prophets of Baal prepare a sacrifice? And after the sacrifices were prepared he said, "You call on the name of your gods, and I will call on the name of the LORD; and the God who answers by fire, He is God" (1 Kings 18:24). Today, a similar stage has been set for a contest between the god of Islam and the God of Israel. Joel prophesied about this contest and its resulting signs, "And I will show wonders in the heavens and in the earth: blood and fire and pillars of smoke." What will cause this blood and fire, and pillars of smoke?

Remember how Zephaniah prophesied about what is going to happen to Moab and Ammon in this coming battle. The arrogant threats from Moab and Ammon are going to be answered,

> "I have heard the reproach of Moab, and the insults of the people of Ammon, with which they have reproached My people, and made arrogant threats against their borders. Therefore, as I live," says the LORD of hosts, the God of Israel, "Surely Moab shall be like Sodom, and the people of Ammon like Gomorrah." (Zeph. 2:9)

The Lord said Moab and Ammon would meet the same fate Sodom and Gomorrah suffered. Then in Psalm 83, the destruction that will come upon the Lord's enemies among whom are Moab and Ammon, we see fire is again part of the storm that accompanies the LORD when He comes in a great whirlwind of His anger.

> O my God, make them like the whirling dust, like the chaff before the wind! As the fire burns the woods, and as the flame sets the mountains on fire, so pursue them with Your tempest, and frighten them with Your storm. (Ps. 83:13–15)

Ezekiel also describes how the Lord will answer these forces with fire: "I will rain down on him, on his troops, and on the many peoples who are with him, flooding rain, great hailstones, fire, and brimstone" (Ezek. 38:22). Ezekiel and Joel described an event that will take place in the latter days: "And it will come to pass in the last days… that I will show wonders in the heavens and in the earth: blood and fire and pillars of smoke" (Acts 2:17,19). These verses agree with each other that a storm of fire shall fall on God's enemies. Remember what Elijah said? Let the God who answers by fire be God! It appears God intends to answer by fire and show Himself to be GOD!

It will be a great wonder and an awesome SHOW to see God demonstrate that He is God when He answers by fire and reduces to nothing all the gods of the earth. All nations and peoples will worship Him because they will know that the LORD is the Most High over all the earth! For it is written, "At the name of Jesus every knee should bow, of those in heaven, and of those on earth, and of those under the earth, and that every tongue should confess that Jesus Christ is Lord, to the glory of God the Father" (Phil. 2:10–11). This show of God's power will be so great and so awesome that men of all other religions will realize they have inherited lies and worthless things. God will turn the hearts of many nations back to Himself as the Lord God of Israel.

Many prophetic words have been spoken by the Lord God almighty that point to a culmination of this age, a Grand and Final SHOW of His great and awesome power. It will be the greatest contest between gods the world has ever seen, and the Lord will humble the pride of all man's glory.

> The loftiness of man shall be bowed down and the haughtiness of men shall be brought low, the LORD alone will be exalted in that day but the idols He shall utterly abolish (completely put an end to)... In that day a man will cast away his idols of silver and his idols of gold which they made, each for himself to worship to the moles and bats. (Isa. 2:17–18, 20)

In that day, all will respect the Holy One of Israel and the nations shall worship the LORD.

> The nations on every shore will worship Him, everyone in its own land. (Zeph. 2:11 NIV)

> Many nations shall be joined to the LORD in that day, and they shall become My people. (Zech. 2:11)

> Now it shall come to pass in the latter days that the mountain of the LORD's house shall be established on the top of the mountains and shall be exalted above the hills, and all nations shall flow to it. Many people shall come and say, "Come, and let us go up to the mountain of the LORD, to the house of the God of Jacob." (Isa. 2:2–3)

In a world where Allah and all other gods have been reduced to nothing, the house of the God of Jacob will be built in its place on His holy mountain in Jerusalem. And all nations will go up to pray before the Lord, "For My house shall be called a house of prayer for all nations" (Isa. 56:7).

The truth shall be revealed when the veil is removed. All questions such as, "Where is God? Why doesn't God do something about all the wickedness taking place in the world today? Whose god is God, the Muslims or the Christians or the Jews, or some other god?" will be answered. For, "He will destroy on this mountain the surface of the covering cast over all people, and the veil that is spread over all nations" (Isa. 25:7). His mighty hand will destroy the covering over all people that has blinded them to the truth—that He is the LORD God Almighty—and they will come to worship Him.

> Thus says the LORD of hosts: "Peoples shall yet come, inhabitants of many cities; the inhabitants of one city shall go to another, saying, 'Let us continue to go and pray before the LORD, and seek the LORD of hosts. I myself will go also.' Yes, many peoples and strong nations shall come to seek the LORD of hosts in Jerusalem, and to pray before the LORD." (Zech. 8:20–22)

> Even them I will bring to My holy mountain and make them joyful in My house of prayer. (Isa. 56:7)

> And it will be said in that day: "Behold, this is our God; we have waited for Him, and He will save us. This is the LORD; we have waited for Him; we will be glad and rejoice in His salvation." For on this mountain the Hand of the LORD will rest. (Isa. 25:9–10)

The LORD shall cause them to know His power and His might, and He will reduce to nothing all the gods of the earth so that He alone is exalted in the earth! As it is written, "I will be exalted among the nations, I will be exalted in the earth!" (Ps. 46:10). "The LORD alone shall be exalted in that day" (Isa. 2:11). Then the nations shall know, "All who have come before Him are thieves and robbers" (John 10:8). They shall know the truth and the truth shall set them free! (Jn. 8:32)

CHAPTER 6

The Plundering

Several things God accomplished in Moses's days were types and a foreshadowing of what is to come. His magnificent show of power was a judgment against the wicked and treacherous manner in which Pharaoh was dealing with His chosen people, who had served him faithfully in peace. Having judged Pharaoh for his deeds, God ordained that His people, Israel, should receive the wealth of Egypt. They plundered the Egyptians of their precious possessions; they plundered those who had plundered them.

> Now the children of Israel had done according to the word of Moses, and they had asked from the Egyptians articles of silver, articles of gold, and clothing. And the LORD had given the people favor in the sight of the Egyptians, so that they granted them what they requested, thus they plundered the Egyptians. (Ex. 12:35–36)

Israel had favor in the sight of the Egyptians because the Egyptians had seen the power of Israel's great God and feared Him; they considered the children of Israel His servants.

The plundering of the Egyptians had been in God's plan all along. God told Abraham hundreds of years before, "And also, the nation whom they serve I will judge; afterward they shall come out with great possessions" (Gen. 15:14). It was God's plan for Israel to plunder its enemies because they had plundered the Israelites. Egypt was destroyed, their riches were plundered by slaves, and their gods did nothing. But Israel's God did mighty things for them as God had said years earlier that it should happen. It was another demonstration of God's power in the sight of the nations.

The Lord has more than once permitted the Israelites to plunder their enemies for hostilities against them. In the days of Jehoshaphat, king of Judah, a great multitude came to battle against Jehoshaphat without cause. It was the house of their father, Moab, Ammon, and Mount Seir. These came up against Jehoshaphat, but he prayed to the Lord, and the Lord delivered them into Jehoshaphat's hands. The Lord confused them so much that Judah's enemies destroyed each other, and the Israelites spent three days gathering the spoils (2 Chron. 20). When God blesses a nation, it is blessed!

All these things were types and a foreshadowing of what is to come for Israel in the last days after its people bore their shame for their transgressions against the Lord: "Who gave Jacob for plunder, and Israel to the robbers? Was it not the LORD, He against whom we have sinned? For they would not walk in His ways, nor were they obedient to His law" (Isa. 42:24). The Lord gave them into the hand of their enemy to plunder them, and they were plundered. This has occurred more than once, but now it is time for them to plunder those who plundered them.

What does the plundering of the Egyptians in the days of Moses tell us about the plundering of His people today? Could it be in God's plan that Israel plunders those people who for the last two thousand years have plundered them? Most people do not realize that many of the Arab Islamic countries of the Middle East in the late 1800s had large, thriving Jewish communities in them while the Holy Land was desolate without inhabitants just as it was written: "I will make the cities of Judah a desolation without inhabitant" (Jer. 34:22). At the end of World War I, a homeland for the Jewish people began to fall into place. However, the idea was not pleasing to the Arab nations. Radical Islamic groups despised the idea of having a sovereign Jewish state in their midst. They fought against the establishment of a Jewish state way before it came to be.

We cannot understand why the Muslims hate the sovereign Jewish state in their midst without learning something about Islam. In Islam, any people subjugated during a conquest who did not convert to Islam were permitted to live among them if they accepted one of two choices—become the lower citizen status called *dhimmi* or death. The choice was left up to the conquered party. That was applied to Jews and Christians as well as members of other religions. The dhimmi had to pay a special tax to the Muslim government that was a writ of protection from Muslim superiors, but it did not always work out that way. The dhimmi had to wear a tag on their clothes so Muslims would know they had paid their tax. The dhimmi had a status that was lesser than that of Muslim citizens. If a dhimmi was riding a donkey and a Muslim was coming from the other direction, the dhimmi had to get off the animal till the Muslim had passed. They had to show complete submission. A dhimmi could not ride a horse, which was considered a noble animal. If a dhimmi was accused of touching a Muslim woman, there was but one penalty—death.

It is with how the dhimmi status affected the relationship between Muslims and Jews that we are concerned. A Jew living in a Muslim country had to live in complete submission to their superiors. Jews in Arab countries permitted to build a synagogue could not build it higher than a mosque. The Muslims in some countries treated the dhimmi not much better than dogs, and in many cases, they used them to vent their anger. Knowing these things helps us understand why the Muslims around Israel cannot live with a sovereign Jewish state in their midst; they consider that provoking and unacceptable. The pride of their supreme religion as they call it will not permit them to rest until Israel is wiped off the map and the Jews are brought back into subjection as dhimmis.

But God's plan will turn His enemies' worlds upside down. Now that the Jews or Israel have borne their shame, now that they have received from the Lord's hand double for all their sins, and now that the time of their punishment has come to an end, the time of their favor has begun.

> For thus says the LORD: "Just as I have brought all this great calamity on this people, so I will bring on them all the good that I have promised them." (Jer. 32:42)

> "The Gentiles shall know that the house of Israel went into captivity for their iniquity; because they were unfaithful to Me, therefore I hid My face from them. I gave them into the hand of their enemies, and they all fell by the sword. According to their uncleanness and according to their transgressions I have dealt with them and hidden My face from them." Therefore, thus says the Lord GOD: "Now I will bring back the captives of Jacob and have mercy on the whole house of Israel." (Ezek. 39:23–25)

> Instead of your shame you shall have double honor, and instead of confusion they shall rejoice in their portion. Therefore, in their land they shall possess double, everlasting joy shall be theirs. (Isa. 61:7)

> You will arise and have mercy on Zion, for the time to favor her, Yes, the set time, has come … This will be written for the generation to come that a people yet to be created may praise the LORD. (Ps. 102:13, 18)

These prophecies were given thousands of years ago of a set time of favor that would come to Israel so that when a people yet to be created at the time of the prophecy see it come to pass, they will praise the name of the Lord. Glory to God!

After World War I, primarily through the campaign of Lawrence of Arabia, the British won all the Middle East countries including the Holy Land from the Ottoman Turk Empire. Great Britain liberated the Arab Muslims from the Turkish Muslims, but not many have taken note of that. Under the Ottoman Turks according to maps dated before World War I, the Holy Land had three territories, Akka in the north, Nablus in the middle, and El Kuds (the holy city) a territory which contained Jerusalem, in the south. This is important to note because there was no province, or state called Palestine. The British named the territory Palestine because they were concerned about Arab oil. It seemed wiser to avoid an Arab revolt which might result from naming the land Israel. Through the League of Nations, the Palestine Mandate legalized Great Britain's temporary rule of Palestine.

A certain Jew who had greatly contributed to the war effort on the side of the British had persuaded the British foreign secretary, Arthur James Balfour, to write a declaration in favor of the establishment of a national homeland for the Jewish people in Palestine. That declaration is known as the Balfour Declaration. It reserved all of what is Israel and Jordon today as a national homeland for the Jewish people. However, there was great hostility among the Arab nations against this declaration, and the British were more concerned about Arab oil than pleasing the Jews. Therefore, the British began to show favor to the Arab cause and opposed Jews trying to immigrate to their homeland.

After the Balfour Declaration in 1917, Arab countries encouraged the immigration of Arabs to Palestine in an effort to claim the land promised to the Jews. The declaration limited Jewish immigration but set no restraints on Arab immigration. Many Arabs having moved in and settled parts of the Holy Land began to resist the British presence and the immigration of Jews to the land. It was not that the Arab nations did not have enough land; the problem was that they didn't want the Jews to have any. The battle for the land began and the stage was set for all the fighting and conflicts we have seen today in the Middle East.

Arabs and Jews were moving into the Holy Land, each group resisting the British presence as well as each other. Arabs of all the surrounding nations were very angry with the British for double-dealing the land. They had promised the land to the Jews as well as to them during the war. In an attempt to appease Arab anger, Winston Churchill cut off three-quarters of the land in 1921 and gave it to the Arab Hashemite Kingdom, which became the country we know today as Jordan.

There was intense sporadic fighting from 1917 to 1948 for control of the Holy Land. The fighting was so troublesome for Great Brittan that it handed the problem back to the United Nations. On November 29, 1947, the United Nations voted on a partition plan for Palestine hoping to appease the Arabs and satisfy the Jews. The UN partition plan passed; the small remaining piece of Palestine was to be divided again between the Jews and the Arabs.

The League of Nations mandate for Britains temporary rule of Palestine was to end on May 14, 1948. Against all odds, Israel with the authority of the United Nations, proclaimed to the world the establishment of the state of Israel. The Arabs rejected the partition plan while Israel accepted it. It was a joyous time for Jews worldwide, but it was a day of catastrophe for the Arabs. After the establishment of the state of Israel, Jews in all the Arab nations were severely persecuted; the Arabs vented their anger on the Jewish populations in their midst and began to kill and plunder them.

Jews who had lived in Arab countries for thousands of years, some from the time of the Babylonian captivity –around 2,500 years ago– had their properties, businesses, and bank accounts seized and plundered by their Arab governments. All their dhimmi taxes did not do them any good in the Arab nations. In Baghdad, some wealthy prominent Jews were accused of spying for Israel and hanged publicly in the city square, while behind the scenes, all they had was plundered by their Arab government. As a result of these trying times, wealthy Jews were considered very fortunate if they managed to leave the country of their nativity with the clothes on their backs. It was a great injustice done to the Jewish citizens of Arab countries.

Jews in Arab countries were fleeing for their lives, leaving their homes and nearly everything they had, while the Arabs were claiming the land of Israel in the name of nomadic Arabs who had lived there only a few decades. The Arab nations plundered the large Jewish communities that lived among them without mercy, without a cause, and without justice.

Not being content with that, the day after Israel proclaimed its independence, it was attacked by five surrounding Arab nations. Upon preparing to invade Israel, the Arabs announced over the airways that what Hitler did to the Jews was nothing compared to what they were going to do. They boasted great things and declared their intent to kill every Jew, and those who escaped they would drive into the sea. Their raging desire was to murder the Jews and plunder their land.

From the beginning of the conflict, the Arabs around Israel have dealt very treacherously with the people of the Lord. And the scripture says: "The treacherous dealers have dealt treacherously, indeed, the treacherous dealers have dealt very treacherously" (Isa. 24:16). "Woe to you who deal treacherously, though they have not dealt treacherously with you! When you make an end of dealing treacherously, they will deal treacherously with you" (Isa. 33:1). As they have done to Israel, so shall it be done to them. The Lord is bringing His people home, and the surrounding nations are enraged at Him.

We can easily see the workings of a stage very similar to that of the children of Israel in Egypt in the days of Moses. A people dealt treacherously with God's anointed people back then, and a multitude of people are dealing treacherously with them now. Certainly, the radical Islamic terrorists today have filled up the cup of the Lord's anger and the great judgment we see in the prophets is about to come.

It appears the Lord is planning to do a great and mighty work in these last days; and we can be sure it is in all the prophets: "The Lord GOD will do nothing unless He reveals His secret to His servants the prophets" (Amos 3:7). The Lord knows the surrounding Arab nations have plundered His people, and He tells us what He will do.

> Thus says the LORD of hosts: "He sent Me after glory, to the nations which plunder you; for he who touches you touches the apple of His eye. For surely, I will shake My hand against them, and they shall become spoil for their servants. Then you will know that the LORD of hosts has sent Me." (Zech. 2:8–9)

Another translation says; "They shall become plunder for those who served them" (Zech. 2:9 AMP). The Arab nations have plundered unjustly the people of the Lord, the apple of His eye, at a time when their punishment had come to an end. Israel entered a time of favor when they proclaimed their independence on May 14, 1948, and the desert lands of Israel began to blossom as the rose. Therefore, the Lord will execute judgments on His enemies round about Israel, and the nations shall see His people plunder those who plundered them.

Notice the Messiah is in this passage: "Then you will know that the Lord of hosts has sent Me." As we have noticed before, God's people today are looking for the coming of their Messiah, and this passage speaks of His coming. Notice that there are two members of the trinity in this passage; the Lord of hosts is God the Father, and the One He sent is the Messiah. At the beginning of this passage, He said, "He sent Me after glory." God the Father sent Jesus after glory to the nations that plundered His people. Then He says: "Then you will know that the Lord of hosts has sent Me." Jesus spoke of Himself to the Pharisees in the same manner.

> While the Pharisees were gathered together, Jesus asked them, saying, "What do you think about

the Christ? Whose Son is He?" They said to Him,
"The Son of David." He said to them, "How then
does David in the Spirit call Him 'Lord,' saying:
'The LORD said to my Lord, "Sit at My right
hand, till I make Your enemies Your footstool"'? If
David then calls Him 'Lord,' how is He his Son?"
(Matt. 22:41–45)

Of course, they could not answer Him. But notice how He
pointed out that there were two members of the Trinity in this
passage: "My Lord said to my Lord." Likewise, in this passage in
Zechariah, He is pointing out that Israel will know that the Lord
of hosts has sent Jesus, their Messiah, to them when this thing
happens. It appears God the Father will send Jesus in a glorious
appearing, probably with a multitude of angel horses and chariots
of fire like those that helped Elisha (2 Kings 6:17), and in a great
SHOW of power enter this battle and destroy those who plundered
His brethren. Then they will know that the Lord of hosts sent Jesus
their Messiah to them and it is He who fights for them in this battle.

Israel will know and believe that Jesus is their Messiah; for, the
Lord will be seen over them, they will look upon Him whom they
pierced, He will plead His case with them face to face and bring
them into the bond of the covenant; thus, all Israel will be saved.
Just as it was written by the apostle Paul: "And so all Israel will be
saved, as it is written: 'The Deliverer will come out of Zion, and He
will turn away ungodliness from Jacob; for this is My covenant with
them, when I take away their sins'" (Rom. 11:26–27). The words of
the prophets indicate that Jesus is coming to deliver His people from
their sins and from those who hate them! Then they will plunder
those who plundered them.

Some will wonder within themselves, "When is this going
to happen?" But the Lord says: "'Wait for Me,' says the LORD,
'Until the day I rise up for plunder, My determination is to gather
the nations to My assembly of kingdoms, to pour on them My

indignation, all My fierce anger'" (Zeph. 3:8). The Lord has an appointed time, and it is coming soon. The Lord God is angry with the nations that have killed and plundered His people: For He says: "My fury will show in My face ... in the fire of My wrath I have spoken" (Ezek. 38:18–19). They will know in that day that it is the Lord's people they have been killing and plundering.

Just as in the days of Moses, the Lord will turn it around and have His people plunder those who have plundered them. The Lord says the whirlwind of His anger has gone forth in fury; it will not turn back, nor be quenched until it is released on all the nations who have despised and plundered His people. In Ezekiel, we will see that plunder is the inspiration of all the nations under the influence of Gog in the latter days. They shall go up against Israel to plunder it; the stage is set.

The Lord shall deal with all who afflict and plunder the apple of His eye. Woe to those who murder and plunder without a cause and deal treacherously with His people! The Lord is waiting patiently while they fill to the full measure the cup of His fury. When the appointed time has finally arrived, the scripture says: "O LORD, be gracious to us; We have waited for You. be their arm every morning, our salvation also in the time of trouble. At the noise of the tumult the people shall flee; When You lift Yourself up, the nations shall be scattered; And Your plunder shall be gathered" (Isa 33:2-4).

Again, the Lord says, "Now I will rise," says the Lord; "Now I will be exalted, Now I will lift Myself up!" (Isa. 33:10) "The Lord of hosts shall be exalted in judgment!" (Isa. 5:16) "In that day a man will look to his Maker and his eyes will have respect for the Holy One of Israel" (Isa. 17:7). People will worship God, and Israel will plunder their enemies: "'Then those who dwell in the cities of Israel ... will plunder those who plundered them, and pillage those who pillaged them,' says the Lord GOD" (Ezek. 39:9–10).

The Lord's judgment will come upon all those who have plundered His people. When you see all these things set in order in the latter days, you will know and understand perfectly that it is near, at the very door!

CHAPTER 7

The Day of the Lord upon the Nations

From this side of the great prophetic mountain, we see through the Lord's eyes another view of this great event. It is important to understand this view, so we do not confuse it with other judgments in God's Word that are called the Day of the LORD. The Day of the LORD would first come upon Israel when it had pushed God's anger to the point that there was no remedy. Then after Israel had borne its punishment, the Day of the LORD would come upon the nations whom God used to punish Israel. God would use the nations to punish His people, but the nations were not without sin themselves, so they also had punishment to bear. Then the final Day of the LORD is a judgment that is called the great and terrible Day of the LORD. It is also called the day of wrath and revelation of the righteous judgment of God. (Rom. 2:5-6) Each of these is a Day of the LORD judgment, but the final one is the judgment at the end of the age that Jesus spoke of in His parables. We will focus on the Day of the LORD upon the nations, but we need to understand all three to rightly divide the prophetic Word of God.

The epicenter of the many prophecies referring to the Day of the LORD upon the nations is in Ezekiel 38–39. In these two chapters, the Lord paints a picture of how His fury is poured out in such a way that all nations may know that He is the LORD God of Israel. All that will be accomplished on that day can be found in these two chapters, but first, we need a good understanding of the Lord's judgments to discern the Lord's plan concerning this event.

The Lord describes the Day of the LORD that would come upon Israel in the following verses:

> I will cut off man from the face of the land, says the LORD. I will stretch out My hand against Judah, and against all the inhabitants of Jerusalem ... For the Day of the LORD is at hand ... Therefore, their goods shall become booty and their houses a desolation. (Zephaniah 1:1–13)

> Consecrate a fast, call a sacred assembly; gather the elders and all the inhabitants of the land into the house of the LORD your God, and cry out to the LORD. Alas for the day! For the Day of the LORD is at hand; It shall come as destruction from the Almighty. (Joel 1:14–15)

God's judgment on Israel, the Day of the Lord, came only after He warned the people many times.

> And the LORD God of their fathers sent warnings to them by His messengers, rising up early and sending them, because He had compassion on His people and on His dwelling place. But they mocked the messengers of God, despised His words, and scoffed at His prophets, until the wrath of the LORD arose against His people, till there was no remedy. (2 Chron. 36:15–16)

The Lord was dealing with a stubborn and rebellious people.

> Thus says the LORD: "Behold, I am fashioning a disaster and devising a plan against you. Return now everyone from his evil way and make your ways and your doings good." And they said, "That is hopeless! So we will walk according to our own plans, and we will every one obey the dictates of his evil heart." (Jer. 18:11–12)

God dealt with Israel like this repeatedly until they filled up the cup of His wrath, so He had no choice but to judge them.

> Who gave Jacob for a spoil, and Israel to the robbers? Did not the LORD, he against whom we have sinned? For they would not walk in his ways, neither were they obedient to his law. Therefore, He hath poured upon him the fury of His anger, in the strength of battle. (Isa. 42:24–25)

The Lord allowed Israel's enemies to defeat it, drive the people from their land, and plunder their goods because they refused to heed Him. Afterward, the Lord executed judgment on the nations that had scattered and plundered Israel because these nations were not without sin; they thought themselves above Israel because the Lord had used them to execute His judgment on Israel and plunder their goods. But they were corrupt and wicked themselves and therefore, also had judgment to bear.

The Lord would judge Israel first and then the nations. This is a principle we find in scripture. Paul said in Romans 2:8–9, "Indignation and wrath, tribulation and anguish, on every soul of man who does evil, *of the Jew first and also of the Gentile.*"

Notice what the Lord said in Jeremiah 25:8–14.

"Because you have not heard My words ... behold, I will send ... Nebuchadnezzar the king of Babylon, My servant ...against this land, against its inhabitants, and will utterly destroy them, and make them an astonishment, a hissing, and perpetual desolation's. Then it will come to pass, when seventy years are completed, that I will punish the king of Babylon and that nation, the land of the Chaldeans, for their iniquity," says the LORD; "and I will make it a perpetual desolation. For many nations and great kings shall be served by them also; and I will repay them according to their deeds and according to the works of their own hands."

After the Lord used Nebuchadnezzar to judge Israel, He judged Babylon.

"For behold, I begin to bring calamity on the city which is called by My name, and should you be utterly unpunished? You shall not be unpunished, for I will call for a sword on all the inhabitants of the earth," says the LORD of hosts. (Jer. 25:29)

This could also be translated, "all the inhabitants of the land." The day of the Lord would come upon the Jew first and then upon the Gentile. We see this principle again when the Lord said to Israel,

Thus says your Lord ... See, I have taken out of your hand the cup of trembling, the dregs of the cup of My fury. You shall no longer drink it. *But I will put it into the hand of those who afflict you*, who have said to you, lie down, that we may walk over you.

> And you have laid your body like the ground, and as
> the street, for those who walk over. (Isa. 51:22–23)

After God's anger was spent on His people, He would then judge those nations that destroyed and plundered His people because they did it with wholehearted joy and spiteful minds. Even after Israel had borne God's anger and their punishment ended, these nations would not cease their hatred and anger against Israel. Does this sound like something we see in our world today? And here it is in the days of the Old Testament.

In Obadiah, the Lord says:

> You should not look down on your brother in the day of his misfortune, nor rejoice over the people of Judah in the day of their destruction, nor boast so much in the day of their trouble. You should not march through the gates of my people in the day of their disaster, nor look down on them in their calamity in the day of their disaster, nor seize their wealth in the day of their disaster. You should not wait at the crossroads to cut down their fugitives, nor hand over their survivors in the day of their trouble. *"The day of the LORD is near for all nations.* As you have done, it will be done to you; your deeds will return upon your own head. (Obad. 12–15 NIV)

Another translation says: "For the day of the LORD upon all the nations is near." (NKJV) This is a prophecy that the Day of the LORD upon the nations is coming without fail. It is a judgment dedicated to those who not only plundered their goods but also their land. Ezekiel 36 describes a judgment on those who have taken possession of the ancient heights of Israel and consider the LORD's land to be theirs. The LORD has issued many warnings to these peoples around Israel so that He makes this final warning by raising His hand in an oath that He is going to execute this judgment.

> "And you, son of man, prophesy to the mountains of Israel, and say, 'O mountains of Israel, hear the word of the LORD!'" Thus, says the Lord GOD: "*Because the enemy has said of you, 'Aha! The ancient heights have become our possession,'* therefore prophesy, and say, 'Thus says the Lord GOD: "Because they made you desolate and swallowed you up on every side, so that you became the possession of the rest of the nations, and you are taken up by the lips of talkers and slandered by the people"—therefore, O mountains of Israel, hear the word of the Lord GOD! Thus, says the Lord GOD to the mountains, the hills, the rivers, the valleys, the desolate wastes, and the cities that have been forsaken, which became plunder and mockery to the rest of the nations all around—therefore thus says the Lord GOD: "Surely, I have spoken in My burning jealousy against the rest of the nations and against all Edom, who gave My land to themselves as a possession, with whole-hearted joy and spiteful minds, in order to plunder its open country." "Therefore, prophesy concerning the land of Israel, and say to the mountains, the hills, the rivers, and the valleys, 'Thus says the Lord GOD: "Behold, I have spoken in My jealousy and My fury, because you have borne the shame of the nations." 'Therefore, thus says the Lord GOD: "*I have raised My hand in an oath that surely the nations that are around you shall bear their own shame.*" (Ezek. 36:1–7)

The Lord was speaking against the enemy, the nations all around, the rest of the nations, and against all Edom. (Edom was the name given to the descendants of Esau, Jacob's brother, and it refers to a territory in Jordan today.) The Word of the Lord is against the nations around Israel that have said, "The ancient heights have become our possession …the nations all around that gave My land to themselves as a possession, with whole-hearted joy and spiteful minds, in order to plunder its open country." These scriptures are from ancient times, but they speak to all those who are found around Israel today who want to destroy the people of the Lord and plunder their land. Have they not said that the ancient heights—the West Bank—have become their possession? The day of the Lord upon the nations is at hand.

Once this judgment of the Lord is understood, it is seen in too many passages in scripture to be ignored. In Zechariah, we again see this principle of the Lord judging those people whom He used to judge Israel.

> Then the Angel of the LORD answered and said, "O LORD of hosts, how long will You not have mercy on Jerusalem and on the cities of Judah, against which You were angry these seventy years?" And the LORD answered the angel who talked to me, with good and comforting words. So the angel who spoke with me said to me, "Proclaim, saying, 'Thus says the LORD of hosts: "I am zealous for Jerusalem and for Zion with great zeal. I am exceedingly angry with the nations at ease; For I was a little angry, and they helped—but with evil intent." (Zech. 1:12–15)

Moffatt's translation says, "I am deeply wroth with the arrogant nations. For while I was slightly angry with Israel, they pushed My anger for their own evil ends." This again expresses the righteousness of God, for these people did not judge Israel in righteousness but in greed and spite. In some passages, this judgment was directed toward those who had plundered and robbed God's people on the day of their judgment, while in other passages, it included those around Israel that despised them and were inflamed with a desire to destroy God's people.

Remember, this is not the great and terrible day of the Lord that will come upon all humanity who are not saved and delivered from the wrath to come. The great and terrible day of the Lord is known by several names and is said to come at the end of the age. The Lord describes the great and terrible Day of the Lord in Isaiah 13. Notice it is a global wide judgment, the sun, moon, and stars are all darkened, the earth will move out of her place in this judgment.

> Behold, the *Day of the LORD* comes, cruel, with both wrath and fierce anger, to lay the land desolate. And He will destroy its sinners from it. For the stars of heaven and their constellations will not give their light. The sun will be darkened in its going forth, and the moon will not cause its light to shine. "*I will punish the world for its evil, and the wicked for their iniquity.* I will halt the arrogance of the proud and will lay low the haughtiness of the terrible. I will make a mortal more rare than fine gold, a man more than the golden wedge of Ophir. Therefore, I will shake the heavens, and *the earth will move out of her place*, in the wrath of the LORD of hosts and in the *Day of His Fierce Anger.*" (Isa. 13:9–14)

Again, in Zephaniah, He said,

> *The Great Day of the LORD* is near; It is near and hastens quickly. The noise of the day of the LORD is bitter; there the mighty men shall cry out. That day is a day of wrath, a day of trouble and distress, a

> day of devastation and desolation, a day of darkness
> and gloominess, a day of clouds and thick darkness,
> a day of trumpet and alarm against the fortified
> cities and against the high towers. "I will bring
> distress upon men, and they shall walk like blind
> men, because they have sinned against the LORD.
> Their blood shall be poured out like dust, and their
> flesh like refuse. *Neither their silver nor their gold
> Shall be able to deliver them in the Day of the LORD's
> Wrath*; But *the whole earth shall be devoured by the
> fire of His jealousy*, for He will make speedy riddance
> of all those who dwell in the earth. (Zeph. 1:14–18)

The great and terrible day of the Lord will have a noise so great that the mighty men shall cry out in terror. Peter said, "But the day of the Lord will come as a thief in the night, in which the heavens will pass away with a *great noise*, and the elements will melt with fervent heat; both the earth and the works that are in it will be burned up" (2 Peter 3:10). You know what a great noise sounds like and how terrifying it can be if you have ever been in a thunderstorm. I have felt the ground shake under me at the sound of great thundering. Imagine a sound that God says is great; the earth can shake at the sound of His voice!

Joel said, "The sun shall be turned into darkness, and the moon into blood, before the coming of the *Great and Terrible Day of the LORD*" (Joel 2:31–32). The sun being turned into darkness and the moon into blood is what we see at the opening of the sixth seal in Revelation. This is what the last day will look like for those who are not delivered from the wrath to come.

> I looked when He opened the sixth seal, and
> behold, there was a *great earthquake*; and *the sun
> became black as sackcloth of hair, and the moon
> became like blood*. And the stars of heaven fell to

the earth, as a fig tree drops its late figs when it is shaken by a mighty wind. Then the sky receded as a scroll when it is rolled up, and *every mountain and island was moved out of its place.* And the kings of the earth, the great men, the rich men, the commanders, the mighty men, every slave and every free man, hid themselves in the caves and in the rocks of the mountains, and said to the mountains and rocks, "Fall on us and hide us from the face of Him who sits on the throne and from the wrath of the Lamb! For the *Great Day of His Wrath* has come, and who is able to stand?" (Rev. 6:12–17)

The sun being turned into darkness and the moon into blood appears to be immediately before the great and terrible day of the Lord. This day of the Lord judgment is found in the Psalms and the prophets and is what is called by Jesus and Paul the day of judgment, the day of wrath, and the day of wrath and revelation of the righteous judgment of God, who will render justice to all people based on their deeds (Rom. 2:3–11; Matt. 11:20–24). The prophet said in Psalm 96:13, "For He is coming, for He is coming to judge the earth. He shall judge the world with righteousness and the peoples with His truth."

The first two Day of the LORD judgments are upon the flesh for its deeds, but the great and terrible Day of the LORD is a spiritual judgment on all those who remain after the church is gone: "In those days men will seek death and not find it, they will desire to die, and death will flee from them" (Rev. 9:6). It is a supernatural punishment that is called outer darkness, the furnace of fire; there will be weeping and gnashing of teeth. It is punishment according to each one's deeds. God's judgment is just.

As a preliminary to the great and terrible Day of the LORD, there will be this Day of the LORD upon the nations. There are several reasons the Lord will execute this judgment in the last days. One is to judge those who plundered and destroyed His people because in their arrogance and the pride of their heart they were not without sin either, and another is to judge all those around Israel who hate and despise them without a cause in the last days. The Lord also permitted these nations to have their way with Israel, so He might show His great power by delivering Israel from greater and mightier nations as in the days of old.

> Break forth into joy, sing together, you waste places of Jerusalem! For the LORD has comforted His people, He has redeemed Jerusalem. The LORD has made bare His holy arm *in the eyes of all the nations*; and *all the ends of the earth shall see the salvation of our God*. (Isa. 52:9–10)

The Lord will bring great and mighty nations against His small nation to shame them: "God has chosen the weak things of this world to put to shame the things which are mighty" (1 Cor. 1:27). At the sight of His power and the manifestation of His judgment, fear will seize the souls of those who do not know God and do not obey the gospel of our Lord Jesus Christ.

> The sinners in Zion are afraid; Fearfulness has seized the hypocrites: "Who among us shall dwell with the devouring fire? Who among us shall dwell with everlasting burnings?" He who walks righteously and speaks uprightly, He who despises the gain of oppressions, Who gestures with his hands, refusing bribes, Who stops his ears from hearing of bloodshed, And shuts his eyes from seeing evil: He will dwell on high; His place of defense will be the fortress of rocks; Bread will be given him, His water will be sure. (Isa. 33:14–16)

The Lord will gain respect and be hallowed by many nations as His fury is poured out on His enemies. We have seen what the Lord has spoken, and shall we not take it to heart? Has the Lord spoken, and shall we not declare it?

> A lion has roared, who will not fear. The Lord God
> has spoken who can but prophesy! (Amos 3:8)

> You have heard, see all this, and will you not
> declare it? I have made you hear new things from
> this time even hidden things, and you did not
> know them. They are created now and not from
> the beginning, and before this day you have not
> heard them. (Isa. 48:6–7)

These are new things that have been kept hidden for this hour to prepare His people. You have come to the kingdom for such a time as this: "Behold, the former things have come to pass and new things I declare, before they spring forth I tell you of them" (Isa. 42:9). Many scriptures have been spoken concerning this event. They have been brought together as a result of searching to and fro in the book of the Lord without which no one can know His will. These prophecies have been kept sealed up until the time of the end, when many shall go to and fro through the scriptures, and knowledge of God's plan and His purposes as found in the prophets will increase (Dan. 12:4). "Search from the book of the LORD and read! Not one of these shall fail, not one shall lack her mate. For My mouth has commanded it, and His Spirit has gathered them" (Isa. 34:16).

The Lord is about to muster the armies for battle; the day of the Lord upon the nations is near.

> I will also gather all nations and bring them down
> to the Valley of Jehoshaphat and I will enter
> into judgment with them there on account of

> My people, My heritage Israel whom they have scattered among the nations, they have also divided up My land. (Joel 3:2)

> The LORD shall go forth like a mighty man, He shall stir up His zeal like a man of war! He shall cry out, yes, shout aloud! He shall prevail against His enemies. "I have held My peace a long time, I have been still and restrained Myself. Now I will cry like a woman in labor, I will pant and gasp at once. (Isa. 42:13–14)

> The noise of a multitude in the mountains, like that of many people! A tumultuous noise of the kingdoms of nations gathered together! The LORD of hosts musters the army for battle. - Wail, for the day of the LORD is at hand! It will come as destruction from the Almighty. (Isa 13:4,6)

Not one of these prophecies shall fail; not one shall lack its mate. He has commanded it to make himself known to all nations. It is a grand and awesome event, for He says, "In that day a man will look to his Maker and his eyes will have respect for the Holy One of Israel" (Isa. 17:7). On the day of the Lord, people will respect the Holy One of Israel because of what they see.

The Lord said He would gather all nations for this battle, but His anger is against all the nations who are striving against His plan and purpose for Israel in the last days. In 1897, Theodore Herzl began a movement—Zionism—for the establishment of a national homeland for the Jewish people in Palestine because of growing anti-Semitism in Europe. Zion is the mountain of the Lord in Jerusalem on which the city of David was built. (2 Sam. 5:7) It was later used to refer to Jerusalem and then used in a much broader sense to refer to the whole land and people of Israel. Psalm 137:1 was written when

Israel was carried away captive to Babylon, and there, they reflected on where they had come from: "By the rivers of Babylon, there we sat down, yea, we wept when we remembered Zion." The land is referred to as Zion, and the people are referred to as Zion.

> When the LORD brought back the captivity of Zion, we were like those who dream. Then our mouth was filled with laughter, and our tongue with singing. Then they said among the nations, "The LORD has done great things for them." (Ps. 126:1–2)

This scripture is referring to the return and restoration of God's people to their land.

The nations around Israel are striving against the return and restoration of God's people to the land of their ancestors. If you listen to the ranting of the Arab nations against Israel, you will hear them refer to Zionism; they say the Zionist regime is evil and falsely accuse them of horrible things. You will hear them equate Zionism with Nazism when the reverse of it is the truth. The leaders of Iran have accused the Zionist regime of seeking to take over the world. Iran and many other Arab nations have resisted the Zionist movement to the point of bloodshed; they are contending against the plan of God. They have said, "Aha! The ancient heights have become our possession" (Ezek. 36:2). They fight to possess the land although the Lord dwells there. There is a controversy among the nations because of Zionism; many of the nations are contrary to God's plan for His people.

Isaiah gives us a prophecy of the day of the Lord's vengeance on the nations for their controversy with Zion; the Lord's anger is hot against these nations for all the controversy and striving against Zionism. Israel is small, but all the nations are drawn into the conflict over this land one way or another because of Arab oil or coercion through terrorism. The Word says He will cause His people to return to their own land, so why don't the Arab nations let Israel alone? Why don't they give them the small piece of land that is the only land the Jewish people can call their own?

The Lord directed this announcement to the nations and put them all on notice that He would release His anger on the nations who fought against Him and His plan for Israel.

> Come near you nations to hear and heed you people! Let the earth hear and all that is in it, the world and all things that come forth from it. For the indignation of the LORD is against all nations, and His fury against all their armies. He has utterly destroyed them He has given them over to the slaughter. Also their slain shall be thrown out, their stench shall rise from their corpses and the mountains shall be melted with their blood … For My sword shall be bathed in heaven, indeed it shall come down on Edom and on the people of My curse for judgment … For it is the day of the LORD's vengeance and the year of recompense for the cause of Zion. (Isa. 34:1–3, 5, 8)

The King James Version says, "For it is the day of the LORD's vengeance, and the year of recompense for the controversy of Zion" (Isa. 34:8).

Isaiah revealed a specific reason this day of the Lord is coming upon these nations. These peoples have continually afflicted Israel in one way or another—suicide bombings, missile attacks, stabbings, accusing them at the United Nations of one evil thing or another. The Arabs are accusing the Jews on the international media of being an apartheid country when the Arab countries have driven out all their Jewish citizens! Hypocrites! The people all around them have been filling the cup of God's fury. By opposing the ancient Jewish dream of returning to the Holy Land and building their holy city, Jerusalem, they have added one more reason that this judgment should come on all nations that contend with the cause of Zion.

Even after Israel's judgment has been fulfilled, these nations continue to push His anger for their own evil ends. They have hated Israel with an ancient hatred; they refuse to forgive them and live together in peace. They oppose God and make arrogant threats against His plan for His people and the Holy Land. They attack and murder in the name of a god that cannot see or hear, or speak, or deliver. Therefore, God has raised His hand in an oath, that these nations shall bear their own shame and their god shall be reduced to nothing.

The day of the Lord upon the nations will come upon all the nations that are contrary to Zionism and thus contrary to God. It shall take place on the mountains of Israel.

> You shall fall upon the mountains of Israel. (Ezek. 39:4)

> The mountains will melt with their blood. (Isa. 34:3)

> O mountains of Israel, hear the word of the Lord GOD! Thus says the Lord GOD to the mountains, the hills, the rivers, the valleys, the desolate wastes, and the cities that have been forsaken, which became plunder and mockery to the rest of the nations all around. (Ezek. 36:4)

> Therefore prophesy concerning the land of Israel, and say to the mountains, the hills, the rivers, and the valleys, "Thus says the Lord GOD: 'Behold, I have spoken in My jealousy and My fury, because you have borne the shame of the nations.' Therefore thus says the Lord GOD: 'I have raised My hand in an oath that surely the nations that are around you shall bear their own shame.'" (Ezek. 36:6–7)

> After many days you will be visited. In the latter
> years you will come into the land of those brought
> back from the sword and gathered from many
> people on the mountains of Israel. (Ezek. 38:8)

This battle is coming upon all of Israel's enemies. This is not the battle of Armageddon, which is the sixth bowl of God's wrath that is poured out full strength into the cup of His indignation. During the great and terrible day of the Lord, Armageddon will take place in the valley of Megiddo and is referred to as "the battle of that great Day of God Almighty" (Rev. 16:14). The day of the Lord upon the nations is an event staged for the last days. It has a different purpose than the battle of Armageddon. Those who know God know He has a plan and a purpose for everything He does.

Thus we have another view from another side of this great prophetic mountain we see in Ezekiel 38–39. This event is the pinnacle of last days prophecy, a climax, the beginning of the end times. It begins the countdown of the final days before Christ returns for the resurrection on the last day.

CHAPTER 8

God's Grand Finale

We come to the epicenter of the main event on God's calendar. It is time to view and digest what God said in Ezekiel 38–39 with the insight we have from the Word of God and the Holy Spirit.

Once the time has arrived, there will be no turning back; the world will change and never be the same. It is God's Grand Finale. He will demonstrate who He is with a mighty hand and outstretched arm with fury poured out in a great SHOW for all nations, which shall come to know that the Lord is God and there is none like Him.

Our hearts must be prepared for what is to come. The Word of God, if you are willing to receive it, will prepare your heart.

> Therefore, whoever hears these sayings of Mine, and does them, I will liken him to a wise man. (Matt. 7:24)

> Then Jesus said to His disciples, "If anyone desires to come after Me, let him deny himself, and take up his cross, and follow Me. For whoever desires to save his life will lose it, but whoever loses his life for My sake will find it." (Matt. 16:24–25)

> If then you were raised with Christ, seek those
> things which are above, where Christ is sitting at
> the right hand of God. Set your mind on things
> above, not on things on the earth. For you died, and
> your life is hidden with Christ in God. (Col. 3:1–4)

> Meditate on these things; give yourself entirely to
> them, that your progress may be evident to all.
> (1 Tim 4:15)

In the first part of Ezekiel 38, the Lord had Ezekiel prophesy against Gog of the land of Magog, the chief prince of Meshech and Tubal (NIV). Gog is a chief prince in the hierarchy of the kingdom of darkness. Paul explains that there are different levels in this realm: "For we do not wrestle against flesh and blood, but against principalities, against powers, against the rulers of the darkness of this age, against spiritual hosts of wickedness in the heavenly places" (Eph. 6:12). Gog is more than likely a ruler of the spiritual hosts of wickedness in the heavenly places. We do not know much of what is going on in this realm except that there appears to be princes (or rulers) over certain territories and they do fight. An awesome angel appeared to Daniel and opened his eyes of understanding as to what was going on in this realm.

> I lifted my eyes and looked, and behold, a certain
> man clothed in linen, whose waist was girded with
> gold of Uphaz! His body was like beryl, his face like
> the appearance of lightning, his eyes like torches
> of fire, his arms and feet like burnished bronze in
> color, and the sound of his words like the voice of
> a multitude … While he was speaking this word
> to me, I stood trembling. Then he said to me, "Do
> not fear, Daniel, for from the first day that you set
> your heart to understand, and to humble yourself

before your God, your words were heard; and I have come because of your words. But the prince of the kingdom of Persia withstood me twenty-one days; and behold, Michael, one of the chief princes (of God), came to help me, for I had been left alone there with the kings of Persia ... And now I must return to fight with the prince of Persia; and when I have gone forth, indeed the prince of Greece will come." (Dan. 10:11–13, 20)

The great and awesome archangel who appeared to Daniel made him shake and lose his strength. We see that there are more of these super beings in this tangent world that is invisible to us and that they fight over dominion. Notice there was a prince of Persia, a prince of Greece, and the chief prince of God's people, Michael the Archangel.

Evil spirits rule in the kingdom of darkness. Paul listed the ranks of the kingdom of darkness in Ephesians but notice that there are principalities—the territories or the extent of each prince's dominion. The prince of Persia rules over his principality, the prince of Greece rules over his, and Gog rules over his. Gog is a chief prince, the equivalent of an archangel in the hierarchy of the kingdom of darkness, and he presides over Meshech and Tubal in the land of Magog. Meshach and Tubal have been identified as territories in Russia though some believe they are territories in Turkey. Gog's principality more than likely encompasses both territories and stretches to the far north, to the land of Magog, which many believe to refer to Russia today.

In Ezekiel 38:17, the Lord indicated that at the time of the fulfillment of these things, He would say to Gog, "Are you he of whom I have spoken in former days by My servants the prophets of Israel, who prophesied for years in those days that I would bring you against them?" The Lord looks back at when He had Ezekiel prophesy thousands of years ago that this moment would come. This confirms that the Lord was not having Ezekiel prophesy to a human being but to a spiritual being. Gog has been ruling over these peoples and their descendants for thousands of years. All the forces Gog leads against Israel are under the dominion of the kingdom of darkness. Meshach and Tubal would have lower princes over each of them, but Gog would be the chief prince over all the spirits in his principality.

Therefore, the Lord had Ezekiel prophesy to a spirit in the heavenly places. Understanding of these things are given us by divine revelation through the Word of God. These beings sit upon spiritual thrones in the world of things not seen. We cannot see these fallen angels, but they are deceiving and leading the nations to do their will. We see the nations raging and swelling with turmoil, but we cannot see what is driving them to do this in the unseen realm. Ezekiel is instructed to prophesy in the natural realm; against Gog, a being in that realm; prophesy that he would lead these peoples, tribes, and nations into this battle. Although Ezekiel prophesies more than two-thousand years ago, it is only a few days to Gog.

The forces Gog is leading are first Meshech and Tubal; the scripture says, "Persia, Ethiopia, and Libya are with them, all of them with shield and helmet; Gomer and all its troops; the house of Togarmah from the far north and all its troops—many people are with you" (Ezek. 38:5–6). Russia will come from the north, Libya will join the coalition from the west, Persia or Iran will join from the east, Ethiopia will come from the south, and then Gomer and all his troops and the house of Togarmah and all his troops will come. Ezekiel prophesies that an outer circle of nations from more than a thousand miles away from Israel will come to join this battle. Then he says; many nations would come with them that he does not name. He might have been referring to a multitude of people from many nations near and far who will scramble to join forces with Gog once he makes his move.

The Lord says in Ezekiel: "I will turn you around, put hooks into your jaws, and lead you out, with all your army" (Ezek. 38:4). The Lord said He would put hooks in the jaws of Gog and lead him and his forces down to lay siege against Israel. The conflict between Israel and the surrounding nations could be the hooks in the jaws that draws Gog out of the far north. There is an inner circle and an outer circle of nations prepared for battle in this great show of God's power. Gog and all his forces are the outer circle—the nations and people that come from a great distance—and the inner circle consists of the nations around Israel. There are separate judgments prophesied in scripture against each of them. The inner circle of nations are in the conflict for a different reason than the outer circle. The nations around Israel hate them with an ancient hatred; they have declared, "Let us cut them off from being a nation, that the name of Israel be remembered no more." They have boasted, "The ancient heights of Israel, the West Bank, have become our possession." These are the nations God used to judge His people, but because of envy and hatred, they have continued to punish Israel even after their iniquity had ended. The Lord says,

> "Because you have had an ancient hatred, and have shed the blood of the children of Israel by the power of the sword at the time of their calamity, when their iniquity came to an end, therefore, as I live," says the Lord GOD, "I will prepare you for blood" (Ezek. 35:5–6)

> I have heard all your blasphemies which you have spoken against the mountains of Israel, saying, "They are desolate; they are given to us to consume." Thus, with your mouth you have boasted against Me and multiplied your words against Me; I have heard them. (Ezek. 35:12–13)

The Lord has heard the boasting of the nations around Israel and has proclaimed a judgment against them.

Ezekiel 38–39 are prophecies against the outer circle of nations while Ezekiel 35–36 are prophecies against the inner circle. There are more prophecies against the inner circle of nations than there are against the outer circle. It does not appear in scripture that all these nations come against Israel at the same time, but there is indication that they may come against them in phases. It is something the Lord may reserve as a mystery, we cannot and will not know every detail any more than Moses knew every detail when the Lord told him to lead the children of Israel out of Egypt, but we will know what He is doing when we see it come to pass. Some details may be as it was for the Jews when Jesus came out of Galilee, they did not know at the time, but they knew later.

The inner circle of nations appear to be the ones that ignite this battle, but both circles are brought to judgment as the event escalates. They both appear to be a part of this big event in the last days that will take place after Israel is gathered from the nations. We are told how God intends to destroy the multitudes of the outer circle in Ezekiel but the inner circle is explained in Psalm 83, Zephaniah 2, and Isaiah 33 as a fiery judgment like that of Sodom and Gomorrah. There is fire and brimstone in Ezekiel 38 as well; which ties all these prophecies together, so that none will lack their mate.

It all appears to start with the nations around Israel. Psalm 83 is a prophetic pleading of Israel to God against His enemies, those who hate His people. It is a prophetic psalm of Asaph; he is pleading against a confederacy of nations around Israel that despise His sheltered ones. It appears to apply to Israel and their neighbors today and it all agrees with what the prophets have said about the coming battle. We went over this psalm in an earlier chapter but it is worthy of another look.

> Do not keep silent, O God! Do not hold Your peace,
> and do not be still, O God! For behold, Your enemies
> make a tumult; And those who hate You have lifted
> up their head. They have taken crafty counsel against
> Your people and consulted together against Your

sheltered ones. They have said, "Come, and let us cut them off from being a nation, that the name of Israel may be remembered no more. For they have consulted together with one consent; they form a confederacy against You: The tents of Edom and the Ishmaelites; Moab and the Hagrites; Gebal, Ammon, and Amalek; Philistia with the inhabitants of Tyre; Assyria also has joined with them; They have helped the children of Lot … Who said, "Let us take for ourselves the pastures of God for a possession." O my God, make them like the whirling dust, like the chaff before the wind! As the fire burns the woods, and as the flame sets the mountains on fire, so pursue them with Your tempest, and frighten them with Your storm. (Ps. 83:1–8, 13–15)

The majority of the inner circle of nations are of the house of Abraham. The Ishmaelites are the children of Ishmael, Abraham's firstborn by Hagar (Gen. 16). We mentioned before that Ishmaelites and Hagarites are what the early followers of Muhammad were called; they are the people of Arabia who are south of Israel today. Edom is Esau, Jacob's brother; they were called the Edomites, and they were given Mount Seir as an inheritance (Gen. 25:30, 36:8). Moab and Ammon are the sons of Lot, Abraham's nephew (Gen. 19:36–38). Edom, Moab, and Ammon are all territories in Jordan today on Israel's eastern border. Gebal and Amalek are of the house of Esau. Philistia refers to those who call themselves Palestinians today. Tyre is in Lebanon, which would coincide with Hezbollah on Israel's northern border today. Assyria no longer exists, but it could refer to Syria today, which is on Israel's northeast border.

All these nations along with Egypt are Islamic and are the same coalition of nations that attacked the newly formed state of Israel the day after it proclaimed its independence in 1948. They were unified in their intent to wipe the new state of Israel off the map and take the pastures of God for themselves. They attacked Israel although the Lord was there, shepherding His flock. Their goal was to drive the Jews into the sea that the name of Israel may be remembered no more. They shouted as they attacked, "Allah Akbar!" (Great is Allah) But apparently, no one listened, no one heard. The god they all had in common was not great enough to defeat the God of Israel, for it is written: "And the LORD will take possession of Judah as His inheritance in the Holy Land and will again choose Jerusalem" (Zechariah 2:12).

These tribes, peoples, and nations are enemies of Israel today. They are the inner circle of nations and have a key role to play in this awesome event. If any nation of the world today proclaimed it was going to destroy Israel and plunder the land, the nations around Israel would automatically be on their side. The United Nations is pushing Israel to make peace with these radicals, who are not going to rest until they have killed every last Jew in Palestine. How do you negotiate with such a people? They cannot be trusted at all.

Jeremiah warned His people that they should not trust them: "For even your brothers, the house of your father, even they have dealt treacherously with you; Yes, they have called a multitude after you. Do not believe them, even though they speak smooth words to you" (Jer. 12:6). Their brothers, the house of their father, have attacked Israel time after time since it was established. We see the treacherous dealings of these people daily. They spoke smooth words to Israel, and in 2007, they were given the Gaza strip in a land-for-peace deal. Hamas got the land, but Israel received no peace. Only a fool sees trouble and destruction ahead and keeps going. Agreements with the devil are a disaster, and the Gaza strip is a disaster today.

The Lord God almighty addresses these nations directly.

> Thus says the Lord: "Against all My evil neighbors who touch the inheritance which I have caused My people Israel to inherit. Behold, I will pluck them out of their land and pluck out the house of

Judah from among them. Then it shall be, after I have plucked them out, that I will return and have compassion on them and bring them back, everyone to his heritage and everyone to his land. And it shall be, if they will learn carefully the ways of My people ... then they shall be established in the midst of My people. But if they do not obey, I will utterly pluck up and destroy that nation," says the Lord. (Jer. 12:14–17)

Many Arabs in Israel today have Israeli citizenship. Most of them would rather live in Israel than under one of the Arab regimes where Sharia law brutally reigns. They have learned the ways of His people and live among them in peace and prosperity. They have seen the disaster of Arab rule in Gaza and have probably learned something from that. Twenty percent of Israel's population is made up of Arabs who call themselves Palestinians. Speaking to these people the Lord has said that if they obeyed His word, they will be established in the midst of the land with His people. But; if they do not accept, that the land belongs to Israel and it can never be theirs, He says, "I will utterly pluck up and destroy that nation," Says the Lord.

The Lord has gathered His people back to their land against much opposition. It is a miracle that Israel has survived all the attacks of the Arab nations, and no one can deny it. The Palestinians cannot say God has not warned them. It is sad that so many nations are resisting God today, taking counsel together against Israel, and instructing them to give their land to their enemies even though the Lord has proclaimed these things, "Hear the word of the LORD, O nations, and declare it in the isles afar off, and say, 'He who scattered Israel will gather him, and keep him as a shepherd does his flock" (Jer. 31:10).

We are watching the Lord's plan take place today. He is their shepherd, and they are His flock. To overcome Israel, its enemies will have to overcome God, and that is not going to happen. The time is coming when the scripture will be fulfilled: "The LORD shall go forth like a mighty man; He shall stir up His zeal like a man of war. He shall cry out, yes, shout aloud; He shall prevail against His enemies" (Isa. 42:13). He will come against them like a storm, like a great whirlwind of fiery fury, and He will not turn back until He has destroyed His evil neighbors while the rest of the nations watch and see the reward of these treacherous and wicked people.

The Jews were scattered into all nations for around two thousand years because God said it should be so. The Jews have come back to their land because God said it should be so. It is a sign that the Messiah is coming. The Lord says, "How is it that you can discern the face of the sky, but you cannot discern the signs of these times?" It is written,

> In the latter years you will come into the land of those brought back from the sword and gathered from many people on the mountains of Israel, which had long been desolate; they were brought out of the nations, and now all of them dwell safely. (Ezek. 38:8)

The only gathering of Israel to their land in the latter days began in 1948, and it continues to this day. It is important to stress this point because it is an undisputable sign of these times. The spirit of the word is important in this passage as it appears that Israel will dwell in a time of safety. Since its founding in 1948, Israel has become more powerful and secure.

Ezekiel 38:8 says they would dwell safely, but the Hebrew word translated "safely" is also translated "securely." Israel today dwells in strong security. The Israelis have such a high level of security that many nations buy security systems and equipment from them. They are secure and not afraid of their enemies. They have experienced miracles in their favor when the Arab nations have attacked them. However, should a larger nation such as Russia rise against Israel,

Islamic nations would be emboldening to join the confederacy. That is what we see in Ezekiel; Persia, Ethiopia, and Libya are Islamic nations that will come from a thousand miles away or more to join the confederacy. The many peoples mentioned in Ezekiel 38:9 who join the confederacy could refer to the nations around Israel.

Ezekiel 28 gives us a unique view of this event from another side of this great prophetic mountain; it is of a judgment that will come upon all those around Israel who despise them, after they are gathered back from the nations. This meets all the requirements for an event that should take place today. First notice that the Lord instructed His people through Moses and Joshua to drive out all the inhabitants of the land lest they become a thorn in their side and a prick in their eye, but they did not do as the Lord instructed (Judg. 1–2). From that day on, the people around Israel and in their midst have been a thorn in their side when they were gathered back to their land. They resisted Israel coming back from Babylon, and they are resisting Israel coming back to their land today.

In Ezekiel 28, the Lord said there was coming a time when He would remove the thorn in their side from among all who are around them, who despise them. It is another prophetic view of this judgment on people who despise Israel. It is given a time frame, that it should take place after Israel has been gathered back from the nations, and the same prophetic purpose will be fulfilled, that the nations and Israel may know Him. (Ezek. 38:23) This is a prophetic judgment on the inner circle of nations that have their part to play in this end-time event.

> "And there shall no longer be a pricking brier or a painful thorn for the house of Israel from among all who are around them, who despise them. Then they shall know that I am the Lord GOD." Thus says the Lord GOD: "When I have gathered the house of Israel from the peoples among whom they are scattered and am hallowed in them in

the sight of the Gentiles, then they will dwell in
their own land which I gave to My servant Jacob.
And they will dwell safely there, build houses, and
plant vineyards; yes, they will dwell securely, when
I execute judgments on all those around them who
despise them. Then they shall know that I am the
LORD their God." (Ezek. 28:24–26)

Today Israel is gathered back to their land, they are surrounded
by people who despise them, the eyes of the world are fixed upon
what God is doing and they do not even know it!

The prophet Joel agrees that such a judgment should take place;
after the captivity has ended, and Israel has been gathered back to
their land.

When I bring back the captives of Judah and
Jerusalem. I will also gather all nations … Let the
nations be wakened and come up to the Valley
of Jehoshaphat; for there I will sit to judge all the
surrounding nations. (Joel 3:1–2, 12)

We will take a closer look at this prophecy in Joel later, but we can
see a judgment is coming on the inner circle of nations. In Ezekiel's
prophecy the Lord says: "I will execute judgments on all those around
them," and then in Joel: "I will sit to judge all the surrounding
nations." These both agree with what the Lord says in Ezekiel 39:
"I will set My glory among the nations; all the nations shall see My
judgment which I have executed, and My hand which I have laid on
them" (Ezek. 39:21-22). Today, the stage is set for these prophecies
to come to pass. "Who has perceived and heard His word? Who has
marked His word and heard it?" (Jer. 23:18). The Spirit of the LORD
of Hosts says: "Surely, as I have proposed, it shall come to pass."

The gathering of Israel back from the nations is the key element
in these prophecies. As of today, Israel is gathered back from the

nations; they are surrounded by people who despise them, and there is still a thorn in their side; but the Lord has proposed to remove it, then they will know that it is the LORD of the armies of heaven, their King-Messiah who executes judgments on all those around them who despise them.

In Isaiah 17 there are some things that harmonize with Ezekiel 38–39; it contains an oracle from the Lord against Damascus, which is only about 135 miles from Jerusalem. Isaiah 17:1 says, "Behold, Damascus will cease from being a city, and it will be a ruinous heap." Damascus is the capital of Syria. It is believed to be one of the oldest continually inhabited cities in the world—it existed as far back as the days of Abraham. (Gen. 14:15) It has had its walls breached and has been conquered several times, but there is no record of it ever having been destroyed. This prophecy is yet to be fulfilled and may be the hooks the Lords says He will put in the jaws of Gog to lead him down from the north. "I will turn you around, put hooks into your jaws, and lead you out, with all your army..." (Ezek. 38:4).

A nuclear bomb could instantly make Damascus a ruinous heap; Israel is not far from Damascus, and it has a nuclear bomb. As God used these nations to execute His judgments on Israel, He may use Israel to execute His judgments on one or more of these nations with a nuclear strike. Damascus could be destroyed with a large whirlwind of fire or tornado for all we know, but Damascus has an oracle against it that is yet to come, the details belong to the Lord. As you will see later, the judgment of the outer circle—Gog and his forces—appears to include the inner circle or most of it. The Spirit of God assures us, we cannot know everything, and we should never act like we do. "The secret things belong to the Lord our God, but those things which are revealed belong to us" (Deut. 29:29).

If the surrounding nations were to attack Israel—and that is something that could happen any time—Israel could retaliate with a nuclear strike leveling Damascus and maybe a few other enemy cities besides. Should such a destruction explode in Damascus and maybe some surrounding Arab cities, any backing Israel may have enjoyed from its allies would vanish. Such an attack would definitely bring the rebuke of the leading powers of the world against them, and they would stand alone against Gog and all the coming forces.

If Israel were to use a nuclear bomb against what Russia considers its allies, it could be the hooks in the jaws of Gog that would bring him down from the north. The forces of Gog have their eyes fixed on all the plunder lying in wait for them in Israel, they need only an excuse to come and get it. The outer circle of nations come for plunder, but the inner circle come to wipe the Jewish state off the map. God has a way of hiding things; we will not know exactly how He will fulfill His Word until we see it unfold before our eyes. He has given us these things that we may know what is happening as things unfold. "See that you are not troubled; for all these things must come to pass, but the end is not yet" (Matt 24:6).

In Zechariah 12, the Lord describes a situation in which the nations around Israel reel to and fro like drunkards, or stagger at what they see with their eyes, just as they would if Israel used a nuclear weapon on an Arab city. The thing the rest of the world fears to see the most would come to pass, a nuclear weapon introduced in the Middle East. No matter how the Lord chooses to do this, suddenly it will come to pass, to fulfill His plan for His purpose. We are seeing through a glass darkly, but we can see some things ahead.

The Lord makes it clear, that His hand is performing these events when He says; "I will," in several places in this chapter.

> Behold, *I will* make Jerusalem a cup of drunkenness to all the surrounding peoples, when they lay siege against Judah and Jerusalem. And it shall happen in that day that *I will* make Jerusalem a very heavy stone for all peoples; all who would heave it away will surely be cut in pieces, though all nations of the earth are gathered against it … It shall be in that day that *I will* seek to destroy all the nations that come against Jerusalem. (Zech. 12: 2–4, 9)

What brings this passage of scripture into alignment with Ezekiel 38–39 is that the Lord is orchestrating a great show of His power before the eyes of all nations. In chapter 9 of Zechariah an oracle is uttered against Damascus, and then it says: "For the eyes of men and all the tribes of Israel are on the LORD" (Zech. 9:1). In Isaiah 17 the LORD utters an oracle against Damascus and then in verse 7 says: "In that day a man will look to his maker, and his eyes will have respect for the Holy One of Israel." That is the LORD's plan, He is performing this great show in the eyes of all nations to draw all men to Himself.

If the surrounding nations were to lay siege to Israel and Israel were to use nuclear weapons, it would be a cup of drunkenness to all the surrounding nations. They would stagger with fear at the sight of a great Arab city going up in a pillar of smoke. That could be the hooks in Gog's jaws to bring him down from the far north, into the land of Israel. He will come down like a storm upon the mountains of Israel with many nations and with great confidence.

But the Lord will seek to destroy all the nations that come against Jerusalem; it is the same thing He says in Ezekiel: "I will bring you against My land, so that the nations may know Me" (Ezek. 38:16). And again: "I will set My glory among the nations; all the nations shall see My judgment which I have executed, and My hand which I have laid on them" (Ezek. 39:21). Notice all the times the Lord says, "I will." The Lord musters the nations to battle, He is orchestrating this great and awesome SHOW in the last days. It is God's plan and His will for the last days. It is God's Grand Finale!

The Lord could have just wiped these nations off the face of the earth in a single blow; so that when the people of the Lord arose in the morning, there would be corpses lying all around. The Lord has fought Israel's battle before in this manner. In the days of King Hezekiah, the king of Assyria came up against all the fortified cities of Judah and took them. He then sent one of his generals with a great army to King Hezekiah in Jerusalem asking him to submit to the great king of Assyria or be destroyed. He pointed out that the Assyrian army had conquered all the kingdoms around Hezekiah and that their gods could not deliver them from the king of Assyria, and his armies cast their gods into the fire.

Then He asked Hezekiah the wrong question: "Who among all the gods of these lands have delivered their countries from my hand, that the LORD should deliver Jerusalem from my hand?" (Isa. 36:20). He was challenging the power of the Lord to deliver His people from a great army, but his army was only great in the eyes of men. He said: "Do not let your God in whom you trust deceive you, saying, 'Jerusalem shall not be given into the hand of the king of Assyria'" (Isa. 37:10). If Israel had been worshiping idols at that time, it would have been given into the hand of the king of Assyria because their idols would not have been able to deliver them.

But Hezekiah prayed to the LORD his God,

> Truly, LORD, the kings of Assyria have laid waste all the nations and their lands and have cast their gods into the fire; for they were not gods, but the work of men's hands wood and stone. Therefore, they destroyed them. Now therefore, O LORD our God, save us from his hand, that all the kingdoms of the earth may know that You are the LORD, You alone. (Isa. 37:18–20)

Hezekiah pled his case before the LORD, and the LORD heard him. Hezekiah and all Jerusalem saw the salvation of the LORD God Almighty. "Then the angel of the LORD went out and killed in the camp of the Assyrians one hundred and eighty-five thousand; and when people arose early in the morning, there were the corpses all dead" (Isa. 37:36–37). The Lord could do the same thing today, but that would not be a great SHOW of His power! What the Lord has proposed is a great show of His power that will cause trembling in the hearts of all nations, tribes, and peoples so that they might turn to the Lord. We could call this SHOW, God's opening show for end-time activities.

Ezekiel describes the coming battle:

> "You will ascend, coming like a storm, covering the land like a cloud, you and all your troops and many peoples with you" (Ezek. 38:9).

It will be such a multitude that it will look like the shadow of a cloud advancing across the land. Isaiah uses similar words:

> Woe to the multitude of many people who make a noise like the roar of the seas, and to the rushing of nations that make a rushing like the rushing of mighty waters! The nations will rush like the rushing of many waters, but God will rebuke them, and they will flee far away, and be chased like the chaff of the mountain before the wind, like a rolling thing before the whirlwind. Then behold, at eventide, trouble! And before the morning, he is no more. This is the portion of those who plunder us, and the lot of those who rob us. (Isa. 17:12–14)

Note; this is the same chapter that prophesies the destruction of Damascus. Although it says nothing about the last days, we see the same characteristics of our target event that is in the last days. It is a prophecy of Woe to the nations. It says woe to the rushing of nations that make a noise like the roar of the sea, like the rushing of mighty waters. Woe to those who come against the Lord; He will rebuke them in a mighty whirlwind of His anger, so that in the morning they are no more. The LORD is prophesying of the same event through a different prophet. Like many prophecies—only a certain portion of the whole chapter at times applies to the event.

They can speak to a people at the time of the prophecy, as well as to us at the end of the age.

It is a great show of His power, a show of His fury against His enemies, that the nations may, not only know Him, but fear Him: "I will be known in the eyes of many nations" (Ezek. 38:23). Isaiah says the same thing in different words: "In that day a man will look to his Maker, and his eyes will have respect for the Holy One of Israel" (Isa 17:7). We see the same intent, that He might make Himself known in the eyes of the nations. It appears that Ezekiel and Isaiah are describing the same event from a little different point of view.

These prophecies give us the view of a violent storm of nations rushing to lay siege against God's peaceful people. But God will rebuke them with His mighty hand and outstretched arm, with fury poured out, and they will be blown about by the whirlwind of His fury. We see that Jeremiah is in strong agreement with the previous two prophecies and is alive with His intent and His plan for the latter days.

> The whirlwind of the Lord has gone forth in fury,
> a continuing whirlwind. It will fall violently on the
> head of the wicked. The anger of the Lord will not
> turn back until He has executed and performed the
> thoughts of His heart. In the latter days you will
> understand it perfectly. (Jer. 23:19–20)

Jeremiah and Isaiah agree that these forces will be crushed with a whirlwind, and a storm of the Lord's anger in the latter days. (Isa. 17:13). Ezekiel says, "It will be in the latter days that I will bring you against My land so that the nations may know Me" (Ezek. 38:16). A great multitude is coming down against Israel that will be confronted with a whirlwind of the Lord's fury in the latter days.

The Lord describes in Ezekiel the thoughts that would arise and begin to move this storm of nations to action. "On that day it shall come to pass that thoughts will arise in your mind, and you will make an evil plan: You will say, 'I will go up against a land of unwalled villages; I will go to a peaceful people, who dwell safely, all of them dwelling without walls, and having neither bars nor gates to take *plunder* and to take *booty*, to stretch out your hand against the waste places that are again inhabited, and against a people gathered from the nations, who have acquired livestock and goods, who dwell in the midst of the land'" (Ezek. 38:10–12)

It may be that Gog's forces feel justified because they have suffered loss in Damascus, so they are coming to take what they want knowing the rest of the nations will do nothing. But the Lord God has something planned for them. He has spoken long ago that this battle would take place, and here it is. The inner circle of nations around Israel are motivated by hatred and a strong desire to shed innocent Jewish blood; plunder is not their primary motive. The nations in Ezekiel include Persia, Ethiopia, and Libya—Islamic nations—so their motive may be in strong agreement with the inner circle. But Gog is leading his forces down for plunder; they want everything Israel has.

The Lord describes the motive of these forces who come down against His people and explains the main reason this battle would take place in the latter days.

> Therefore, son of man, prophesy and say to Gog, "Thus says the Lord GOD:" On that day when My people Israel dwell safely, will you not know it? Then you will come from your place out of the far north, you and many peoples with you, all of them riding on horses, a great company and a mighty army. You will come up against My people Israel like a cloud, to cover the land. It will be in the latter days that I will bring you against My land, so that the nations may know Me, when I am hallowed in you, O Gog, before their eyes. (Ezek. 38:14–16)

The Lord said, "When My people Israel dwell safely, will you not know it?" This is the point of view of those who come from the far north—Russia.

Russia has seen what has gone on between Israel and the Arab nations since the birth of Israel. Russia has seen the Arab nations declare war against Israel and boast how they would wipe Israel off the map. But every time the Arab nations have attacked Israel, they lost both the war and more land. Russia has this in memory, and therefore, the scripture says, "When My people Israel dwell securely will you not know it?" They know that Israel, though it is a small nation, has never been defeated by their much greater Arab neighbors. Russia will consider its power, which is much greater than all the Arab nations put together, and think that combined with the Arab nations, it should easily win. The first stage of the inner-circle judgment will probably be nuclear, not something perceived as supernatural or Russia would think twice before coming against Israel and their God. But nuclear weapons, Russia has many and would not fear a nuclear attack from Israel.

Therefore, He says: "It will come to pass at the same time, when Gog comes against the land of Israel," says the Lord GOD, "that My fury will show in My face. For in My jealousy and in the fire of My wrath I have spoken" (Ezek. 38:18–19). I don't believe there are any stronger words the Lord could have used to express His great anger at these nations. The Lord has restrained Himself while watching the cruel affliction His people have endured from their Arab neighbors, but the time is coming when He will unleash His anger and fury against those who hate Him! The whirlwind of the Lord has gone forth in fury; a continuing whirlwind of His anger that will not rest until it has been spent on His enemies.

Do these people realize the power of God's anger? The psalmist said, "The nations raged, the kingdoms were moved; He uttered His voice, the earth melted" (Ps. 46:6). The nations rage against Him, and He could with a word make an end of the earth! What if God wanted to make a great show of His wrath? If He has proposed it, He will do it. We see His great anger going forth in Ezekiel 38 against all His enemies that all nations may know Him. The Lord describes the unleashing of His great anger in this chapter:

> "Surely in that day there shall be a great earthquake in the land of Israel, so that the fish of the sea, the birds of the heavens, the beasts of the field, all creeping things that creep on the earth, and all men who are on the face of the earth shall shake at My presence. The mountains shall be thrown down, the steep places shall fall, and every wall shall fall to the ground. I will call for a sword against Gog throughout all My mountains," says the Lord GOD. "Every man's sword will be against his brother. And I will bring him to judgment with pestilence and bloodshed; I will rain down on him, on his troops, and on the many peoples who are with him, flooding rain, great hailstones, fire, and brimstone. Thus, I will magnify Myself and sanctify Myself, and I will be known in the eyes of many nations. Then they shall know that I am the LORD." (Ezek. 38:19–23)

The day is coming when the Lord God Almighty will release His anger on His enemies. This corresponds to what the Lord said in Isaiah: "'Now I will rise,' says the LORD; 'Now I will be exalted, Now I will lift Myself up!'" (Isa. 33:10). The Lord will be exalted among the nations when He is aroused from His holy habitation. It is a day when every eye will see His power and have respect for the Holy One of Israel: "This is the day of which I have spoken" (Ezek. 39:8).

First, there shall be a great earthquake in Israel that will spread throughout the earth. The birds of the heavens, the fish of the sea and the beasts of the fields, and all people who are on the face of the earth will shake at His presence. If that is not enough to get their attention; I don't know what would be. As this horde of nations comes like a storm; the earth beneath them will begin to shake. The mountains around them will fall. The Lord will call for a sword against His enemies and every man's sword will turn against his brother. He will bring them to judgment with pestilence and bloodshed. He will rain down on them flooding rain, great hailstones, fire, and brimstone. Though just one of these actions could destroy His enemies, these could be phases of judgment as God did in Egypt.

In the first phase, every man's sword will be turned against his brother and there will be lots of bloodshed. Ezekiel said, "You shall fall upon the mountains of Israel" (Ezek. 39:4). Isaiah said, "The mountains shall be melted with their blood" (Isa. 34:3). Those who escape the sword will be consumed by the pestilence.

When the first phase of the attack fails to destroy Israel, the second phase will strike, and they will be hit with floods and great hailstones, and they will not prevail. And all the nations will be watching. When the commanders see that the second attack has also failed, they will send all that remains in full attack, and they will be hit with fire and brimstone and be completely destroyed. The nations will be amazed that the great and mighty forces that come against the tiny state of Israel could not prevail.

When every man's sword turns against his brother, it could be perceived as, the troops just get confused and began killing each other. When the flooding rain and great hailstones fall from the sky, it could also be perceived as a natural phenomenon, not God. But when the Lord rains down fire and brimstone and destroys the enemies of Israel, this phenomenon has a history that comes from the Bible. The nations know God destroyed Sodom and Gomorrah when fire and brimstone fell from heaven, and that phenomenon will be perceived as supernatural.

Referring to this event the Lord states that He will suddenly lift Himself up in Isaiah 33, He then describes the aftermath of the fire and brimstone: "And the people shall be like the burnings of lime; like thorns cut up they shall be burned in the fire. Hear, you who are afar off, what I have done; and you who are near, acknowledge My might" (Isa. 33:12–13). The ground beneath them will shake as they watch the marvelous show of God's power. And so, all nations will know there is no god in all the earth like the LORD God of Israel.

Ezekiel states that when this judgment takes place, all men who are on the face of the earth will shake at His presence. Joel's prophecy appears to be connected to this event where the Lord has said He will pour out His Spirit on all flesh and show wonders in the heavens above and signs in the earth beneath; blood and fire and pillars of smoke. The mountains will tremble as every wall falls to the ground.

The walls could refer to the walls between Christian groups or denominations, the walls between different religions, the wall between Christians and Jews, every wall between people will come down. Everyone will be on the same level when the heavens and earth shake. "And it shall be: As with the people, so with the priest; As with the servant, so with his master; As with the maid, so with her mistress; As with the buyer, so with the seller; As with the lender, so with the borrower; As with the creditor, so with the debtor. The land shall be entirely emptied and utterly plundered, for the LORD has spoken this word" (Isa. 24:2-3).

Peter quoted the prophet Joel in Acts 2:19, as a prophecy for the last days: "It shall come to pass in the last days, says God... I will show wonders in heaven above and signs in the earth beneath." Ezekiel 38:20 says: "The birds of the heavens... and all men who are on the face of the earth shall shake at My presence." The shaking of the heavens and the earth would demonstrate God's power according to what is written in the prophets:

> "Once more (it is a little while) I will shake heaven
> and earth, the sea and dry land. And I will shake
> all nations, and they shall come with the Desire
> (Wealth, Treasures,) of all Nations, and I will fill

> this temple with glory," says the LORD of hosts.
> "The silver is Mine and the gold is Mine," says the
> LORD of hosts. (Hag 2:6–8)

This passage references the temple of Jesus's day, but there is a future fulfillment that will be accompanied by the shaking of heaven and earth along with all nations. The glory of the latter temple; refers to the glory of the church, His temple in the Spirit, as Paul taught in Ephesians 2:19–22. The Lord is saying that He will fill His church with glory and that the gold and silver of the nations is all His and He shall fill His temple, His church, with it. Billionaires will turn all their money over to the church, because they will see that all their money will not be able to save them from the day of vengeance of our God.

The Lord is going to shake all the monies loose for His glory and His work. But there will be nothing but fear for those who do not know God: "Men's hearts will be failing them from fear and the expectation of those things which are coming on the earth, for the powers of the heavens will be shaken" (Luke 21:26).

Haggai agrees with the shaking of heaven and earth we see in Ezekiel 38, but notice what else agrees with Ezekiel 38:

> I will overthrow the thrones of kingdoms and destroy
> the power of the kingdoms of the nations. And I
> will overthrow the chariots and their riders, and
> the horses and their riders will go down, everyone
> by the sword of his brother. (Hag. 2:21–22 ASV)

The Lord declared in both of these prophesies that there would be a shaking of the heavens and the earth. None of these prophecies will fail; none will lack its mate. Many will be fulfilled when the Lord shakes not only the earth, but also the heavens. But Haggai also prophesies that the power of these nations will be overthrown, their strength would come down, everyone by the sword of their brother.

Ezekiel prophesies the same thing; there will be a shaking of the heavens and the earth, and every man's sword would be against his brother (Ezek. 38:20-21).

The Lord has used this manner of destroying Israel's enemies before; He smote the enemies of Israel with such confusion that they destroyed each other. When the people of Moab with the people of Ammon, along with Mount Seir came to battle against Israel with a great multitude:

> Jehoshaphat bowed his head with his face to the ground, and all Judah and the inhabitants of Jerusalem bowed before the LORD, worshiping the LORD ... And when he had consulted with the people, he appointed those who should sing to the LORD, and who should praise the beauty of holiness, as they went out before the army and were saying: "Praise the LORD, for His mercy endures forever." Now when they began to sing and to praise, the LORD set ambushes against the people of Ammon, Moab, and Mount Seir, who had come against Judah; and they were defeated. For the people of Ammon and Moab stood up against the inhabitants of Mount Seir to utterly kill and destroy them. And when they had made an end of the inhabitants of Seir, they helped to destroy one another. So when Judah came to a place overlooking the wilderness, they looked toward the multitude; and there were their dead bodies, fallen on the earth. No one had escaped. (2 Chron. 20:18–24)

The whole story is a great demonstration of God's power. The Lord will destroy a number of His enemies in Ezekiel's battle in the same way. Haggai and Ezekiel agree that this is how the Lord will destroy a number of His enemies on that day. Both these prophets agree that there is going to be a shaking of the heavens and the earth, and both agree that every man's sword will turn on his brother, and that the Lord will overthrow the power of the gentile kingdoms. Haggai gives us a different view of the same event—in Haggai we move to another side of this great prophetic mountain—and we pick up some more treasured details.

In Hebrews 12 we come to another prophetic passage that agrees with this great shaking. When God came down on Mount Sinai in the days of Moses; it was covered with thick black clouds, and there were flashes of lightning with peals of thunder. God's voice was like a great trumpet blast that shook the mountain. Referring to this terrifying event, the author of Hebrews says, "See that you do not refuse Him who speaks ... Whose voice then shook the earth, but now He has promised, saying, 'Yet once more I shake not only the earth but also heaven'" (Heb. 12:25–26). This prophecy in Hebrews implies that the heavens and the earth will shake at His voice; just as it did in the days of Moses.

This agrees with what the Lord has said in the prophet Joel: "The LORD also will roar from Zion and utter His voice from Jerusalem; the heavens and earth will shake; but the LORD will be a shelter for His people, and the strength of the children of Israel" (Joel 3:16). In the mouths of two or three witnesses every word shall be established: we have four prophets testifying to this great shaking of heaven and earth; Ezekiel, Joel, Haggai, and Hebrews. The Lord will roar from Zion and utter His voice from Jerusalem when He enters this battle!

Isaiah agrees that the Lord will go forth into battle with a great shout: "The LORD shall go forth like a mighty man; He shall stir up His zeal like a man of war. He shall cry out, yes, shout aloud; He shall prevail against His enemies" (Isa. 42:13). The Lord only spoke to the children of Israel on Mount Sinai; but the whole mountain shook, and it terrified them. The Lord says He will roar and shout aloud as He enters this battle with His enemies. When the Lord God Almighty shouts aloud: I believe the heavens and earth will shake!

The great outpouring of the Spirit accompanied by wonders in heaven above and on earth beneath, with blood and fire and pillars of smoke; in Joel chapter 2: shall be fulfilled in this event. The Lord also introduces something in Joel chapter 3 that is a companion to what is in chapter 2. It is also describing this event that should take place before the great and terrible Day of the Lord, or you could say, in the last days. The shaking of heaven and earth in Joel chapter 3, agrees with what we see through the words of the prophets. We have visited this scripture before, but it will bear another look. Let us climb around to another side of this great prophetic mountain and take another look at the words of the prophet Joel:

> For behold, in those days and at that time, when I bring back the captives of Judah and Jerusalem, I will also gather all nations, and bring them down to the Valley of Jehoshaphat. And I will enter into judgment with them there on account of My people, My heritage Israel, whom they have scattered among the nations. They have also divided up My land. They have cast lots for My people, have given a boy as payment for a harlot, and sold a girl for wine, that they may drink. (Joel 3:1–3)

Where he says: "In those days and at that time"—as Peter points out in Acts chapter 2 when he quotes Joel—is referring to the last days. The next chapter in Joel appears to also contain an event appointed for the last days. We see in Joel a prophetic gathering of the captives of His people that is being fulfilled in the return of Israel we see today. Chapter 3 contains a prophecy of a judgment of the nations that should come to pass in the last days. It shall come upon those who have scattered His people; divided up His land and treated His people spitefully. It is referring to the Day of the Lord upon the nations, as we learned in the last chapter, a judgment that is yet to come.

The nations around Israel have afflicted them for many years. There is great agreement in the words of the prophets with what we see and know concerning Israel and its neighbors today. Many prophecies are about this event because it will be a world-changing event that encompasses the whole world in the last days. It is the Lord's plan that He be magnified and sanctified in the eyes of all nations; it is God's Grand Finale. No wonder it is found in so many places in the prophets. The Lord has kept this event hidden because it is not directly mentioned in Daniel or in the end-time teachings of Jesus, but it is sure found in the holy prophets. Didn't Peter say we should be mindful of the words spoken before by the holy prophets? (2 Peter 3:2).

Though He says: "all nations," it is clear He means those who have plundered, despised, and scattered His people. The word Jehoshaphat means: "Jehovah judges." The phrase the Lord uses here: "the valley of Jehoshaphat," is not referring to a literal valley but a metaphorical valley. As it is written in the prophets: "Every valley shall be exalted, and every mountain and hill brought low" (Isa. 40:4). He was not talking about geography but about people. The Lord says He will gather the nations together all around because it is a judgment on the nations around Israel.

The nations that come against Israel are lifted up in pride and consider themselves a mountain stronghold; more than able to destroy the tiny state of Israel, but they shall be brought very low when Jehovah judges. The Lord calls this judgment the valley of Jehoshaphat to signify the humbling of His enemies when He is exalted in judgment. As it is written, "People shall be brought down, each man shall be humbled, and the eyes of the lofty shall be humbled. But the LORD of hosts shall be exalted in judgment, and God who is holy shall be hallowed in righteousness" (Isa. 5:15–17).

The Lord's people will be feeling very low when these great and mighty forces gather together to cut them off from being a nation, but the Lord will give them praise and fame in every land where they were put to shame. The lowly will be exalted, when Jehovah judges their enemies: "Assemble and come, all you nations, and gather together all around. Cause Your mighty ones to go down there, O Lord. Let the nations be wakened and come up to the Valley of Jehoshaphat. For there I will sit to judge all the surrounding nations" (Joel 3:11–12). Joel agrees with Ezekiel 28—it is a judgment on all those around them who despise them.

Should Gog and his forces see Damascus wiped off the map, they would come down like a cloud to cover the land and the Lord will respond thus: "I will bring him to judgment with pestilence and bloodshed; I will rain down on him, on his troops, and on the many peoples who are with him, flooding rain, great hailstones, fire and brimstone." In Joel and Ezekiel, blood and fire with smoke ascending are a sign of this judgment. When Peter quoted Joel in Acts we see blood, fire, and smoke: "I will show wonders in heaven above and signs in the earth beneath blood and fire and vapor of smoke" (Acts 2:19). Some translations say: "Pillars of smoke." When the Lord rains down fire and brimstone on Israel's enemies, there will be great pillars of smoke ascending to the heavens as when He rained down fire and brimstone on Sodom and Gomorrah.

> And Abraham went early in the morning to the place where he had stood before the LORD. Then he looked toward Sodom and Gomorrah, and toward all the land of the plain; and he saw, and behold, the smoke of the land which went up like the smoke of a furnace. (Gen. 19:27–28)

Therefore, Ezekiel agrees with the words of Joel—there will be blood and fire with pillars of smoke ascending from the fire and brimstone the Lord rains down on His enemies.

The Lord has a grand and awesome event prepared for the last days to grab the attention of everyone; it is no wonder it mentioned by so many prophets. God would not have us ignorant concerning these things, for He says: "Search from the book of the Lord and read! Not one of these shall fail! Not one shall lack her mate. For My mouth has commanded it, and His Spirit has gathered them" (Isa. 34:16).

How can we know what He has said unless we read His Word? We are looking at many prophecies and their companions; they share a common intent, a common goal, and common time to be fulfilled, and they all share a commonality with the epicenter, Ezekiel 38–39. They are linked to each other by the Lord's thoughts and intents. "Who among you will give ear to this? Who will listen and hear for the time to come?" (Isa. 42:23–24). Behold, I have told you all things beforehand; Says the Lord, how is it you cannot discern the signs of these times?

Judgment is justice served. Remember how the people of the Lord have been plundered by their Arab neighbors though they did not plunder them. The Arab nations have dealt very treacherously with their Jewish citizens though their Jewish citizens did not deal treacherously with them. Therefore, the Lord pleads the cause of His people.

> Thus says your Lord, the LORD and your God, who pleads the cause of His people: "See, I have taken out of your hand the cup of trembling, the dregs of the cup of My fury; you shall no longer drink it. But I will put it into the hand of those who afflict you, who have said to you, lie down, that we may walk over you. And you have laid your body like the ground, and as the street, for those who walk over." (Isa. 51:22–23)

The Lord has determined that the cup of His fury shall now be put into the hand of those who have afflicted and plundered His people. When they have ceased plundering, they shall be plundered. Jeremiah agrees with what Isaiah says concerning this judgment: "Take this wine cup of fury from My hand, and cause all the nations, to whom I send you, to drink it. They will drink and stagger and go mad because of the sword that I will send among them" (Jer. 25:15-16). "And if they refuse to take the cup from your hand to drink, then you shall say to them, thus says the Lord of hosts: 'You shall surely drink!'" (Jer. 25:28). His anger will not turn back until He has executed and performed the thoughts of His heart. Today, we understand it perfectly.

We all know the wickedness and grief Israel has endured from their enemies around them and we understand why the Lord is so angry with these arrogant nations. They have been weighed in the balances and found guilty of innocent blood; and of every abomination that the LORD hates, they have rejoiced to do it. The Lord has sent His messengers to proclaim to the nations that He is gathering His people Israel back to their own land, and He is their shepherd, but they have refused His words and despised His prophets. Therefore, the Lord has a controversy with the nations, they are contrary to His plan for His people Israel. When the Lord comes to deliver His people; He will roar out of Zion, His holy habitation, against all these nations.

> "Therefore, prophesy against them all these words, and say to them: 'The LORD will roar from on high and utter His voice from His holy habitation; He will roar mightily against His fold. He will give a shout, as those who tread the grapes, against all the inhabitants of the earth. A noise will come to the ends of the earth — For the LORD has a controversy with the nations; He will plead His case with all flesh. He will give those who are wicked to the sword,' says the LORD." (Jer. 25:30-31)

All the inhabitants of the earth will fear and tremble when He gives a great shout, but it is the wicked that He will give to the sword. Jeremiah says: "'The LORD will roar from on high and utter His voice from His holy habitation." Joel says the same thing as well: "The LORD also will roar from Zion [His holy habitation] and utter His voice from Jerusalem; the heavens and earth will shake" (Joel 3:16). The Lord is coming like a roaring lion, as the Lion of the tribe of Judah He will come and plead His case with Israel and all flesh! The Day of the Lord upon the nations is near, it is coming soon; cruel, with both wrath and fierce anger, He will destroy His enemies before the eyes of many nations. Then they shall know that His name is the LORD!

In the day when the LORD God demonstrates His might and fury, He will bring His people Israel into the bond of the covenant and be their King-Messiah. As it is written in the prophet Ezekiel:

> "As I live," says the Lord GOD, "surely with a mighty hand, with an outstretched arm, and with fury poured out, I will rule over you. I will bring you out from the peoples and gather you out of the countries where you are scattered, with a mighty hand, with an outstretched arm, and with fury poured out. And I will bring you into the wilderness of the peoples, and there I will plead My case with you face to face. Just as I pleaded My case with your fathers in the wilderness of the land of Egypt, so I will plead My case with you," says the Lord GOD. "I will make you pass under the rod, and I will bring you into the bond of the covenant." (Ezek. 20:33–37)

This awesome SHOW of God's power will cause them to honor and revere the LORD and His Messiah. Every knee shall bow, and every tongue confess, that Jesus is the Messiah! The Jews are still living under the old covenant; they are not in the new covenant. But the Lord says He is going to bring them into the new covenant, that means all Israel shall be saved! To come into the new covenant, they will have to except the new and binding contract. A covenant is a binding contract; therefore, He says He will bring them into the bond of the covenant. Their enemies become His enemies; His enemies become their enemies, etc.

Remember how Jesus pled His case over Jerusalem:

> O Jerusalem, Jerusalem, the one who kills the prophets and stones those who are sent to her! How often I wanted to gather your children together, as a hen gathers her chicks under her wings, but you were not willing! See! Your house is left to you desolate; for I say to you, you shall see Me no more till you say, "Blessed is He who comes in the name of the LORD!" (Matt. 23:37–39)

The Lord says He will again plead His case with them face to face, and these words agree with the prophets: "The Lord will be seen over His people" (Zech. 9:14), and "They will look upon Him whom they have pierced" (Zech. 12:10). The latter prophecy was fulfilled when Jesus hung on the cross and they looked upon Him, but that was fulfilled out of context with the rest of the chapter. Now it will be fulfilled in context; when the LORD seeks to destroy all the nations that come against Jerusalem they will look upon Him whom they pierced. He will appear over them and plead His case with them face to face.

Many peoples from many nations go up to Jerusalem today, and it is being said, blessed are those who come in the name of the Lord. Christians from all over the world are welcome in Jerusalem. Now is the time that He should appear to them; now is the time that He should plead His case with them face to face. Now it is time that He should bring them into the bond of the covenant; now is the time that He should destroy their enemies and give them praise and fame among all the nations where they were put to shame. This is the manner in which all Israel shall be saved! This is the Messiah dealing with His kinsmen according to the flesh: "The LORD their God will save them in that day, as the flock of His people. For they shall be like the jewels of a crown, lifted like a banner over His land" (Zech. 9:16).

When the Messiah came the first time, the Jews were looking for a conquering hero to deliver them from the Romans and set up His kingdom, but that didn't happen. Remember that after Jesus was raised from the dead and appeared to the disciples, they asked: "Lord, will You at this time restore the kingdom to Israel?" (Acts 1:6). Today, Israel is still looking for its conquering Messiah. All the prophets and the law testify to this coming of Messiah to conquer their enemies and set up a kingdom which will never be destroyed. Therefore, today, they are still looking for their King-Messiah to deliver them from their enemies and restore the kingdom to Israel.

His people have been pleading with Him for thousands of years for their King–Messiah to come and deliver them: "Hear our cry, O Lord! Look at the treachery of Your enemies! Those who hate You have lifted up their heads! They are like brute wild beasts good for nothing but to be slaughtered! Killing men who should live and permitting men to live who should be put to death! They murder, destroy, and plunder in the name of a god that can neither see, nor hear, nor speak, nor deliver, but You, O Lord, created the heavens. They are ungodly children committing ungodly acts in an ungodly way. Let them drink the wine cup of Your fury! How long, O Lord, until you judge and avenge us on our enemies?"

The Lord of hosts has heard their pleas! For He has said: "Out of Zion, the perfection of beauty, God will shine forth. Our God shall come and not keep silent; a fire shall devour before Him, and it shall be very tempestuous all around Him. He shall call to the heavens from above and to the earth…" He shall come in great splendor and glory! For He also says: "The LORD also will roar from Zion, and utter His voice from Jerusalem; the heavens and earth will shake" (Joel 3:16) He shall execute His judgments on all those around His people—Israel—that have plundered and despised them: "Surely it is coming, and it shall be done," says the Lord GOD. "This is the day of which I have spoken" (Ezek. 39:8).

In the days of Noah, people had become so disgustingly obnoxious to the Lord that they were not considered worth saving. A ship large enough to save thousands of people was reserved for animals instead—the animals on Noah's ark were of more value than the ruthless, brutal people of that time. Now at the end of the age, after thousands of years, people continue in their disgusting and abominable behavior against God; they are like brute wild beasts good for nothing but to be slaughtered. Their flesh is good for nothing except for the birds and the beasts to feast on, and their blood is good for nothing more than drink for the same. To see things through God's Word is to see things through His eyes. After this great slaughter of God's enemies, there will be a great sacrificial meal on the mountains of Israel. The flesh of those who hated God will be fed to the birds of the air and the beasts of the field.

> "And as for you, son of man," thus says the Lord GOD, "speak to every sort of bird and to every beast of the field: "Assemble yourselves and come; Gather together from all sides to My sacrificial meal which I am sacrificing for you, a great sacrificial meal on the mountains of Israel, that you may eat flesh and drink blood. You shall eat the flesh of the mighty, drink the blood of the princes of the earth, of rams and lambs, of goats and bulls, all of them fatlings of Bashan. You shall eat fat till you are full, and drink blood till you are drunk, at My sacrificial meal which I am sacrificing for you. You shall be filled at My table with horses and riders with mighty men and with all the men of war," says the Lord GOD. (Ezek. 39:17–20)

The Lord will destroy the strength of the Gentile nations, their armies and their weapons will be destroyed. The nations will see the reward of the wicked and fear and tremble because of the Lord our

God. After the birds and the beasts have gorged themselves on God's sacrificial meal, the house of Israel will cleanse the land.

> It will come to pass in that day that I will give Gog a burial place there in Israel, the valley of those who pass by east of the sea; and it will obstruct travelers, because there they will bury Gog and all his multitude. Therefore, they will call it the Valley of Hamon Gog. For seven months the house of Israel will be burying them, in order to cleanse the land. Indeed, all the people of the land will be burying, and they will gain renown for it on the day that I am glorified," says the Lord GOD. (Ezek. 39:11–13)

> Then those who dwell in the cities of Israel will go out and set on fire and burn the weapons, both the shields and bucklers, the bows and arrows, the javelins and spears; and they will make fires with them for seven years. (Ezek. 39:9)

Following this judgment, they will be burying the dead bodies of the forces of Gog for seven months; for seven years they will be burning the weapons and instruments of war, left from his destroyed army.

The seven years of burning weapons will begin after this judgment; however, the seventieth week of Daniel is still to come. These last years will begin with the glory of God, and the greatest spiritual revival the world has ever seen. God's Holy Spirit will be poured out on all flesh; there will be great signs in the heavens above and on the earth beneath. The powers of the heavens will be shaken, and all men who are the face of the earth will shake at the presence of God. Those in the church of the LORD Jesus Christ will be so filled with the Holy Spirit that they will blast out into the streets speaking in tongues and prophesying. All the works of Jesus shall be done by the church, His body; healing the sick, raising the dead, and casting out devils will be commonplace.

Even those who have never proclaimed before will be surprised at the boldness with which they shall proclaim the things pertaining to the kingdom of God. It matters not what illness people have; a child of God will look at them and say, "Be made whole in Jesus's name!" and it will happen so that all may marvel at the gracious works the Lord is doing through His people.

The Holy Spirit will take charge of His people and do mighty works giving glory to God. The people who know their God shall be strong and do great exploits before the eyes of many nations. They shall give all glory and all honor to the Lord, who does all these things; and the LORD will be exalted through His people, He will be exalted in the earth. Israel will be accepted into the bond of the covenant and be filled with the Spirit speaking in tongues and prophesying!

> "When I have brought them back from the peoples and gathered them out of their enemies' lands, and I am hallowed in them in the sight of many nations, then they shall know that I am the LORD their God, who sent them into captivity among the nations, but also brought them back to their land, and left none of them captive any longer. And I will not hide My face from them anymore; for I shall have *poured out My Spirit* on the house of Israel," says the Lord GOD. (Ezek. 39:27–29)

> I will pour on the house of David and on the inhabitants of Jerusalem the *Spirit of grace* and supplication; then they will look on Me whom they pierced. Yes, they will mourn for Him as one mourns for his only son and grieve for Him as one grieves for a firstborn. (Zech. 12:10)

As the Lord pled His case with the children of Israel in the land of Egypt, He will plead His case with them again and bring them into the bond of the covenant. According to the prophets, He will also pour out His Spirit on the house of Israel in those days. No, the Lord is not finished with His people Israel, nor has He replaced them with some other people. The scattering and desolation are always followed by the gathering and restoration of Israel, and it is mentioned in scripture more than any other event. It is God's witness to the nations that He is God, because He does all these things in the sight of the nations. It is also how He tells us where we are on His time clock.

Isaiah also says the Spirit will be poured out on Israel. "On the land of My people will come up thorns and briers, yes, on all the happy homes in the joyous city; Because the palaces will be forsaken, the bustling city will be deserted… —Until *the Spirit is poured upon us* from on high, and the wilderness becomes a fruitful field, and the fruitful field is counted as a forest" (Isa 32:13-15). The Spirit will be poured out on the children of Israel and the land will be restored to its former glory. The out pouring of the Spirit mentioned by these three prophets will be the main fulfillment of the out pouring of His Spirit in Joel's prophecy. The Spirit will be poured out on all flesh and the LORD will show us His wonders!

This is God's Grand Finale. It is the greatest manifestation of God's power the world has ever seen. When the time has finally arrived, suddenly, He will spring forth and enter this battle. He has held His peace a long time, He has been still and restrained Himself while His enemies have been filling up to the full measure the cup of His indignation. When His enemies gather themselves together for a final assault on His beloved, the LORD God Almighty's fury will come up in His face. He will roar from Zion and cry out loud like the sound of a great trumpet blast! He will cut loose with the great sound of a battle cry as He goes forth to destroy His enemies! The heavens and earth will shake at the thunderous sound of His voice! The Spirit of God, like a flood, will pour out and cover all flesh!

After this great show of God's power and the outpouring of His Spirit on all flesh the LORD will return to His place to test those who dwell on earth to know what is in their hearts. Will they continue to believe Him? Or will they fall away as soon as persecution arises? Remember how the Lord withdrew from Hezekiah to test him, to know what was in his heart?

When the angel of the Lord struck down one-hundred-and-eighty-five-thousand soldiers of the army of the king of Assyria, ambassadors came from Babylon to inquire about the wonder that was done in the land. Word of the wonder went out to all the countries surrounding Israel. All these nations were also under threat of being destroyed by the great Assyrian army, so when the army of Assyria was destroyed all those countries rejoiced greatly because they were relieved of the threat of that army. Hezekiah, king of Judah, was exalted in the eyes of these nations. They believed he was responsible for the great deliverance and victory. Therefore, the Lord withdrew from him to see whether his heart would remain loyal to Him or he would be turned aside and put his trust elsewhere. The scripture says: "God withdrew from him, in order to test him, that He might know all that was in his heart" (2 Chron 32:31).

So it shall be when God performs this great show in the eyes of all nations. It will be the greatest manifestation of God's power the world has ever seen. However, as it was in the days of Hezekiah; the Lord will afterwards return to His place, to test the people to see what is in their hearts. What will men do after they have seen His great power. Some will believe Him and stand firm till the end, while others at first will believe, but because the LORD returns to His place they will be deceived and fall away. Yes, the Lord will come out of His place, and scatter seed over the face of the whole earth; some will fall on the wayside, some on stony soil, some among thorns, but some will land on good soil and produce abundantly for the harvest! Those who believe will do the works of Jesus and greater works as they preach the gospel in all the world as a witness to all the nations, for the time of the end has begun.

CHAPTER 9

The End of the Age

This chapter addresses the time from the grand finale until Christ' coming for the resurrection at the last day. It will cover at least ten and a half years and maybe a little more, we'll see. While none of us are without error the following is given knowing those things which God has spoken concerning this timeframe. It is the time called by the Lord the end of the age. Daniel calls it the time of the end. Being familiar with prophecies and how they are fulfilled, we will consider all these prophecies in the word of God as things that must be fulfilled. Matthew; in several places noted that something was done, so that the Scriptures might be fulfilled. We will view all the prophecies we are going to visit, that speak of the end of the age, as prophecies that must be fulfilled.

These prophecies are God's plan; they are words and thoughts that are higher than ours, and there is a purpose that we may not see now, but later we will see. It appears we are the last generation in the last days; we will see things no generation before us has seen. When we think about it, in these times, we have already seen things that have not been seen by any generation before us. But the power of God is going to be manifested in ways that have never been seen or heard before as well. More will be given to this generation than any other before, but more will be required of it than any other as well.

The time we will address now will include Daniel's seventieth week and the things that shall take place as the last day approaches. Remember the seventy weeks that were determined for Daniel's people and their holy city Jerusalem? It is an important prophecy. It is divided into three sections; seven weeks, sixty-two weeks, and one week. After the judgment of those around Israel; the first two sections, the seven weeks and the sixty-two weeks, will have run their course and their purpose will have been fulfilled. We must remember what the angel told Daniel in the vision in chapter 9, because after God's Grand Finale, there is still more of this prophecy to come.

The seventy-weeks were divided into three sections for the coming of Messiah. This prophecy was speaking to several generations, the generation of Daniel's day, the generation of Jesus' day, as well as to the last generation. Let's take a look at the whole prophecy and notice the three divisions of time that are given:

> "Seventy weeks are determined for your people and for your holy city, to finish the transgression, to make an end of sins, to make reconciliation for iniquity, to bring in everlasting righteousness, to seal up vision and prophecy, and to anoint the Most Holy. "Know therefore and understand, that from the going forth of the command to restore and build Jerusalem until Messiah the Prince, there shall be seven weeks and sixty-two weeks; the street shall be built again, and the wall, even in troublesome times. "And after the sixty-two weeks Messiah shall be cut off, but not for Himself; and the people of the prince who is to come shall destroy the city and the sanctuary. The end of it shall be with a flood, and till the end of the war desolations are determined. Then he shall confirm a covenant with many for one week; but in the middle of the week He shall bring

an end to sacrifice and offering. And on the wing
of abominations shall be one who makes desolate,
even until the consummation, which is determined,
is poured out on the desolate." (Dan. 9:24-27)

We went over this before, but it is good to refresh our memory.
The angel outlines the whole prophecy at the beginning and we find
there are three chronological parts to the prophecy. (1) To finish the
transgression and make an end to sin. (2) To make reconciliation for
iniquity and bring in everlasting righteousness. (3) To seal up vision
and prophecy, and to anoint the most holy. These are the keys to the
prophecy. The seventy weeks are divided into three sections of time,
and these are the purpose of each section of time.

The sixty-two weeks are explained as for the first coming of
Messiah. It says: After the sixty-two weeks Messiah would be cut
off but not for Himself. This agrees with what Isaiah says: "He was
wounded for our transgressions, He was bruised for our iniquities;
the chastisement for our peace was upon Him" (Isa 53:4-5). All He
endured was not for Himself, it was for us. And verse 8 says: "He was
cut off from the land of the living" Daniel is told the same thing.
He was cut off but not for Himself. We see that the sixty-two weeks
are specifically appointed for Messiah's first coming.

The purpose of this section is to finish the transgression and make
an end to sin. This was fulfilled when the nation of the Jews filled up
to the full measure their sins by committing the greatest level of sin
there is, the unpardonable sin. It was fulfilled when they hated Him
without a cause and put the author of life to death. They finished,
or you could say, completed their transgression; because there is no
greater or higher abomination they could commit. For the Jews who
received Him, He put an end to sin, or you could say, destroyed the
power of sin and death. Thus, the scriptures were fulfilled.

The next coming or appearing over His people will be a great
and tremendous show of His power by which all Israel shall be saved,
and the greatest revival the church has ever seen will begin. When

Israel receives their Messiah; their iniquity is pardoned, they are reconciled to God and everlasting righteousness is obtained through Christ. If their being cast away was the reconciling of the world, their acceptance, their reconciliation to God will result in the greatest revival the world has ever seen!

There are three divisions of time in this prophecy, yes, 3 divisions of time, that are each appointed for a coming of Messiah in a specific manner. We are about to see the second fulfilled. The angel tells Daniel that the purpose for the last week is to seal up vision and prophecy, and to anoint the Most Holy. It means the last week will see the fulfillment of the prophetic visions of His servants the prophets concerning the time of the end, and there will be a great anointing of the Lamb's Most Holy Bride with glory and honor when He comes in that day. The last week ends when Jesus Christ comes in power and great glory to remove His Bride from the earth as the Day of Judgment begins.

When the church is taken out of the earth, we can call it by definition, the rapture. The Bride of Christ will be removed from the earth and taken to Her bridal chambers and the door will be shut. Remember the words of Isaiah: "Come, my people, enter your chambers, and shut your doors behind you; hide yourself, as it were, for a little moment, Until the indignation is past. For behold, the LORD comes out of His place to punish the inhabitants of the earth for their iniquity" (Isa 26:20-21). Then Hosea says: "On the third day He will raise us up, that we may live in His sight" (Hosea 6:2) His Bride will be raised up that she may live in His sight, in His presence, together with Him forever. Paul says: "Then we who are alive and remain shall be caught up together with them in the clouds to meet the Lord in the air. And thus, we shall always be with the Lord" (1 Thess. 4:17-18).

The time frame, from God's Grand Finale until the return of Christ for the resurrection at the last day, we will refer to as the time of the end. To make this clear; following this judgment there will be a burning of weapons for seven years, but Daniel's seventieth week does not begin right after this judgment. It appears that as much as one thousand, two-hundred and sixty days may be required to incubate the conditions needed for the man of sin to be revealed. Till this happens, the revival of God's people will be going strong and gaining strength. Great amounts of money and wealth will come into the hands of the saints so that they become a powerful and organized authority in the earth.

Following God's Grand Finale, the seventieth week will not come immediately, but arrive at its appointed time. There will first be a great outpouring of God's Spirit on all flesh, and a great revival! The coming revival can be seen in scripture in several ways. In Romans 11, Paul explained a mystery concerning Israel that the Lord had kept hidden. It is God's plan for Israel, that through them He might enlighten the church: "Now if their fall is riches for the world, and their failure riches for the Gentiles, how much more their fullness!" (Rom. 11:12). There is coming a fullness of Israel! What would a fullness of Israel be? Paul said, "For if their being cast away is the reconciling of the world, what will their acceptance be but life from the dead?" (Rom. 11:15).

If all Israel will be saved, we can agree that their acceptance would reference their being accepted into the new covenant. Their fullness references all the promises made to them of restoration, fame, and glory that will be fulfilled. Paul said their acceptance would result in their being revived from the dead. If their being cast away was the reconciling of the world, their acceptance will result in the greatest revival the world has ever seen! It is the Lord's doing that no flesh may glory in His presence.

All His promises to adorn them with His glory and restore them spiritually will be fulfilled! Their cup of blessing will completely overflow. Israel will be in the new covenant and grafted back into the natural olive tree that they might partake of the fatness of the root of their inheritance. (Rom. 11:16-23) Isaiah says:

> Arise, shine; for your light has come! And the glory
> of the LORD is risen upon you! The Gentiles shall

come to your light and kings to the brightness of your rising. Lift up your eyes all around, and see: they all gather together, they come to you ... Then you shall see and become radiant and your heart shall swell with joy, because the abundance of the sea shall be turned to you the wealth of the Gentiles shall come to you ... they shall bring gold and incense and they shall proclaim the praises of the LORD. (Isa. 60:2–6)

Surely the coastlands shall wait for Me; and the ships of Tarshish will come first, to bring your sons from afar, their silver and their gold with them, to the name of the LORD your God, and to the Holy One of Israel, because He has glorified you. (Isa. 60:9)

And Zephaniah says:

"For I will give you fame and praise among all the peoples of the earth" Says the LORD. (Zeph. 3:20)

All the scriptures concerning God's promises to Israel will be fulfilled. The fullness of Israel is coming ... revival is coming!

The silver and gold are the Lord's, and He has promised to fill His temple with glory. When the Lord demonstrates His supreme majesty with a great show of His mighty power, His promise to pour out His Spirit on all flesh will explode upon the earth! It will be the main fulfillment of the prophecy in Joel 2. This outpouring of His Spirit will cover the earth; a flood of His Spirit will be poured out on all peoples, tribes, tongues, and nations. The earth will shake at the sound of His voice when He roars from on high against His enemies, it will shake as a flood of His Spirit covers the earth. The floodgates of heaven will open, and a flood of the river of life will pour down and cover the earth like a caramel apple, and the whole earth will begin to shake at His presence: "The floodgates of the heavens are opened, the foundations of the earth shake" (Isa. 24:18 NIV).

All Israel shall be saved and filled with the same Spirit that raised Christ from the dead. Glory to God! It will be a time of great glory for the children of Israel not because of their good deeds but for His holy name's sake. At first, they will be grieved and ashamed for all their evil ways. But the nations will come from all over the earth bringing their wealth to the name of the Lord and to the people in whom He delights to honor: "The wealth of the sinner is stored up for the righteous" (Prov. 13:22). Billionaires will be saved and turn all their money over to the children of God to send the gospel of the Kingdom of Heaven to the four corners of the earth. We're talking about some of the wicked ones who have obtained great wealth by fraud and corruption; they will turn from darkness to light and from dead works to serving the living God. It will be understood that all the money in the world will not deliver anyone in the day of the Lord's wrath, which is still to come.

The scriptures speak a word of warning directly to the rich in these last days.

> Come now, you rich, weep and howl for your miseries that are coming upon you! Your riches are corrupted, and your garments are moth-eaten. Your gold and silver are corroded, and their corrosion will be a witness against you and will eat your flesh like fire. You have heaped up treasure in the last days. (James 5:1–4)

> Neither their silver nor their gold shall be able to deliver them in the day of the LORD's wrath. (Zeph. 1:18)

Billionaires will release all their finances to the work of God in the last days. The church will become so powerful, they will have no lack of finances whatsoever. Missionaries will be sent to preach the gospel in all the world as a witness to all the nations, and then the end will come. Yes, all people will see the glory of God's power and the destruction of His enemies, but they must hear His Word. Their hearts will turn back to God, but they must be born again. They will ask, "What must we do to be saved?" And they will say, "You must be born again." They must hear the gospel. And whoever calls on the name of the Lord shall be saved!

Through this great show of God's power, the hearts of many will turn back to the Lord and will come into His house and worship Him: "Many nations shall be joined to the LORD in that day, and they shall become My people" (Zech. 2:11). The Lord plans to turn the hearts of many nations back to Him, and they will come to His house and worship Him. As it is written:

> Now it shall come to pass in the latter days that the mountain of the LORD's house shall be established on the top of the mountains and shall be exalted above the hills; and all nations shall flow to it. Many people shall come and say, "Come, and let us go up to the mountain of the LORD, to the house of the God of Jacob." (Isa. 2:2–3)

Many will come from the ends of the earth to worship the Lord on His holy mountain in Jerusalem: "People from nations around the world shall worship the Lord" (Zeph. 2:11 NLT). The words of the prophets shall be fulfilled: "I will be exalted among the nations, I will be exalted in the earth!" (Ps. 46:10). They will turn to Him with all their heart, soul, and strength and give their wealth to the work of the Lord. The wealth that comes into the house of God will be holy to the Lord, it will not be stored away for safe keeping, but will flow to those who live before the Lord, to eat sufficiently and for fine clothing. But the Lord will be a swift witness against all those who do wickedly. The fear of the Lord is the beginning of wisdom—remember Ananias and Sapphira?

The temple mount in Jerusalem has a 36-acre platform that Herod the Great built as a foundation to build the temple on. I see a massive structure built on it that covers the whole platform which has the appearance of a sanctuary fortress because it is so big. It is the House of God in Jerusalem which is built on His holy hill, so that people from all nations may come to worship the Lord in Jerusalem. "Many people shall come and say, "Come, and let us go up to the mountain of the LORD, to the house of the God of Jacob; He will teach us His ways, and we shall walk in His paths." For out of Zion shall go forth the law, and the word of the LORD from Jerusalem" (Isa 2:3).

People from all over the world will come to the house of God and pray before the Lord. His house shall be called a house of prayer for all nations, and all nations will be joyful in His house of prayer. "Great is the LORD, and greatly to be praised in the city of our God, in His holy mountain. Beautiful in elevation, the joy of the whole earth is Mount Zion on the sides of the north, the city of the great King" (Ps. 48:1–2) The Lord shall be praised and exalted in all the earth and on His holy mountain, mount Zion, the city of the great King. "And He will destroy on this mountain the surface of the covering cast over all people, and the veil that is spread over all nations" (Isa. 25:7) Then the eyes of the nations will be opened, and they shall see whose god is God, for the veil shall be removed. "I will bring the blind by a way they did not know; I will lead them in paths they have not known. I will make darkness light before them, and crooked places straight. These things I will do for them and not forsake them" (Isa. 42:16).

Israel will be center stage of this event and the glorious times that follow. Nations will come to them, not because of anything they will do but because of the Lord their God, the Holy One of Israel: "And nations who do not know you shall run to you, because of the LORD your God, and the Holy One of Israel; for He has glorified you" (Isa 55:5). The Lord shall glorify them and give them the wealth of the Gentiles. The fear of the Lord shall be in their hearts, and they shall distribute this wealth as any has need. Thus, the Word of the Lord shall be fulfilled: "He who gathered much had nothing left over and he who gathered little had no lack" (Ex. 16:18). The wealth of the nations will be turned over to the people of the Lord and the saints of the Most High, and His holy people will become a powerful presence in the earth.

In the New Testament, the temple of the Lord is not made with hands. As it is written:

> However, the Most High does not dwell in temples made with hands, as the prophet says: 'Heaven is My throne, and earth is My footstool. What house will you build for Me? says the LORD, or what is the place of My rest? Has My hand not made all these things? (Acts 7:48–50)

> God, who made the world and everything in it, since He is Lord of heaven and earth, does not dwell in temples made with hands. (Acts 17:24)

The Lord does not dwell in temples made with hands. Heaven is His throne and the earth is His footstool. He dwells in His people. The holy people of the Lord are the temple of the living God and His holy of holies. It is a spiritual house and a holy temple not made with hands: "For you are the temple of the living God, as God has said, 'I will dwell in them and walk among them. I will be their God, and they shall be My people'" (2 Cor. 6:16).

> Coming to Him as to a living stone, rejected indeed by men, but chosen by God and precious, you also, as living stones, are being built up a spiritual house, a holy priesthood, to offer up spiritual sacrifices acceptable to God through Jesus Christ. (1 Peter 2:4–6)

God's temple on earth is His people. Where does He instruct His people to build Him a third temple? He doesn't.

The Lord has a temple in heaven that was not made with hands, it is mentioned several times in Revelation: "Then the temple of God was opened in heaven, and the ark of His covenant was seen in His temple" (Rev. 11:19). It is a temple, but it too was not made with human hands. Why do we hear of building a temple with hands and reintroducing animal sacrifices neither of which God has commanded? It is because people will do what they want rather than seek God's plan.

If they sacrifice animals and sprinkle blood, it will not be accepted as an offering before the Lord. Those things were just a shadow of the good things to come: "For it is not possible that the blood of bulls and goats could take away sins" (Heb. 10:4). It is not God's plan to go back to the old ways and back to the old covenant: "I will make a new covenant with the house of Israel and with the house of Judah … In that He says, 'A new covenant,' He has made the first obsolete" (Heb. 8:8, 13). Sacrifices and worship in the old covenant are obsolete. That is not what the Lord instructs His people to do today.

It is prophesied by Isaiah the prophet that the Lord's holy house would be established on the top of the mountains and exalted above the hills, and all nations would come there to worship and pray before the God of earth. We must take note that His house is just a house or a building until His holy people fill His house; then, it could be called a temple and that only because His people are in it.

In the new covenant, God's people offer up spiritual sacrifices in holiness. The apostle Peter said we are a royal priesthood and a holy nation, God's special people whom He created that we may proclaim praises to Him for calling us out of darkness and into His marvelous light. (1 Peter 2:9) We are a people so precious to God that everything we do has His attention, and it affects whether He is joyful over us or grieved. Yes, He can be grieved when we do things against His will, because, in the end it hurts us. But He is blessed by our spiritual sacrifices and the praise we offer Him, so let the fruit of our lips continually give thanks to His name. (Heb. 13:15–16) We live in a new covenant that has a new way of worship in a new temple. As a royal priesthood, let us worship in spirit and in truth for the Father seeks such to worship Him. Let us live before Him joyfully giving and sharing because He is well pleased with such sacrifices. "I beseech you therefore, brethren, by the mercies of God, that you present your bodies a living sacrifice, holy, acceptable to God, which is your reasonable service" (Rom 12:1). The Amplified translation says: "Which is your spiritual worship."

The time is coming when the church shall enter its glory and perform great exploits. Multitudes will be saved, filled with the Spirit, speak in tongues, and prophesying. There will be prophesying here and prophesying there. Teachers who know the Word of God will teach multitudes; people will not live by bread alone but by every Word that proceeds from the mouth of God. The Word of God will grow mightily in His people and their communities; and it will be preached, taught, and received like never before.

As the Lord has promised, He will be working with them confirming the Word with signs and wonders following as a witness to all nations. His glory will be revealed to all nations; all flesh shall see it together. The church will be so filled with the glory and power of the Spirit that they will begin to see into the spirit realm. Hosts of angels will appear to His people and minister to them. Yes, it will be a glorious time for the people of the Lord, but it will gradually usher in a time of great persecution. Although the wicked will see many great signs and wonders, as time goes by, they will fall away in unbelief.

When the Lord filled His temple with glory in the book of Acts, it was great and marvelous, but it was also not pleasing to the world around them. In Acts 7:55–58, when Steven gave testimony before the Sanhedrin, he did not speak his own words but those the Lord gave him for that hour, and the leaders of God's people hated him for the Word of God and rejected him vehemently. But the way

God sees it, they did not reject man but Himself: "He who hears you hears Me, he who rejects you rejects Me, and he who rejects Me rejects Him who sent Me" (Luke 10:16). They were so offended by his words that they gnashed their teeth at him and stoned him. But Steven saw the glory of God; heaven opened, and he saw Jesus standing at the right hand of God. This is the only place in scripture where Jesus is seen standing at the right hand of God. Great glory is attributed to those who have endured great persecution.

The Lord explained how this persecution would come, and He quoted the prophet Daniel.

> Therefore, when you see the "abomination of desolation," spoken of by Daniel the prophet, standing in the holy place then there will be great tribulation, such as has not been since the beginning of the world until this time, no, nor ever shall be. And unless those days were shortened, no flesh would be saved; but for the elect's sake those days will be shortened. (Matt. 24:15–22)

Daniel says:

> At that time Michael shall stand up, the great prince who stands watch over the sons of your people; and there shall be a time of trouble, such as never was since there was a nation, even to that time. And at that time your people shall be delivered, everyone who is found written in the book. And many of those who sleep in the dust of the earth shall awake, some to everlasting life, some to shame and everlasting contempt. (Dan 12:1-2)

Daniel called this great tribulation a time of trouble the likes of which there had not been before, but the Lord's people will be delivered out of it. There will never be such a time of great tribulation for the elect again because their days on earth will end. The trouble Daniel described, and the tribulation Jesus spoke of take place at the time of the end, before the day of wrath and revelation of the righteous judgment of God. The great tribulation is a time of great persecution like that which the church experienced in Acts 8, however, it is not the day of wrath and judgment.

Jesus gave some pretty hard instructions concerning these times, but many will listen to neither God nor man concerning these things. They put only the scriptures they like into their comfortable, little boxes. The whole counsel of God cannot be found in their box. However, God's thoughts are higher than ours and His ways are higher than ours. He cannot be put into a box; we cannot limit the Holy One of Israel.

Remember when Jesus spoke to His disciples about His death? They could not believe what He was saying. There was a great gap between what God's plan was, and what the disciples were believing and planning.

> From that time Jesus began to show to His disciples that He must go to Jerusalem and suffer many things from the elders and chief priests and scribes, and be killed, and be raised the third day. Then Peter took Him aside and began to rebuke Him, saying, "Far be it from You, Lord; this shall not happen to You!" But He turned and said to Peter, "Get behind Me, Satan! You are an offense to Me, for you are not mindful of the things of God, but the things of men" (Matt. 16:21–23)

Jesus had just confirmed to all the disciples that He was the Christ, the Son of the living God. Their dreams appeared to be within their grasp. The disciples had plans to see the kingdom restored to Israel so that they could rule with Jesus in a kingdom on earth, but His words did not agree with their vision and the plans they were creating in their hearts. Notice how James and John had planned to sit in authority with Jesus in this new kingdom:

> Then James and John, the sons of Zebedee, came to Him, saying, "Teacher, we want You to do for us whatever we ask." And He said to them, "What do you want Me to do for you?" They said to Him, "Grant us that we may sit, one on Your right hand and the other on Your left, in Your glory." (Mark 10:37)

The disciples knew Jesus was the Christ, the long-awaited Messiah, and He would be King of Israel, and they were out to secure their place in His kingdom. So when they heard Jesus say He would be put to death, they saw all their plans vanish like vapor. That is how the natural mind of man thinks; we want things to go according to our plan, and when we find out God's plan is different than ours, we get upset and want to straighten Him out. However, we are not called to do our own will or pursue our own plan but the will and plan of Him who sent us. When tribulation comes, the prayer of Jesus should always be first in our heart, "Father, if it be your will take this cup from me, nevertheless not my will but yours be done."

From the passage in Matthew 16, we learn that even the Lord's closest disciples could be swayed by Satan and be an offense to God. If we think the end times ought to follow a plan that is easy for us, or should be one we like, we could be found to agree with Satan, and that is an offence to God. The disciples did not see their plan come to pass; God's plan came to pass, the disciples had to just stop complaining and get onboard with what was obviously God's plan. Because, what may be highly esteemed among men may be an offence to God.

Some say you must seek to save your life in the last days, and that we need to store up food and prepare to survive. When God's people do not listen to Him, they get things in a mess. Paul said, "For the love of Christ compels us, because we judge thus: that if One died for all, then all died; and He died for all, that those who live should live no longer for themselves, but for Him who died for them" (2 Cor. 5:14–15). Our love of Christ compels us to do His will. As Jesus said, "If you love Me, keep My Word" (John 14:15).

We have died so that we will no longer live for ourselves but for Him because He died for us. Why should a dead man fear death? "It is the Spirit that gives life, the flesh profits nothing" (John 6:63). The flesh is condemned to death because of the sin that put Jesus on the cross. He had to be put to death in the flesh that we might live in the spirit. He paid for us with His life, and our lives belong to Him to do His will. Paul said:

> If then you were raised with Christ seek those things which are above, where Christ is sitting at the right hand of God. Set your mind on things above, not on things on the earth. For you died, and your life is hidden with Christ in God. (Col. 3:3)

Paul said, "You died." Dead men do not fear death. They don't fear anything! That is how Christ wants us to live for Him. If One died for all, then all have died for the One. Our lives are not our own. We were bought with a price, and we can glorify God with our bodies in life and death. Have you never read what Jesus our Lord said to Peter? "Most assuredly, I say to you, when you were younger, you girded yourself and walked where you wished; but when you are old, you will stretch out your hands, and another will gird you and carry you where you do not wish." This He spoke, signifying by what death he would glorify God. And when He had spoken this, He said to him, "Follow Me" (John 21:18-19). He who is able to accept it, let him accept it.

The Word of God instructs us so that we might be prepared to glorify God, if or when the time comes. We only get one shot at this and it determines how we will enter eternity. We can glorify God when we exit this world; when we leave the world and go to the Father, or we can seek to save our life, which robs us of eternal glory. Following Jesus is the greatest thing we can do with our lives here on earth! Remember how He spoke about His death? "I came forth from the Father and have come into the world. Again, I leave the world and go to the Father" (John 16:28).

How we leave the world and go to the Father is up to us, we choose how we go. Only don't be offended at His words because you don't agree.

> Then they will deliver you up to tribulation and kill you, and you will be hated by all nations for My name's sake. (Matt. 24:9)

These things will happen for His name's sake; they will kill His people because they hate Him. His followers love Him more than their own life, and the world will be enraged at His holy people, because they follow Him. Therefore, He said: "And do not fear those who kill the body but cannot kill the soul. But rather fear Him who is able to destroy both soul and body in hell" (Matt. 10:28). We should not fear those who hate us. We are so filled with His Holy Spirit when this great persecution comes that we will not even fear death. Our love of Christ is so great that we are eager to present our body a living sacrifice for all He has done for us.

He is not saying we have to be martyrs for Him; He is saying we should not fear death! We are peculiar and strange to this world when we do not fear death because the people of this world are controlled by the fear of death. Jesus told us; do not fear death, in several places, that is the Lord's word for this generation. We are to live for Him as seeing that which is not visible; we are to live for eternity and not for this life which is passing away. It is a stone of stumbling and a rock of offense for some, but to this we were called.

The Lord Jesus set an example that we should follow. He was

obedient unto death, putting the Father's will before His own. But there was a joy in it for Jesus, and we can tap into it. The scripture says that we should look to Jesus, the author and finisher of our faith: "Who for the joy that was set before Him endured the cross, despising the shame, and has sat down at the right hand of the throne of God" (Heb. 12:2). The joy of the Lord was His strength; it gave Him strength to endure the cross. We must also have His joy that we may also have His strength to endure all things and to sit with Him on His throne! As it is written: "To him who overcomes I will grant to sit with Me on My throne, as I also overcame and sat down with My Father on His throne" (Rev. 3:21). Glory to God! If that doesn't give you joy, you must be dead even while you live!

Persecution and tribulation have been happening since the beginning of the church age; there will just be an increase of what has always been in the last days because of the glory of God that will be poured out upon His people. The glory of God was seen on His people in Acts, then great persecution arose against them. When Stephen was accused falsely, his face was seen as the face of an angel. (Acts 6:15) The glory of God was seen on him! If it happened to them it will happen to us. Notice what happened to the early church when Steven spoke the wisdom of God to the religious leaders of that day:

> When they heard these things, they were cut to the heart, and they gnashed at him with their teeth. But he, being full of the Holy Spirit, gazed into heaven and *saw the glory of God*, and Jesus standing at the right hand of God, and said, "Look! I see the heavens opened and the Son of Man standing at the right hand of God!" Then they cried out with a loud voice, stopped their ears, and ran at him with one accord; and they cast him out of the city and stoned him. And the witnesses laid down their clothes at the feet of a young man named Saul.

> And they stoned Stephen as he was calling on God
> and saying, "Lord Jesus, receive my spirit." Then he
> knelt down and cried out with a loud voice, "Lord,
> do not charge them with this sin." And when he had
> said this, he fell asleep. (Acts 7:54–60)

Then: "At that time a great persecution arose against the church" (Acts 8:1). The glory of God will bring great persecution. Steven did not fear those who could destroy the body but could do nothing beyond that. He did not seek to save his life but spoke the Word of God with boldness even though it would result in his death.

As a flower is crushed to produce a beautiful fragrance, so Steven suffered the death of his flesh; he was crushed, and a beautiful fragrance came forth: "Lord, do not charge them with this sin." He had no hate in his heart for his executioners. Too often when we are attacked and in great pain, vile and nasty things come out of us. Not so with those who walk in the Spirit and do not fulfill the lusts of the flesh. Love suffers long and is kind. Be zealous therefore, and repent, begin to practice the word.

Steven had to be filled with the Holy Spirit and joy to endure these things and release the beautiful fragrance that came forth in his great trial of affliction. He had prepared himself by praying in the Spirit and walking in love toward his enemies. It does not come naturally; it comes by walking, praying, and worshiping in the spirit and abiding in His Word. It is time we *prepare* ourselves to be a beautiful fragrance and not a stench. It may be required of us as we transition from this age to the next. We cannot ignore what the Lord has said to us and expect to be a beautiful fragrance; we must *prepare* ourselves.

Referring to what happened to Steven, Acts 11:19 says, "Now those who were scattered after the persecution that arose over Stephen traveled as far as Phoenicia, Cyprus, and Antioch, preaching the word." The Greek word translated "persecution" here in Acts 11:19 is not the same Greek word translated "persecution" in Acts

8:1; it is the Greek word translated "tribulation" in all the prophetic passages in the New Testament. Tribulation and persecution are used interchangeably in the New Testament; they have a shared meaning. In Matthew 24, when Jesus referred to the end times, He said there would be great tribulation; He was quoting Daniel 12:1. But Daniel called it a time of trouble. The Hebrew word translated "trouble" in Daniel 12:1 is also translated "tribulation," "distress," "anguish," and "affliction." The Greek word translated "tribulation" is also translated "persecution," "trouble," "affliction," and "anguish." It is in no way referring to the great and terrible day of God's wrath from which we have been delivered.

The passage that is our point of interest is the great tribulation Jesus spoke of in His end-time discourse in Matthew 24. If the early church went through great tribulation, it is given that we also will see great tribulation when the glory of God is poured out on us. The early disciples were scattered after the great persecution and tribulation that arose over Steven. Therefore, toward the time of the end, because of great glory, there will be an unprecedented time of great persecution and tribulation against the church of God that will never be again for their sojourn on earth will end. Jesus said that it should happen at the time of the end.

When the glory of God is present; and millions come to the Lord and are saved, and the power of the holy people grows strong, the profits of the wicked will rapidly decline, while the finances of God's people will increase greatly. They won't like that. According to prophecy, the Lord will fill His church with glory and billions of dollars and millions of people will enter His kingdom. However, after some time, persecution will arise against the saints. As we see in Acts, when the glory of God is revealed, great persecution will arise.

In the seven years that follow God's grand finale, the wicked will see that the prosperity they once enjoyed is gone. When the glory of God is present to heal, save, and deliver, people won't want the products of the wicked any more. They won't want pornography, liquor, tobacco, or gambling, pharmaceutical drugs are no longer needed, things that have given the wicked much prosperity will all be gone, and the wicked will be filled with wrath. It will happen according to what we see in Acts. When no one is buying their goods anymore, they will gather together a counsel and say, "If we leave the Christians alone like this, we will eventually have nothing." Therefore, they will stir up persecution against the church of God.

In Acts, we see a type and a foreshadowing of what will come. In Acts 19, when Demetrius the silversmith saw that what Paul was preaching and teaching would destroy his business, he gathered men of like trades and said,

> "Men, you know that we have our prosperity by this trade. Moreover; you see and hear that not only at Ephesus, but throughout almost all Asia, this Paul has persuaded and turned away many people, saying that they are not gods which are made with hands. So not only is this trade of ours in danger of falling into disrepute, but also the temple of the great goddess Diana may be despised, and her magnificence destroyed, whom all Asia and the world worship." Now when they heard this, they were full of wrath and cried out, saying, "Great is Diana of the Ephesians!" So the whole city was filled with confusion. (Acts 19:25–29)

We must understand that when the early church was filled with the glory of God, great persecution arose against them. What we see in Acts is a type of what will happen in the last days. Great glory will be poured out on the whole world, and at first, the wicked will be confused and caught off guard and believe for a small moment. But in the seven years that follow God's grand finale, they will fall back into their wicked ways and begin to plot against the people of the Lord.

The Lord will come out of His place for a moment to make Himself known, then return to His place, and let people make their decision; whom will they believe, whom will they serve. They have seen His glory and power; what will they do? It is a time of decision as the prophet Joel has said: "Multitudes, multitudes in the valley of decision! For the day of the LORD is near in the valley of decision" (Joel 3:14). Then later the Lord comes out of His place again to punish the inhabitants of the earth for their iniquity. (Is. 26:21)

It will be the last chance God gives people to turn from dead works to serve Him before the great day of His wrath comes. People will know God's presence; hear His Word and see a great and mighty show of His power, and then He will return to His place. Then as time goes by there will also be a counterfeit and deceptive move drawing people away from God. Some will explain away the mighty works of the Lord. They will give theories and explanations of all the people have seen. Then; when they have their attention and the deception is working, they will offer them the pleasures of this life. Depending on what people decide in those days will determine whether they are taken or left behind. The great and terrible day of the Lord is near in the valley of decision.

All peoples, tribes, and nations shall see the glory of God almighty, and many miracles, signs, and wonders will be done by His people, but many will persist in their unbelief. Though the people of the Lord will issue many warnings from the Word of the Lord, many will turn away in unbelief. Remember this warning in Hebrews 3:12: "Beware, brethren, lest there be in any of you an evil heart of unbelief in departing from the living God." Because of great persecution, many will fall away from the faith, do evil, and enjoy the passing pleasures of sin. The Spirit expressly says that in latter times some will depart from the faith, giving heed to demons. You can't depart from the faith unless you were in it. These are Christians who will be led away because they were never grounded in the Word of God and the things of God.

Those who depart from the faith will be led away by deceiving spirits. False prophets who are led by these spirits will arise and do great signs and wonders by the power of the demons, whose purpose it is to lead people away from the faith: "False christs and false prophets will rise and show great signs and wonders to deceive, if possible, even the elect" (Matt. 24:24). Some will be deceived because they do not know the false from the true prophets because of signs and wonders. The Lord has informed us that we would not know a prophet of God by signs and wonders because the false prophets would also show great signs and wonders. Notice what the Lord instructed the children of Israel concerning false prophets in the days of Moses.

> If there arises among you a prophet or a dreamer of dreams, and he gives you a sign or a wonder, and the sign or the wonder comes to pass, of which he spoke to you, saying, 'Let us go after other gods which you have not known' and let us serve them,' you shall not listen to the words of that prophet or that dreamer of dreams, for the LORD your God is testing you to know whether you love the LORD your God with all your heart and with all your soul. (Deut. 13:1–3)

This could be applied to our days in that false prophets do not say, "Let us go after other gods," but they lead people away from the truth with deceptive words; and turn many away from the Word of God by deceiving them with twisted scriptures and signs and wonders. They can give a prophetic word and it comes to pass, but that does not mean the prophet is of God. Therefore, we need to emphasize that we will not know the false from the true prophets by signs and wonders or even prophetic words that come to pass. Jesus teaches us how we will know the true prophet from the false.

> Beware of false prophets, who come to you in sheep's clothing, but inwardly they are ravenous wolves. You will know them by their fruits. Do men gather

grapes from thorn bushes or figs from thistles? Even
so, every good tree bears good fruit, but a bad tree
bears bad fruit. A good tree cannot bear bad fruit,
nor can a bad tree bear good fruit. (Matt. 7:15–18)

We will know them by their fruit. False prophets will be
inwardly ravenous wolves who pursue their own gain while honoring
themselves and leaving a trail of pain and suffering behind them.
Wolves do not always kill sheep; they often times will just rip and
tear on them and leave them bleeding. Jesus said that we would
know them by their fruit, their works. The fruit of the Spirit will
not be present in them, and the works of the flesh that drive them
cannot be hidden.

Peter described the false prophets' and teachers' tactics and
characters.

But there were also false prophets among the
people, even as there will be false teachers among
you, who will secretly bring in destructive heresies,
even denying the Lord who bought them, and
bring on themselves swift destruction. And many
will follow their destructive ways, because of
whom the way of truth will be blasphemed. By
covetousness they will exploit you with deceptive
words … They are those who walk according to
the flesh in the lust of uncleanness and despise
authority. They are presumptuous, self-willed.
They are not afraid to speak evil of dignitaries …
They are spots and blemishes, carousing in their
own deceptions while they feast with you, having
eyes full of adultery and that cannot cease from sin,
enticing unstable souls. They have a heart trained
in covetous practices … For when they speak great
swelling words of emptiness, they allure through

the lusts of the flesh, through lewdness, the ones
who have actually escaped from those who live in
error. (2 Peter 2:1–3, 10, 13–14, 18)

Peter said they would exploit God's people with deceptive words,
teachings, and doctrines. They would walk according to the flesh
and be presumptuous, self-willed, and not afraid to speak evil of
dignitaries. They would entice unstable souls; that they might fill
their pockets to satisfy their covetous hearts. They would speak
great and swelling but empty words that are like junk food for the
spirit, they do not produce healthy mature saints. They would offer
teachings that accommodated lustful desires, self-promotions, and
sinful practices of hidden agendas. Where he says they would deny
the Lord, this could be taken as Paul says to Titus: "They profess to
know God, but in works they deny Him" (Titus 1:16).

In Galatians 5, the works of the flesh and the fruit of the spirit
are listed. I'm not going to list them all but just enough to give you
an idea of what Jesus was talking about: "Now the works of the
flesh are evident, which are: adultery, fornication, hatred, jealousies,
outbursts of wrath, selfish ambitions, envy, drunkenness" (Gal.
5:19–21). These can be easily discerned in a person's character. There
is no genuine care for others, and they are irritable and get angry if
they are not believed. They are greedy for money and ambitious for
self-promotion. They have a spiritual poison in them that is deceit.

They will know the scriptures and use them to get what they
want. No one would ever listen to them if they didn't quote the
Bible, so they will lure their victims away with the Word of God,
but then, they will begin to twist the Word of God to make it say
things it does not say. It's like this—you cannot get a dog to eat strait
poison, but if you put it in a little meat, he will swallow it without
hesitation. False prophets will know the scriptures, but they will
twist them and use them along with signs and wonders to deceive.

The fruit of the Spirit will be present in the saints and easily
discernable: "The fruit of the Spirit is love, joy, peace, longsuffering,

kindness, goodness, faithfulness, gentleness, self-control" (Gal. 5:22–23). These are things we look for in everyone we meet, and it does not take much effort to discern when they are absent.

And again, John says:

> Beloved, do not believe every spirit, but test the spirits, whether they are of God; because many false prophets have gone out into the world. By this you know the Spirit of God: Every spirit that confesses that Jesus Christ has come in the flesh is of God, and every spirit that does not confess that Jesus Christ has come in the flesh is not of God. And this is the spirit of the Antichrist, which you have heard was coming, and is now already in the world. (1 John 4:1-3)

These times will be marked by deception on every corner by those who are perishing. We are instructed to test the spirits, whether they are of God. When false prophets are doing signs and wonders by the power of the demons that is when the spirit by which they do these things must be tested. If they cannot say Jesus Christ is Lord and has come in the flesh that spirit is not of God but is the spirit of the antichrist, which is already at work in the world today through his children. The Holy Spirit was sent to guide us into all truth and tell us things that are to come. To be led away, we must be deceived, so the Lord has given us the Spirit of truth to teach us all things and bring to our remembrance all that the word of God says. Draw near to Him and He will draw near to you. Love, joy, and peace will be found only in those whose treasures are in heaven, while the fear of losing treasures will be found among those whose minds are set on things on the earth.

Paul mentions how those who were his companions were joyful when they suffered loss. We need to have this same intent: "For you had compassion on me in my chains, and joyfully accepted the plundering of your goods, knowing that you have a better and an enduring possession for yourselves in heaven. Therefore, do not cast away your confidence, which has great reward. For you have need of endurance, so that after you have done the will of God, you may receive the promise: "For yet a little while, and He who is coming will come and will not tarry. Now the just shall live by faith; but if anyone draws back, My soul has no pleasure in him." (Heb 10:34-38)

These are God thoughts, His wisdom and understanding, not the thinking of the natural man; for the natural man is enmity with God. Therefore: "We should no longer be children, tossed to and fro and carried about with every wind of doctrine, by the trickery of men, in the cunning craftiness of deceitful plotting" (Eph. 4:14–15). Some prophets out there are wolves in sheep's clothing who take advantage of ignorant and gullible Christians for their own profit. Those who follow them will suffer harm and loss. But the Word of God has told us beforehand how we will know them.

The Spirit specifically says that the time is coming when people will not listen to sound doctrine, but according to their own desires and having itching ears, they will gather around teachers who will tell them what they want to hear. False teachers will lead them away from the truth and aside to heresies. In a wisdom that is earthly, sensual, and demonic, they will turn many away from the truth. Whoever speaks the truth of God's Word will be persecuted in those days.

As persecution increases, people will turn away from the faith and choose to believe a lie. The wicked will begin to lie and deceive and even murder to get what they want. As they do lawlessness will abound and the heart of many will grow cold.

> Now the Spirit expressly says that in latter times some
> will depart from the faith, giving heed to deceiving
> spirits and doctrines of demons, speaking lies in
> hypocrisy, having their own conscience seared with

a hot iron, forbidding to marry, and commanding to abstain from foods which God created to be received with thanksgiving. (1 Tim. 4:1-3)

Persecution and tribulation will arise to an intense level never seen before by God's people; because of which many will renounce their faith. The Roman persecution of the early church is a model of what to expect. Roman centurions were sent to the home of one who was accused of being a Christian; and they asked them if they were Christian, if they answered yes, the question was asked again adding capital punishment. If they persisted they were put to death. The Romans were the children of the prince who is to come. His children will begin to hunt down Christians and kill them because they do not resist evil with evil. It is on this stage that the man of sin is revealed.

When the transgressors have reached their fullness, a king shall arise, having fierce features, who understands sinister schemes. His power shall be mighty, but not by his own power; He shall destroy fearfully and shall prosper and thrive; He shall destroy the mighty, and also the holy people" (Dan 8:23-24).

The wicked will begin to persecute the saints mildly at first but steadily increasing until they begin to openly kill them, then the man of sin, the lawless one, will rise up and seize power. Paul says the falling away will come first, then the man of sin will be revealed. We see a pattern of persecution growing with an intensity, many depart from the faith to escape the persecution, which continues to grow to an intense level, then the lawless one will be revealed.

For that Day will not come unless the falling away comes first, and the man of sin is revealed, the son

of perdition, who opposes and exalts himself above
all that is called God or that is worshiped, so that he
sits as God in the temple of God, showing himself
that he is God (2 Thess. 2:3-4)

The Greek word translated, *falling away*, is apostacy. It means
the renouncing of a religious faith, or the departure from a religious
faith. Some will not be able to endure the persecution and will
renounce their faith. They were saved and had become Christians—
they could not renounce the faith if they were never in it—but
because of persecution and their desire for pleasures of this world,
they renounce their faith. Daniel mentions them as those who
forsake the holy covenant.

The man of sin is referring to the antichrist. "Anti" means,
"against." He opposes Christ, he is against Christ, he is against
Christians—His followers. He is revealed as the leader of those who
are already filled with the spirit of antichrist that is at work in our
world now. Remember what Jesus said, "He who is not with Me, is
against Me" (Matt. 12:30). Concerning the antichrist, Daniel says
a vile person shall arise: "To whom they will not give the honor of
royalty; but he shall come in peaceably and seize the kingdom by
intrigue. With the force of a flood they [his opposition] shall be
swept away from before him and be broken, and also the prince of
the covenant. And after the league [covenant] is made with him he
shall act deceitfully" (Dan 11:21-23). There will be fighting among
the wicked as they strive for power and position. The only way the
man of sin can be exalted above other contenders, is if he has the
power of Satan working in him. Paul said,

The coming of the lawless one is according to the
working of Satan, with all power, signs, and lying
wonders, and with all unrighteous deception among
those who perish, because they did not receive the
love of the truth, that they might be saved. And for

> this reason, God will send them strong delusion,
> that they should believe the lie, that they all may
> be condemned who did not believe the truth but
> had pleasure in unrighteousness. (2 Thess. 2:9–12)

These people have seen the awesome power and righteous judgment of God, but as time goes by they forget His mighty works and turn aside to have pleasure in unrighteousness and do not receive the love of the truth they were hearing preached every day; even while persecution was becoming intense. These people have seen and know all God has done, but they turn against Him and renounced their faith to take pleasure in lustful desires and the passing pleasures of sin. Once they have renounced their faith they must swear allegiance to the antichrist and worship him. At this point there no longer remains a sacrifice for sin but a certain and fearful expectation of fiery judgment.

Daniel says of the man of sin, whom we call the antichrist:

> And after the league is made with him he shall
> act deceitfully, for he shall come up and become
> strong with a small number of people. He shall
> enter peaceably, even into the richest places of the
> province; and he shall do what his fathers have not
> done, nor his forefathers: he shall disperse among
> them the plunder, spoil, and riches; and he shall
> devise his plans against the strongholds, but only
> for a time. (Dan 11:23-24)

The church is too powerful to deal with at first, so this league is made to buy time, while deceitfully he is behind the seines plotting to overthrow them. After World War I the victor nations formed the League of Nations to maintain peace. A league is like a covenant in that it is an agreement between nations for a common purpose, to live in peace. Once the man of sin is revealed he confirms a covenant or league with many only to appear to promote peace and stability while through his cunning craftiness and deceitful plotting he pursues power. He will become strong with a small number of faithful followers. Pretending to come in peace he will enter the wealthiest of the countries, over throw them, plunder their riches and goods and distribute it to his loyal subjects.

During the church's days of glory, they will build a great sanctuary house of God in Jerusalem so that all nations may flow to it. They will come to worship God and pray before the Lord on His holy mountain in Jerusalem, it is the desire of many nations. "So it shall be in that day: the great trumpet will be blown; they will come... And shall worship the LORD in the holy mount at Jerusalem" (Isa 27:13). The covenant he confirms allows true worship, but only so he can buy time to gain the power necessary to overthrow them. It will take him three and a half years to accomplish his goal, then he will make his move. He shall cause the sacrifice of praise and offering of worship to cease in the house of the Lord. He will come in exalting himself above all that is called god, or that is worshipped. It is an abomination that causes desolation throughout the world.

> So he shall return and show regard for those who forsake the holy covenant. And forces shall be mustered by him, and they shall defile the sanctuary fortress; then they shall take away the daily sacrifices, and place there the abomination of desolation. Those who do wickedly against the covenant he shall corrupt with flattery; but the people who know their God shall be strong and carry out great exploits. (Dan 11:30-33)

The church is a powerful force he will want to eliminate. Their great exploits are competition to his great signs and wonders he does through Satan's power. When he commits the abomination of desolation; they will refuse to worship him, so persecution of

Christians will be legalized and war against the saints will break out, they will begin to kill them indiscriminately. As it is written of him: "I was watching; and the same horn was making war against the saints and prevailing against them" (Dan 7:21). And again: "It was granted to him to make war with the saints and to overcome them" (Rev. 13:7). It is a time of the Devil's wrath, when he divides families against each other: "Now brother will betray brother to death, and a father his child; and children will rise up against parents and cause them to be put to death. And you will be hated by all for My name's sake. But he who endures to the end shall be saved" (Mark 13:12-13). "Whoever desires to save his life will lose it, but whoever loses his life for My sake will find it" (Matt 16:25). The antichrist and his forces are given power to make war with the saints and overcome them. His kingdom is exceedingly dreadful, one which devours the whole earth and brakes it in pieces.

For three and a half years the antichrist and his forces are at war with the Christians, killing them and plundering their goods. "And those of the people who understand shall instruct many; yet for many days they shall fall by sword and flame, by captivity and plundering. Now when they fall, they shall be aided with a little help; but many shall join with them by intrigue. And some of those of understanding shall fall, to refine them, purify them, and make them white, until the time of the end; because it is still for the appointed time" (Dan 11:33-35).

"Then I, Daniel, looked; and there stood two others, one on this riverbank and the other on that riverbank. And one said to the man clothed in linen, who was above the waters of the river, "How long shall the fulfillment of these wonders be?" Then I heard the man clothed in linen, who was above the waters of the river, when he held up his right hand and his left hand to heaven, and swore by Him who lives forever, that it shall be for a time, times, and half a time; and when the power of the holy people has been completely shattered, all these things shall be finished" (Dan 12:5-7).

After three and a half years of war with the saints they destroy the power of the holy people. When their power has been completely shattered and the kingdom of the antichrist believe they have won, the end will come like a storm. The end of the antichrist's reign will come without human aid; all the power of his fleshly army cannot help him. All the power and authority Satan gave him cannot help him, and he comes to an end. The Lord comes on that day in flames of fire to take vengeance on him and his children. And He destroys the antichrist with the words of His mouth and the consuming fire of His anger. As it is written of him: "For the mystery of lawlessness is already at work; only He who now restrains will do so until He is taken out of the way. And then the lawless one will be revealed, whom the Lord will consume with the breath of His mouth and destroy with the brightness of His coming" (2 Thess. 2:7-8).

According to the visions of Daniel, the prophecies of Jesus and the apostles we have one view of the time of the end, which is the acts of the antichrist and his destruction on the last day. But John, in the book of Revelation, gives us another view that completes our understanding of the time of the end. When and where the last day is found in Revelation is determined by a completely different means. Great tribulation is only mentioned once in the prophecies of Revelation, and it is where a great multitude has come out of it. From that point on there are numerous references to God's wrath and judgment, which is the main content of the book.

We know that at the end of the three-and-a-half-year great persecution the Lord comes to take His saints out of this world. As it is written: "Immediately after the tribulation of those days... they will see the Son of Man coming on the clouds of heaven with power and great glory. And He will send His angels with a great sound of a trumpet, and they will gather together His elect from the four winds, from one end of heaven to the other" (Matt 24:29-31). At the same time, He comes in flames of fire to take vengeance on those who have been killing His saints.

In Revelation there is a picture of the Lord God Almighty sitting on His throne in heaven, and He has in His right hand a scroll or book sealed with seven seals. The scroll cannot be opened unless the seven seals are loosened. Once the scroll is opened its contents can then be observed and executed.

> And I saw in the right hand of Him who sat on the throne a scroll written inside and on the back, sealed with seven seals. Then I saw a strong angel proclaiming with a loud voice, "Who is worthy to open the scroll and to loose its seals?" And no one in heaven or on the earth or under the earth was able to open the scroll, or to look at it. So I wept much, because no one was found worthy to open and read the scroll, or to look at it. But one of the elders said to me, "Do not weep. Behold, the Lion of the tribe of Judah, the Root of David, has prevailed to open the scroll and to loose its seven seals." And I looked, and behold, in the midst of the throne and of the four living creatures, and in the midst of the elders, stood a Lamb as though it had been slain, having seven horns and seven eyes, which are the seven Spirits of God sent out into all the earth. Then He came and took the scroll out of the right hand of Him who sat on the throne. (Rev 5:1-7)

Now when He had taken the scroll, the four living creatures and the twenty-four elders fell down before the Lamb, each having a harp, and golden bowls full of incense, which are the prayers of the saints. And they sang a new song, saying:

"You are worthy to take the scroll,
And to open its seals;
For You were slain,
And have redeemed us to God by Your blood

Out of every tribe and tongue and people and nation,
And have made us kings and priests to our God;
And we shall reign on the earth."
(Rev 5:8-10)

The scroll which cannot be opened by anyone but the Lamb who was slain; is the written judgment. The reason no one but Jesus can loosen the seals and open the scroll is because all judgment has been committed to Him. As it is written: "For the Father judges no one but has committed all judgment to the Son" (John 5:22). Several books are mentioned in scripture that are in heaven, the Book of Life is one (Rev. 20:12), and there is a book of remembrance (Mal. 3:16), and the book or scroll the Lamb takes from the right hand of God. This book appears to be the written judgment; because, when it is opened the day of wrath and judgment begins.

There are more books mentioned, but these are enough to make the point that God writes things down in heaven, there are books in heaven. Notice that the written judgment is mentioned in this Psalm: "Let the saints be joyful in glory; Let them sing aloud on their beds. Let the high praises of God be in their mouth, and a two-edged sword in their hand, to execute vengeance on the nations, and punishments on the peoples; to bind their kings with chains, and their nobles with fetters of iron; to execute on them the *written judgment* — This honor have all His saints" (Ps 149:5-9).

The only one found worthy in heaven and earth to loosen the seals and open the scroll is Jesus, the Lamb who was slain from the foundation of the world. Yes, the Father has committed all judgment to the Son. Even so, Jesus said, "I can of Myself do nothing. As I hear I judge, and My judgment is righteous, because I do not seek My own will but the will of the Father who sent Me" (John 5:22, 30). All judgment is committed to Jesus on the Day of Judgment, and we are His body, so we will have a part to play. That day is a day of wrath and vengeance, but the saints will only do what they hear the

Father say, for they are the body of Christ. The Day of Judgment is the execution of the written judgment.

Therefore, the seals are events that must take place before the scroll or book can be opened and the contents executed. When the first seal was opened John wrote:

> Now I saw when the Lamb opened one of the seals; and I heard one of the four living creatures saying with a voice like thunder, "Come and see." And I looked, and behold, a white horse. He who sat on it had a bow; and a crown was given to him, and he went out conquering and to conquer. (Rev. 6:1–2)

Jesus is the only one seen in scripture on a white horse as He goes into battle. (Rev. 19:11-16) In the prophets, Israel's King, the Messiah, has a bow as He goes fourth to conquer His enemies, where it is written: "Bow down Your heavens, O LORD, and come down; touch the mountains, and they shall smoke. Flash forth lightning and scatter them; shoot out Your arrows and destroy them" (Ps. 144:5–6). Then Zechariah says: "For I have bent Judah My bow, fitted the bow with Ephraim. Then the LORD will be seen over them, and His arrow will go forth like lightning" (Zech. 9:13–14). The Messiah is coming to battle their enemies with His weapons of war. His arrows will shoot forth like lightning; He will prevail against His enemies and make a quick work of them.

Zechariah painted a clear picture of the Lord using a bow when He enters this battle. His people, Israel, are His weapon in this battle. For He said Judah would be His bow, He would fit the bow with Ephraim, and His arrows would fly forth like lightning. Just as the Lord used the nations as His weapon to destroy and scatter Israel and bring their land to desolation, so in these last days will He use Israel to a certain degree as His weapon to destroy His enemies. A nuclear missile could be perceived as an arrow that shoots forth and flashes like lightning when it hits

its target. His people will understand perfectly when they see His Word fulfilled.

The Messiah will deliver His people, Israel, from mighty forces that come against them in these last days in a great and awesome show. Remember in Zechariah chapter 2 where the Lord sends Jesus after glory against the nations who had plundered His people and land? The prophets say that GOD the Father will send Jesus, Israel's King-Messiah to completely conquer their enemies. All those who have plundered and destroyed His people will know that the LORD is GOD in heaven above and on the earth beneath, there is no other! People in all nations will rejoice when they see the destruction of those who hate His people, Israel.

Jesus, the Messiah, is crowned King-Messiah: "In that day the LORD of hosts will be for a crown of glory and a diadem of beauty to the remnant of His people" (Isa. 28:5). When Israel accepts their King, the Messiah, He becomes the great king they have been waiting for, He becomes their King of Glory. A crown is the symbol of ruling. Ezekiel the prophet says the LORD would rule over them, meaning, as their King–Messiah; when He demonstrates His power with a mighty hand, with an outstretched arm, and with fury poured out. (Ezek. 20:33) This is the manner in which the Jews of Jesus's day expected their King-Messiah to come. It will be glorious when their Messiah comes and the whole earth rejoices and is glad: "'Sing and rejoice, O daughter of Zion! For behold, I am coming, and I will dwell in your midst,' says the LORD. 'Many nations shall be joined to the LORD in that day, and they shall become My people'" (Zech. 2:10–11).

The Lord is coming a conquering King and will dwell in their midst, many nations and multitudes of people shall be joined to the Lord that day. They will turn from darkness to light, from the power of Satan to God. It will be a worldwide revival, an awesome show of God's power the likes of which the world has never seen. This show of God's power will move many nations as well as the whole house of Israel to come to the Lord Jesus and be saved. And His Spirit shall be poured out on all flesh—there will be a great harvest at the end of the age. Isn't that what is written in the Word of God? The harvest is the end of the age! (Matt. 13:9).

Therefore, God's Grand Finale is the first seal to be removed and begin the process that will open the scroll and begin the Day of Judgment. The first seal begins a series of three-and-a-half-year periods that frame the final years of this age. There are three ways the scriptures announce this prophetic measure of time: 1,260 days (Rev. 11:3, 12:6), forty-two months (Rev. 11:2, 13:5), and a time, times, and half a time (Dan. 7:25; Rev. 12:14). And it appears there are three of these three-and-a-half-year periods; one follows God's Grand Finale, one following the confirmation of a covenant, and the last one begins when the abomination of desolation is set up.

It also appears that there are two; one–week or seven-year periods involved in the time of the end that overlap each other. The first week begins when the Jews start burning weapons for seven years after the bloody battle of Ezekiel 38-39. Then in the middle of the first seven-year period—which would be three and a half years into it—the man of sin will confirm a covenant with many for one week—seven years. Then when the first seven-years expire, and His people cease burning weapons it will be in the middle of Daniel's seventieth week, when the abomination of desolation is set up. Some of the scriptures we are going over have been previously cited, but to understand where and how they belong in the book of Revelation we need to hear them again.

When the antichrist sets up the abomination that causes desolation he demands to be worshipped. In World War II Hitler did not demand worship but he did demand the allegiance of his subjects. He obtained the allegiance of the people by invoking scripture into what he was doing. The population of the country were told that the Third Reich would usher in the Millennial reign and last a thousand years. He twisted scripture to gain their allegiance. Anyone who spoke out against him, was accused of being a traitor and put to death. To swear allegiance to Hitler the people had to put him before God, and that was an abomination that caused the desolation of their land.

When the abomination of desolation is set up, there will be great persecution such as has not been since there was a nation, even till that time, and it will continue for forty-two months. As it is written: "And he was given a mouth speaking great things and blasphemies, and he was given authority to continue for forty-two months... It was granted to him to make war with the saints and to overcome them. And authority was given him over every tribe, tongue, and nation. All who dwell on the earth will worship him, whose names have not been written in the Book of Life" (Rev. 13:5–8). And again: "Then the saints shall be given into his hand for a time and times and half a time" (Dan. 7:25). We see that the reign of antichrist lasts forty-two months, which is three and a half years. The man of sin will not only make it illegal to worship God but add to the violation capital punishment. His disgustingly unpleasant acts will cause desolations and famine throughout the earth. Remember, his kingdom shall devour the whole earth, trample it and break it in pieces. (Dan. 7:23)

Jesus says: "Therefore when you see the 'abomination of desolation,' spoken of by Daniel the prophet, standing in the holy place... then there will be great tribulation, such as has not been since the beginning of the world until this time, no, nor ever shall be. And unless those days were shortened, no flesh would be saved; but for the elect's sake those days will be shortened" (Matt 24:15,21-22). When the abomination of desolation is set up in the holy place, murder is justified by the antichrist for anyone who resists him. His brutal dictatorship begins, and at that point peace is taken from the earth.

The antichrist revokes his covenant of peace and instructs his forces to kill anyone who refuses to, not only swear allegiance to him, but worship him. People will begin to violently kill one another like they have not since the beginning of the world until this time. Thus, the second seal is opened:

> When He opened the second seal, I heard the second
> living creature saying, "Come and see." Another
> horse, fiery red, went out. And it was granted to the
> one who sat on it to take peace from the earth, and
> that people should kill one another; and there was
> given to him a great sword. (Rev 6:3-4)

Peace is taken from the earth, and people begin to kill one another. "Then they will deliver you up to tribulation and kill you, and you will be hated by all nations for My name's sake" (Matt 24:9). Many of God's people will leave the world as Jesus did, and go to the Father rejoicing with exceedingly great joy, because they were counted worthy to suffer for His name sake! And a white robe, the martyrs robe, will be given to each of them.

The abominations the antichrist promotes on earth will cause desolations throughout the world, and till the end of his war with the saints, desolations are determined. The destruction caused by his ambitions will cause a shortage of many things around the world. Food and necessities of life become rare, and when they are found the price is too high to buy them. Thus, the third seal is opened:

> When He opened the third seal, I heard the third
> living creature say, "Come and see." So I looked,
> and behold, a black horse, and he who sat on it had
> a pair of scales in his hand. And I heard a voice in
> the midst of the four living creatures saying, "A
> quart of wheat for a denarius, and three quarts of
> barley for a denarius; and do not harm the oil and
> the wine. (Rev 6:5-6)

Famine and inflation follow his destructive forces around the world. It comes to a point where a day's wages can only purchase enough food for a day. Due to the desolation and destruction left behind his advancing army, many lands and countries are not able to produce food and goods like before. His kingdom will devour the whole earth, trample it down, break it in pieces, and crush it.

The great persecution and tribulation divides those who walk with God from those who walk away from Him. There is a great division in the masses, the bad will not mingle with the good, as iron does not mix with clay. Daniel says of the last kingdom: "As you saw iron mixed with ceramic clay, they will mingle with the seed of men; but they will not adhere to one another, just as iron does not mix with clay" (Dan 2:43). Families will be divided, those who do not believe God against those who do.

> Do not think that I came to bring peace on earth. I did not come to bring peace but a sword. I have come to 'set a man against his father, a daughter against her mother, and a daughter-in-law against her mother-in-law'; and 'a man's enemies will be those of his own household.' He who loves father or mother more than Me is not worthy of Me. And he who loves son or daughter more than Me is not worthy of Me. And he who does not take his cross and follow after Me is not worthy of Me. He who finds his life will lose it, and he who loses his life for My sake will find it. (Matt 10:35-39)

And again: "You will be betrayed even by parents and brothers, relatives and friends; and they will put some of you to death. And you will be hated by all for My name's sake. But not a hair of your head shall be lost. By your patience possess your souls" (Luke 21:16-19). "Whatever I tell you in the dark, speak in the light; and what you hear in the ear, preach on the housetops. And do not fear those who kill the body but cannot kill the soul. But rather fear Him who is able to destroy both soul and body in hell" (Matt. 10:27-28). "If you are reproached for the name of Christ, blessed are you, for the Spirit of glory and of God rests upon you. On their part He is blasphemed, but on your part, He is glorified" (1 Peter 4:14).

The forces of the antichrist will hunt down the children of God through those of their own household who betray them. And the neighbor they once trusted will lie in wait to take their life and plunder their goods. The killing will increase and become great. Death will be everywhere as many of the saints are murdered. Thus, the fourth seal is opened:

> When He opened the fourth seal, I heard the voice of the fourth living creature saying, "Come and see." So I looked, and behold, a pale horse. And the name of him who sat on it was Death, and Hades followed with him. And power was given to them over a fourth of the earth, to kill with sword, with hunger, with death, and by the beasts of the earth. (Rev 6:7-8)

These things must take place till the Word of God has been fulfilled. The fifth seal tells us what is happening in heaven as these things are taking place on the earth. We are given a picture of what all these saints are doing in heaven after they have been martyred. The fifth seal is opened:

> "When He opened the fifth seal, I saw under the altar the souls of those who had been slain for the word of God and for the testimony which they held. And they cried with a loud voice, saying, "How long, O Lord, holy and true, until You judge and avenge our blood on those who dwell on the earth?" Then a white robe was given to each of them; and it was said to them that they should rest a little while longer, until both the number of their fellow servants and their brethren, who would be killed as they were, was completed" (Rev 6:9-11)

The fifth seal tells us that the Day of Judgment is still to come. They say: "How long, O Lord, holy and true, until You judge and avenge our blood on those who dwell on the earth?" because the Day of Judgment and vengeance is not yet come. Their brethren and fellow servants are being killed on the earth just like they were, but they must wait till the number of the martyrs of Jesus is complete. "And unless the Lord had shortened those days, no flesh would be saved; but for the elect's sake, whom He chose, He shortened the days" (Mark 13:20). The fifth seal in Revelation indicates that there is a specific number of martyrs that must be reached. Zechariah 13 agrees that there is a specific count that will be reached:

> I will turn My hand against the little ones. And it shall come to pass in all the land, "Says the LORD," that two-thirds in it shall be cut off and die, but one –third shall be left in it: I will bring the one –third through the fire, will refine them as silver is refined, and test them as gold is tested. They will call on My name, and I will answer them. I will say, "This is My people"; And each one will say, "The LORD is my God." (Zechariah 13:7-9)

Two thirds will be cut off and die, just like their Lord was also cut off from the land of the living and was put to death. As He suffered many things and was rejected by His generation, it appears that His body of believers must also suffer many things and be rejected by this generation. (Luke 17:25) Now we have a better understanding of why the wicked will see the Lord coming on the last day in flames of fire to take vengeance! And why He will consume the antichrist with the breath of His mouth and destroy him with the brightness of His coming. The great persecution and tribulation will take place in a span of three and a half years.

The Bride of Christ, in the state that she is in now, is not ready to meet her Bridegroom. Therefore, the word of God indicates that it will take this much time for her to make herself ready. As She enters Her time of purification, many shall fall, to refine them, purify them, and make them white, until the time of the end; because it is still for the appointed time. (Dan. 11:35) The goal is to be conformed into the image of Christ, who gave himself to the will of God and was obedient to death. It may take some chastening to bring the Bride into the image of Christ. "Now no chastening seems to be joyful for the present, but painful; nevertheless, afterward it yields the peaceable fruit of righteousness to those who have been trained by it" (Heb 12:11).

Now, to be certain about what is coming, there are three different kinds of wrath found in scripture; the wrath of God, the wrath of man, and the wrath of the Devil. Revelation 12:12 says the Devil has come down, having great wrath. And it is said of his man of sin that; he shall prosper till the wrath has been accomplished. (Dan. 11:36) The Devil must accomplish his wrath; what has been determined, through his children; then the wrath of God will come.

At the end of Daniel's seventieth week, after the antichrist has run his course, and accomplished the wrath, and his forces have crushed the power of the holy people, the Lord Jesus will be seen by them coming with His mighty angels in flames of fire to take vengeance. The Day of Wrath and revelation of the Righteous Judgment of God has suddenly come upon them. Thus, the sixth seal is opened:

> I looked when He opened the sixth seal, and behold, there was a great earthquake; and the sun became black as sackcloth of hair, and the moon became like blood. And the stars of heaven fell to the earth, as a fig tree drops its late figs when it is shaken by a mighty wind. Then the sky receded as a scroll when it is rolled up, and every mountain and island was moved out of its place. And the kings of the earth, the great men, the rich men, the commanders, the

mighty men, every slave and every free man, hid
themselves in the caves and in the rocks of the
mountains, and said to the mountains and rocks,
"Fall on us and hide us from the face of Him who
sits on the throne and from the wrath of the Lamb!
For the great day of His wrath has come, and who
is able to stand? (Rev 6:12-17)

After this view of what is taking place on the earth the sixth
seal also gives us a look at things taking place in heaven. There is a
preparation for what is about to come, and the revealing of a great
multitude that had just come out of great tribulation.

After these things I saw four angels standing at the
four corners of the earth, holding the four winds
of the earth, that the wind should not blow on the
earth, on the sea, or on any tree. Then I saw another
angel ascending from the east, having the seal of
the living God. And he cried with a loud voice to
the four angels to whom it was granted to harm the
earth and the sea, saying, "Do not harm the earth,
the sea, or the trees till we have sealed the servants
of our God on their foreheads." And I heard the
number of those who were sealed. One hundred
and forty-four thousand of all the tribes of the
children of Israel were sealed... After these things
I looked, and behold, a great multitude which no
one could number, of all nations, tribes, peoples,
and tongues, standing before the throne and before
the Lamb, clothed with white robes, with palm
branches in their hands, and crying out with a loud
voice, saying, "Salvation belongs to our God who
sits on the throne, and to the Lamb!" All the angels
stood around the throne and the elders and the four

living creatures and fell on their faces before the throne and worshiped God, saying: "Amen! Blessing and glory and wisdom, thanksgiving and honor and power and might, be to our God forever and ever. Amen." Then one of the elders answered, saying to me, "Who are these arrayed in white robes, and where did they come from?" And I said to him, "Sir, you know." So he said to me, "These are the ones who come out of the great tribulation, and washed their robes and made them white in the blood of the Lamb. Therefore, they are before the throne of God, and serve Him day and night in His temple. And He who sits on the throne will dwell among them. They shall neither hunger anymore nor thirst anymore; the sun shall not strike them, nor any heat; for the Lamb who is in the midst of the throne will shepherd them and lead them to living fountains of waters. And God will wipe away every tear from their eyes." (Rev 7:1-4,9-17)

The sixth seal reveals that on earth they are running to hide themselves in the caves and rocks of the mountains because they see that the great day of God's wrath has come and there is no escape. Then our attention is turned to what is taking place in Heaven. Preparations are being made for the day of judgment; the holding back of the four angels that they should not harm the earth yet, and the sealing of those of the twelve tribes of Israel, for what will follow. We see now that the time of God's wrath has come and at the same time a great multitude has come out of great tribulation. As we have seen when we studied the last day in chapter 2, the last day is the transitioning point from the time of the end and the tribulation, to the great day of God's wrath and judgment.

The foundation laid in chapter 2 is needed here in Revelation. Remember that on the last day the resurrection and the rapture will take place, and at the same time God's wrath and judgment have come? And that the last day is a fixed point in time whereby the events of the end of the age are determined to be either before this day, or after it. The great persecution and tribulation from the antichrist are before this day; and the resurrection and rapture are on this day. Then the day of judgment and wrath will begin on this day and continue after it, until all that is written in the word of God has been fulfilled.

Therefore, as we go through what has been given us in revelation, the only sure way we can determine where the rapture takes place in Revelation is by finding where the day of wrath and judgement begins. We have been delivered from the wrath to come, therefore, when we see the day of God's wrath begin, that is where the rapture will take place.

At the opening of the sixth seal, the great day of God's wrath has come, and that is when we see a great multitude that has been taken out of great tribulation. This great multitude is the raptured saints. They are seen in heaven before the throne of God giving thanks for His salvation! If you can imagine it, we will be omni present after we are glorified, it is our inheritance to be as He is. As it is written: "We know that when He is revealed, we shall be like Him, for we shall see Him as He is" (1 John 3:2). Our whole understanding of things from this point on has to change, because at that time, we will be changed. We can't be dogmatic about any of these things because, no matter how much we know, we still only know a very small fraction of how things are going to be at that time.

Notice that this great multitude we see before the throne of God in this passage are worshiping like the saints were when Jesus entered Jerusalem. Remember when He went riding into Jerusalem on a donkey's colt? "The next day a great multitude that had come to the feast, when they heard that Jesus was coming to Jerusalem, took branches of palm trees and went out to meet Him, and cried out: "Hosanna! 'Blessed is He who comes in the name of the LORD!' The King of Israel!" Then Jesus, when He had found a young donkey, sat on it; as it is written: "Fear not, daughter of Zion; behold, your King is coming, sitting on a donkey's colt" (John 12:12-15).

A great multitude took palm branches and went out to meet Him crying out Hosanna! Hosanna means: Lord save us! In contrast to this great multitude, the great multitude in Revelation 7 also having palm branches are crying out with a loud voice: "Salvation belongs to our God and to the Lamb." One great multitude was waving palm branches and crying out, Lord save us! And the other great multitude is waving palm branches and singing that the Lord has saved us, for salvation belongs to the Lord. These are the only places in the New Testament where palm branches are mentioned, and I believe in both places they are being used as instruments of worship by the saints.

The Greek word translated, *salvation*, is also translated, *delivered*. The great multitude in Revelation 7 were taken out of, or you could say, delivered out of great tribulation; and at the same time, they were delivered from the wrath to come. Therefore, they sang: "Salvation belongs to Him who sits on the throne!" We can also sing that deliverance belongs to Him who sits on the throne and to the Lamb! It is a great deliverance! Having the understanding that we are delivered from the wrath to come, when the seventh seal is opened, seven trumpet judgments are revealed. They are the execution of the Day of Wrath and Revelation of the Righteous Judgment of God; who, will render to everyone according to their works. (Rom. 2:5-6)

There are four angels that are told not to harm the earth, the sea, or any tree till the servants of God are sealed, when the sixth seal was opened; then when the seventh seal is opened there are seven trumpet judgments revealed. The first four trumpets are on the creation, the trees, the sea, and rivers and springs of water, and the sun and moon, so that a third of them are stricken. The remaining three trumpets are three woes that are to come upon the inhabitants of the earth. This is when the Lord comes out of His place to punish the inhabitants of the earth for their iniquity. (Is. 26:21) "Say to those who are fearful-hearted, "Be strong, do not fear! Behold, your God will come with vengeance, with the recompense of God; He will come and save you" (Isa 35:4).

The scripture says that the Lord Jesus is coming back for a glorious church, without spot or wrinkle or any such thing, but that she shall be holy and without blemish. (Eph. 5:27) However, the church today is not in such a state; without purity she is not ready to attend her wedding. The words of the angel in Daniel 12:10 come to mind:

> Go your way, Daniel, for the words are closed up and sealed till the time of the end. Many shall be purified, made white, and refined, but the wicked shall do wickedly; and none of the wicked shall understand, but the wise shall understand. (Dan. 12:9–10)

The great persecution will purify many; make them white and refined for what is about to come, the marriage of the Lamb. Now, I will tell you a mystery, one that has been kept secret from the foundation of the world—the city of our God, the New Jerusalem, and Zion, is coming down out of heaven from God for the wedding. It will look like a great star in the distance, but we will know what it is. When we are taken up into the clouds to join our Lord, there will be a great cloud of witnesses with Him, and we will all ascend up to the New Jerusalem to be seated at the banquet tables in front of this great city: "He brought me to the banqueting house and his banner over me was love" (Song 2:4). The city of God is coming! Notice we are not alone in our hope.

> By faith he (Abraham) dwelt in the land of promise as in a foreign country, dwelling in tents with Isaac and Jacob, the heirs with him of the same promise; for he waited for the city which has foundations, whose builder and maker is God. (Heb. 11:9–10)

We are strangers and sojourners on earth; we are not of this world but citizens of a heavenly country and a heavenly city. We believe the promises of God, so God is not ashamed to be called our God; for He has prepared a city for us. (Heb. 11:16)

> Then one of the seven angels ... talked with me, saying, "Come, I will show you the bride, the Lamb's wife." And he carried me away in the Spirit to a great and high mountain, and showed me the great city, the holy Jerusalem, descending out of heaven from God, having the glory of God. Her light was like a most precious stone, like a jasper stone, clear as crystal. Also, she had a great and high wall with twelve gates, and twelve angels at the gates, and names written on them, which are the names of the twelve tribes of the children of Israel: three gates on the east, three gates on the north, three gates on the south, and three gates on the west. Now the wall of the city had twelve foundations, and on them were the names of the twelve apostles of the Lamb. And he who talked with me had a gold reed to measure the city, its gates, and its wall. The city is laid out as a square; its length is as great as its breadth. And he measured the city with the reed: twelve thousand furlongs. Its length, breadth, and height are equal. Then he measured its wall: one hundred and forty-four cubits, according to the measure of a man, that is, of an angel. The construction of its wall was of jasper; and the city was pure gold, like clear glass. The foundations of the wall of the city were adorned with all kinds of precious stones: the first foundation was jasper, the second sapphire, the third chalcedony, the fourth emerald, the fifth sardonyx, the sixth sardius, the seventh chrysolite, the eighth

beryl, the ninth topaz, the tenth chrysoprase, the
eleventh jacinth, and the twelfth amethyst. The
twelve gates were twelve pearls: each individual gate
was of one pearl. And the street of the city was pure
gold, like transparent glass. (Rev. 21:9–21)

This is the city we are promised and are waiting for. Its builder
and maker is God. She is the Lamb's bride, and she is coming to
receive us for the wedding supper of the Lamb: "Then I, John, saw
the holy city, New Jerusalem, coming down out of heaven from God,
prepared as a bride adorned for her husband" (Rev. 21:2).

Mount Zion, the city of the living God, the New Jerusalem,
shall be stationed out in space a little way out from the earth. After
we are caught up to meet the Lord in the clouds, we will ascend up to
this great and beautiful building and be seated at the banquet tables
before it for the wedding supper of the Lamb! We will be clothed in
clean and bright linen garments that are trimmed in all the colors of
the rainbow. Then we will hear a great announcement!

And I heard, as it were, the voice of a great
multitude, as the sound of many waters and as the
sound of mighty thunderings, saying, "Alleluia! For
the Lord God Omnipotent reigns! Let us be glad
and rejoice and give Him glory, for the marriage of
the Lamb has come, and His wife has made herself
ready!" And to her it was granted to be arrayed in
fine linen, clean and bright, for the fine linen is
the righteous acts of the saints. Then he said to
me, "Write: 'Blessed are those who are called to the
marriage supper of the Lamb!' "And he said to me,
"These are the true sayings of God." (Rev. 19:6–9)

The view will be spectacular at the wedding supper of the
Lamb! Then we will crown Jesus King of Kings and Lord of Lords!

And there will be the voice of a great multitude, as the sound of mighty thunderings, saying, "Alleluia! For the LORD our God reigns! To Him be the glory and the power and the dominion for ever and ever, amen!"

The Lord's plan is about to take place! His servant and watchman was instructed to write the vision down, as He says in Habakkuk: "Write the vision and make it plain on tablets, that he may run who reads it. For the vision is yet for an appointed time; but at the end it will speak, and it will not lie. Though it tarries, wait for it; because it will surely come, It will not tarry" (Hab. 2:2-3). The Lord has taken his servant and watchman up in the Spirit on a great and high mountain, so that He might show him all these things, that he might go and give warning to His people of what is about to come. And now, He has also taken you up in the spirit on a high and prophetic mountain through the spirit of His Word and shown you all these things about to take place that are written in the prophets, in the psalms, and spoken by our Lord, and the apostles of the Lamb concerning the last days, that you may have an understanding of the times.

Be prepared; the end of all things is at hand. The words are not sealed up because the time is at hand. All these things were written for your instruction and admonition and encouragement. You are a carrier and possessor of the oracles of God. You are a custodian of the mysteries of God and of the presence of the Holy Spirit. Be faithful and fulfill what God has called you to do. Do not be afraid but take courage; God is with you wherever you go and whatever you do. Therefore, whatever you do, do all for the glory of God. All praise, all glory, and all honor be to God who sits on the throne and to the Lamb who sits at His right hand! May the grace of our Lord Jesus Christ be with you all, amen!

APPENDIX

To inform you of some things that have greatly influenced the writing of this book; this appendix is added. As I mentioned in chapter 3, "The Messianic Cycle," the Lord instructed me to look at His first coming for answers to His second coming; as I did, I noticed something I consider very important to this generation. When Christ came the first time, He sent a messenger to prepare the way for Him that the scripture might be fulfilled which says: "Behold, I send My messenger, and he will prepare the way before Me" (Mal 3:1).

Many have voiced their opinion of how God should fulfill this prophecy, but what the Lord says about it captures my attention. He has determined how this scripture should be fulfilled. In Luke 1, the archangel Gabriel told Zacharias that his son, John, would "go before Him in the spirit and power of Elijah, 'to turn the hearts of the fathers to the children,' and the disobedient to the wisdom of the just, to make ready a people prepared for the Lord" (Luke 1:17). There was a special anointing on John the Baptist to go before the Lord and prepare the people to meet Him.

Jesus explained in Matthew 11 that two specific prophecies were fulfilled in John the Baptist; these prophecies describe the anointed office in which John the Baptist was sent. Jesus said of John, "What did you go out to see? A prophet? Yes, I say to you, and more than a prophet. For this is he of whom it is written: 'Behold, I send My messenger before Your face, who will prepare Your way before You'" (Matt. 11:9–10).

The Lord sent John to prepare the people for His coming. John was a messenger and a prophet sent to make ready a people prepared to meet the Lord. Then Jesus said of John, "And if you are willing to receive it, he is Elijah who is to come" (Matt. 11:14). In case the people had not heard what was said to Zacharias some thirty years before about John; Jesus confirmed that John had come in the spirit and power of Elijah. He was saying that the prophecy in Malachi 4:5 which says: "Behold, I will send you Elijah the prophet before the coming of the great and dreadful day of the Lord," was fulfilled in John the Baptist.

We must take note that the Lord's messenger was sent in the spirit and power of Elijah; a literal coming of Elijah the prophet was not the intent of the prophecy. But notice that Jesus said, "If you are willing to receive it, he is Elijah who is to come." To say; if you are willing to receive it, disconnects all argument from the conversation. Either you are willing to receive, or you are not. There is no argument to be had. There will always be some who do not believe or receive what God is doing because it is not the way they have it set in their mind. But we must go with what God has revealed to us by His Spirit and the precedence He has set in His Word. The words John the Baptist spoke were anointed with the Spirit and power of Elijah to prepare the people, that was his purpose. Flesh and blood cannot reveal this kind of thing to the heart of man; but only the Father.

Someone might say, "That's great! The scriptures were fulfilled, and that's the end of the matter." But Jesus is coming again. Wouldn't He again want to send a messenger to prepare the way before Him? After Jesus, Peter, James, and John had just been visited by Moses and Elijah on the mount of transfiguration Jesus indicated in His conversation with His disciples that He intends to do so. When Jesus and the disciples were coming down from the mount of transfiguration and the memory of seeing Moses and Elijah, still filled their minds they asked Jesus,

"Why then do the scribes say that Elijah must come first?" Jesus answered and said to them, "Indeed,

Elijah is coming first and will restore all things. But I say to you that Elijah has come already, and they did not know him but did to him whatever they wished ..." Then the disciples understood that He spoke to them of John the Baptist. (Matt. 17:10–13)

Jesus said Elijah was coming first and would restore all things; but then He says that Elijah had come already, and they did not know him. He was speaking of two comings of Elijah in this passage, one is in the future and the other in the past. The Lord is telling us in His own way that He would again send His messenger before His face; and as in the previous time, we can expect that His messenger would come in the spirit and power of Elijah to prepare His people to meet Him. Just as the Lord sent John the Baptist in the spirit and power of Elijah with a message that came from God, we should be looking for nothing less than the same.

Jesus set a precedent with John the Baptist concerning His messenger and the coming of Elijah. Such a messenger would come with a powerful message that will prepare our hearts to meet the Lord. John did not come speaking on his own authority, but the Father who sent him. John came doing no miracles, but Jesus called him more than a prophet, and said of him, "Assuredly, I say to you, among those born of women there has not risen one greater than John the Baptist" (Matt. 11:11). Jesus said John was greater than all the prophets. Therefore, miracles are not necessary to demonstrate the spirit and power of Elijah. Isaiah, Jeremiah, and Ezekiel are considered the greatest of the prophets, but their ministries were all about the words and visions of God—they performed no mighty miracles.

If the Lord were to send a messenger to us today, would we know him? Would we be looking for miracles or a message that would prepare our hearts? Jesus said that Elijah had come already, and they did not know him but did to him whatever they wished. If the Lord should send a messenger again in our times in the spirit and power of Elijah, would we know him, or would we make the same mistake?

Would we do to him whatever we wished and grieve the Holy Spirit? Or, would we listen to him whom God has sent? No matter what His people would do the Lord would still be faithful and send His messenger to prepare His people. The biggest reason we have to look for such a one is our understanding of the times. We are living in a time that calls for such a messenger to prepare His people because they sure do need it.

I believe His messenger has already come and they did not know him but did to him whatever they wished. Most of God's people do not have an understanding of the times in which we live and are not preparing their selves by fixing their minds on things above and eternal life. Therefore, lest we continue in unbelief, we need to take to heart what Jesus said concerning those whom He has sent: "Most assuredly, I say to you, he who receives whomever I send receives Me, and he who receives me receives Him who sent Me" (John 13:20).

Dr. Percy Collett was a missionary in the Amazon jungles, putting his life on the line for the gospel's sake, for around 48 years. He was an Orthopedic surgeon and one of the leading specialist's in the world on jungle diseases. He spoke all over the world to leaders in the medical field on these subjects. He was well recognized in governments all over the world having degrees in International law and legal documents. But he was also a man of the Holy Ghost, he was a man of God.

At age 73 the Lord took him up to heaven for five and a half days. I had heard of Percy's testimony through a certain minister and I was filled with desire to hear him speak. The first time I got to heard him speak was at Jubilee Christian Center in San Jose, California, in 1984. He talked about heaven as if he had been there just yesterday. I had heard testimonies of several people who had been to heaven for God's purpose, but Percy's testimony was quite an upgrade from what I had heard before. After hearing him speak about heaven I was standing at Percy's table stacked with albums of tapes with the big words at the top: "I Walked In Heaven With Jesus," when I heard this scripture: "The kingdom of heaven is like treasure hidden in a field, which a man found and hid; and for joy over it he goes and sells all that he has and buys that field" (Matt 13:44). At that moment I would have given everything I owned to buy one of his albums of tapes! I did and listened to every one of them over and over and over. I know his testimony, the whole thing. Some of God's people believe and receive it while some do not.

He said in heaven Jesus just called him Percy, no doctor, no initials before or after your name in heaven, all those go away. He was given a divine tour of heaven by the Lord Jesus with a group that included apostles, prophets, and patriarchs. God is not the God of the dead but of the living; they are all alive and with Him. Percy was shown many things in heaven, and how gigantic heaven is. He says, "Your first million years is going to be spent just looking the place over." Yes, that is how big it is! There is no night there, so you're going 24 hours a day enjoying the Lord and His most beautiful creation.

Without getting into all the great and marvelous things he saw and experienced in heaven, I want to get to the main point of his visit. At the end of his five-and-a-half-day tour, the Lord Jesus took Percy up to the golden altar before the throne of God. They were before God the Father with all of heaven looking on, and Jesus took a coal from the altar of God and placed it on Percy's mouth; and said, "You are called, ordained, and sent, an apostle from heaven to earth for what is about to happen in the earth. There is about to be a great explosion of God's power in the earth. Tell My people to be ready." As the coal was touched to his mouth in a manner similar to what the angel did to Isaiah in Isaiah 6:6–7, the Lord Jesus said, "You are going back with heaven in your mouth. Go and tell My people all you have seen and heard."

Jesus informed us that He would send messengers with His instructions and encouragement, and we should listen to them as though they were the Lord Jesus Himself. As it is written: "He who hears you hears Me, he who rejects you rejects Me, and he who rejects Me rejects Him who sent Me" (Luke 10:16). "He who receives a prophet in the name of a prophet shall receive a prophet's reward. And he who receives a righteous man in the name of a righteous man shall receive a righteous man's reward" (Matt. 10:41). Do you want a reward? As John the Baptist was sent by the Lord at an appointed time to prepare for what was coming, so the Lord has sent Percy to prepare His people for what is about to come.

Percy was instructed to record his whole testimony, all he had seen and heard, on albums of tapes, twelve tapes in an album. Remember how the angel said in Revelation 19:10, "For the testimony of Jesus is the spirit of prophecy." This testimony was given, ordained, and sent by the Lord Jesus. Percy testifies of what he has seen and heard. If you are hungry for the things of God and want to listen to his testimony, you can at no cost. As it is written in the prophets:

> Ho! Everyone who thirsts, come to the waters; and you who have no money, come, buy and eat. Yes, come, buy wine and milk without money and without price. Why do you spend money for what is not bread, and your wages for what does not satisfy? Listen carefully to Me, and eat what is good, and let your soul delight itself in abundance. Incline your ear, and come to Me. Hear, and your soul shall live. (Isa 55:1-3)

Percy's testimony is on YouTube. His albums on YouTube have a photo of him and are titled, "I Walked in Heaven with Jesus." I have uploaded his first and second albums on YouTube. If you search for my name on YouTube the albums should come up. Each audio is about an hour long and there are twelve audios in each album. So, there are about 24 hours of his testimony available on YouTube.

If you are willing to receive it, Percy's testimony will take you into heaven by the spirit of prophecy and prepare your heart for what is to come. The Word instructs us, "If then you were raised with Christ, seek those things which are above, where Christ is sitting at the right hand of God. Set your mind on things above, not on the things on the earth" (Col. 3:1–2). This testimony will change the minds and hearts of millions because it is the spirt of prophecy and is anointed with the Spirit of God. Percy describes the place Jesus has prepared for us. As it is written: "In My Father's house are many mansions… I go to prepare a place for you" (John 14:2). He has sent His messenger to tell us what is being prepared for us that we might be prepared for Him!

This testimony is medicine for the soul because it is the Word God sent by His messenger, and His words are spirit and life everlasting. But His words must be mixed with faith or they will profit you nothing. Faith is the evidence of things not seen, and we walk by faith and not by sight. The Lord instructs us to look at things not seen: "While we do not look at the things which are seen, but at the things which are not seen. For the things which are seen are temporary, but the things which are not seen are eternal" (2 Cor. 4:18). The Lord has sent this testimony, a window into the realm of things not seen with human eyes, to set our minds on things above, so that our hearts might be prepared for everlasting life.

Percy says that the main purpose he was sent back to earth was to warn the world of what is about to happen—the great explosion of God's power—and how it would take place. He says Jesus walked him over to the river of life, which had trees all along both banks, and took a leaf from one of the trees and placed it on his chest and said: "These are for the healing of the nations." Jesus led him to the head of the river of life at the base of the throne, just like is says in Revelation: "And he (the angel that spoke with John), showed me a pure river of water of life, clear as crystal, proceeding from the throne of God and of the Lamb" (Rev. 22:1).

Jesus showed him the head of the river of life at the throne, and there were great floodgates holding back a flood of the river of life. Jesus pointed to the waters of the river of life, which were slowly rising, and said: "When the waters of this river rise up and begin to overflow its banks, My Father will open the floodgates and release a great flood of the waters of the river of life, and the waters will flood all over heaven." Jesus told him that these waters will flow out of a window in heaven, flow down through space and hit the earth and completely cover the earth!

It is a flood of the Spirit of God, a flood of the life of God, and a flood of the power of God. It was explained to him that when the flood of the waters of life cover the earth, the earth would begin to shake at the presence of God. That agrees with what Ezekiel said: "All men who are on the face of the earth shall shake at My presence" (Ezek. 38:20). We should prepare ourselves for such a great manifestation of God's power by listening to Percy's testimony, which the Lord Jesus has told him to tell us. It will set our minds on things above, not on the things on earth, which will perish. Our children, families, and works for the Lord are the greatest things we possess because they will ascend with us.

This great explosion of God's power will usher in the greatest revival the world has ever seen. The Spirit of God will be poured out on all flesh, and the earth will shake! It is written, "You shall receive power when the Holy Spirit has come upon you, and you shall be witnesses to Me" (Acts 1:8). God's power will be manifested through His people, and they will do the works of Jesus: "Most assuredly, I say to you, he who believes in Me, the works that I do he will do also; and greater works than these he will do, because I go to My Father" (John 14:12). His church will be filled with power and glory as they bear witness to all the wonderful things God has done for us. And this gospel will be preached in all the world as a witness to all nations, and then the end will come.

One of the first things Jesus showed Percy was Zion, the city four-square. (Rev. 21:16) Jesus took him before this great city and said to him, "This is Zion. Your room is seven hundred miles up. Would you like to see your room?" Here is what the scriptures say about Zion: "But you have come to Mount Zion and to the city of the living God, the heavenly Jerusalem" (Heb. 12:22). Zion is the city of the living God, the heavenly Jerusalem. Abraham looked for the promise of this city because God told him about it: "By faith Abraham ... waited for the city which has foundations, whose builder and maker is God" (Heb. 11:8, 10). The patriarchs of old had this anchor in their souls, that God has prepared a place for them.

> These all died in faith, not having received the promises, but having seen them afar off were assured of them, embraced them and confessed that they were strangers and pilgrims on the earth. For those who say such things declare plainly that they seek a homeland. And truly if they had called to mind that country from which they had come out, they would have had opportunity to return. But now they desire a better, that is, a heavenly country. Therefore, God is not ashamed to be called their God, for He has prepared a city for them. (Heb. 11:13–16)

We have also received these promises, but now, they are very near. Shall we not also embrace them and confess that we are strangers and pilgrims on earth? Should we seek our abode in a heavenly country and a heavenly city? Of course! And God is not ashamed to be called our God because He has prepared a city for us. Jesus has gone to prepare a place for us in this great city, and Jesus is coming down with this great city to deliver us from the hands of those who hate us; as it is written, "The Deliverer will come out of Zion" (Rom. 11:26). He is coming to deliver us out of the world because the wrath of God is coming upon it: Therefore, He instructs us to: "Wait for His Son from heaven, whom He raised from the dead, even Jesus who delivers us from the wrath to come" (1 Thess. 1:10).

The Lord also showed John that Zion was coming down out of heaven from God, but He did not show John when that would take place. Without the teaching of the Holy Spirit, we can only assume we know anything. We do have a pretty good idea when the deliverer will come out of Zion and all Israel will be saved. The prophet Joel gave us a more intense picture of the deliverer coming out of Zion, the New Jerusalem: "The LORD also will roar from Zion and utter His voice from Jerusalem; The heavens and earth will shake" (Joel 3:16). Therefore, Zion is coming down; Percy and the scriptures agree with this.

> Then I, John, saw the holy city, New Jerusalem, coming down out of heaven from God, prepared as a bride adorned for her husband. (Rev. 21:2)

> Then one of the seven angels ... talked with me, saying, "Come, I will show you the bride, the Lamb's wife." And he carried me away in the Spirit to a great and high mountain, and showed me the great city, the holy Jerusalem, descending out of heaven from God, having the glory of God. (Rev. 21:9–11)

Zion is coming down as a bride adorned with beauty and glory as described in Revelation: "The construction of its wall was of jasper; and the city was pure gold, like clear glass. The foundations of the wall of the city were adorned with all kinds of precious stones" (Rev. 21:18–19). She is the bride adorned with the glory of God for her husband; she is our home, and she is the Lamb's wife!

Jesus took Percy to his mansion room in Zion and explained what God is going to do with Zion, the city of the living God. Jesus told him that Zion would be picked up literally out of heaven and brought down into outer space near earth. That scientists would see it and announce they have found a new star; hence, the cover photo of this book. He was told that after the church was caught up in the clouds to meet the Lord in the air, they would then go up to Zion for the wedding supper of the Lamb. He was told that the banquet tables would be prepared out in front of the great and beautiful city of Zion for the wedding banquet. There is enough space up there in space to accommodate everyone too!

Notice what a great announcement God our Father has made before all creation for the wedding supper of the Lamb.

> And I heard, as it were, the voice of a great multitude, as the sound of many waters and as the sound of mighty thunderings, saying, "Alleluia! For the Lord God Omnipotent reigns! Let us be glad and rejoice and give Him glory, for the marriage of the Lamb has come, and His wife has made herself ready." And to her it was granted to be arrayed in fine linen, clean and bright, for the fine linen is the righteous acts of the saints. Then he said to me, "Write: 'Blessed are those who are called to the marriage supper of the Lamb!'" And he said to me, "These are the true sayings of God." (Rev. 19:6–9)

Percy was told that at the marriage supper of the Lamb, we, the church, would crown Jesus King of Kings and Lord of Lords. The Lord has sent this testimony that we might be divorced from this world to prepare us for our marriage to the Lamb. It will be a great ceremony with rejoicing like the sound of mighty thunderings, and a multitude would shout, "Alleluia! For the Lord God omnipotent reigns!" Jesus showed Percy the crown of many crowns on a royal velvet-covered golden table; it was the crown that we, the Lamb's wife, would put on Jesus at the marriage supper of the Lamb! Hallellujah!

Percy was shown the white angel horses of heaven, and he was taken to Jesus's horse, a most beautiful white steed shivering with power and ready to go forth! As he pet the neck of this beautiful horse, it turned back to look at Percy and said, "Praise God." Everything that has breath in heaven praises the Lord! After the wedding supper of the Lamb, Jesus will go forth on His white steed to judge and make war. The armies of heaven clothed in linen clean and white will follow Him on white horses to earth for the battle of that great Day of the Lord God Almighty, Armageddon. Jesus treads the winepress of the fierceness and wrath of almighty God (Rev. 19:11–16). "Do you not know that the saints will judge the world?" (1 Cor. 6:2). This is when it will happen. We will go with Jesus in this battle, but we will not have to fight because the battle is the Lord's. Great and very awesome are insufficient to describe the things that lie ahead for God's people.

The Lord our God has given us this testimony to prepare His people and set our minds on things above, where Christ is seated at the right hand of God. These things have been kept secret since the world began, but now, they have been made known to His people for the appointed time has come. Tell your friends and neighbors about this message—get the word out! The Lord is coming to do great things for His people and the whole world. "Watch therefore and pray always that you may be counted worthy to escape all these things that will come to pass, and to stand before the Son of Man" (Luke 21:36). Pray, prepare, and be ready, for the Lord Jesus has said,

> Because you have kept My command to persevere, I also will keep you from the hour of trial which shall come upon the world, to test those who dwell on the earth. Behold, I am coming quickly! Hold fast what you have, that no one may take your crown. (Rev. 3:10–12)

> To him who overcomes I will grant to sit with Me on My throne, as I also overcame and sat down with My Father on His throne. He who has an ear, let him hear what the Spirit says to the churches. (Rev. 3:21–22)

> He who testifies to these things says, "Surely I am coming quickly." Amen. Even so, come, Lord Jesus! The grace of our Lord Jesus Christ be with you all. Amen. (Rev. 22:20–21)

Printed in the United States
by Baker & Taylor Publisher Services